THIS IS MY OWN

LETTERS TO WES & OTHER WRITINGS ON JAPANESE CANADIANS, 1941 - 1948

by Muriel Kitagawa
Roy Miki, ed.

D1556966

Talonbooks   •   Vancouver   •   1985

published with assistance from the Canada Council and
Multiculturalism Canada

Talonbooks
201 / 1019 East Cordova Street
Vancouver
British Columbia V6A 1M8
Canada

This book was typeset in Garamond Book by Pièce de
Résistance and printed in Canada by Hignell Printing Ltd.

First printing: December 1985

Canadian Cataloguing in Publication Data

Kitagawa, Muriel, 1912-1974.
    This Is My Own: letters to Wes & other writings on Japanese
Canadians, 1941-1948

ISBN 0-88922-231-2 (bound.). — ISBN
    0-88922-230-4 (pbk.)

1. Kitagawa, Muriel, 1912-1974. 2. Japanese
Canadians - Evacuation and relocation, 1942-1945.*
3. World War, 1939-1945 - Personal narratives,
Canadian. I. Miki, Roy Akira, 1942-
II. Title.
FC106.J3K57 1985   940.54'72'71   C85-091423-X
D768.15.K57 1985

for her words
Tsukiye Muriel Kitagawa
(1912-1974)

•

for my father
Kazuo Miki
(1907-1969)

•

for his community spirit
Motoi Iwanaka
(1909—1985)

•

and for all Nisei
who dared to dream

Nisei! If we must suffer this humiliation, let us suffer with dignity! Let us do nothing that will be held against us now or ever afterwards. Let us always remember . . . that there are many, many Occidentals who think that this treatment is a "damned shame."

Yes, we are bitter, with a bitterness we can never forget, which will mark us for the rest of our lives, but we are not fools. This is not the end, but only the beginning. If we rant and rave and give up hope now, what reserve shall we have left to endure the still darker days to come? This is the time to tighten our belts, to gird our courage, to condition ourselves to every kind of privation and endure . . . endure . . . and still endure. We must survive this phase of our history to emerge stronger with the resilience of tempered steel.

Whatever comes, whatever happens, let us forge a record of dignity and endurance to leave as a proud heritage for our sons and daughters to come.

("A Record of Dignity," *New Canadian*, March 1942)

CONTENTS

Editor's Note

Muriel Kitagawa was a prolific writer, and the majority of her numerous contributions to the *New Canadian* from 1940 on, signed either "T.M.K." (the initials for her full name, Tsukiye Muriel Kitagawa) or "Sue Sada" (a pen name taken from her maternal grandmother), were in the form of columns. Readers of the *New Canadian* knew her as the colourful and provocative writer of such columns as "Water 'Neath the Bridge," "For All That," and "Hello There." In these pieces, Muriel presented her community with a variety of topical subjects—arranged marriages, for instance—or she ruminated on intellectual and emotional values. At other times, when the community was threatened by racist individuals, politicians or groups, she would challenge their views and defend her community's commitment to her native land, Canada. In more pensive moods, she wrote poems which were published under the pen name "Dana," and there were many narratives, such as short stories, historical vignettes, and domestic incidents by "T.M.K." and "Sue Sada."

This Is My Own gathers together the relevant material written on Japanese Canadians during and after World War II, from 1941 to 1948, starting with the amazing series of private letters Muriel wrote to her brother Wes Fujiwara in Toronto. These are documents that are the direct products of the upheaval caused by government action in the early months of 1942 to remove the entire Japanese Canadian community from the B.C. coast. After the Kitagawa family moved to Toronto in June 1942, Muriel continued to write both to protest the government's unjust policies, and to educate Canadians on the history and perceptions of Japanese Canadians. The section "Other Writings," which accompanies the letters to Wes, contains statements, essays, and manuscripts which arose out of that concern. In making my choices, I have drawn from three main sources:

the Muriel Kitagawa Papers in the Public Archives of Canada, the *New Canadian* and *Nisei Affairs*, and the private archives of Ed Kitagawa and Dr. Wes Fujiwara.

With a family of four young children, her twins born right in the midst of the uprooting of her community, it is a wonder that Muriel found time to write as much as she did. She was constantly rushing to write articles against deadlines, often without a chance for revisions. Although many of the letters to her brother Wes were typed, others were written by hand—at top speed, as she tried to write down what was happening around her. Her pregnancy was difficult, and for a time after the twins were born, she was weak. Some of her letters were written while in bed. The manuscripts extant in the Public Archives as well as in the private collections of Ed Kitagawa and Wes Fujiwara reveal that throughout the 1940s, after re-settling in Toronto, Muriel was working on two writing projects, neither of which was completed. One was an account of the wartime uprooting and internment of Japanese Canadians, and the other was an autobiography that explored the growth of her Nisei generation. The latter manuscript was to be called "The Crucible," and fragments of this writing venture published here give us glimpses of what the completed work might have been. Because of the tentative nature of much of these pieces—Muriel somehow never got back to them after 1950 when her life was drawn in other directions—I have taken the liberty as an editor to make those revisions that bring out the energy, beauty, and distinctive style of her writing. As the need arose, the changes at times were minimal, at other times extensive, especially for those manuscripts left in draft form. In the edited letters to Dr. Fujiwara, material of a purely private nature has been deleted with his advice and consent.

R.M.
September 30, 1985
Vancouver, B.C.

Introduction
The Life and Times of Muriel Kitagawa

Monday evening: We left Vancouver 7:35 pm. Gosh but a lot of folks were there to see us off.

The Yamadas, Toyofukus, Eiko, Yaeko, Nori, Hide, Niiko and Frank, Tom, Eiji Yatabe, Jim Suzuki, Harold, Mrs. Nakamura, Mr. Mori, Dr. Nomura, Mr. Hotson, the Miyakes, Miyasakis, Ishiwaras, Katsukakes, Miyo Ishiwata.

I had the queerest sensation of living in some fantastic dream as the train slowly moved out of the station. All along the tracks, wherever they could, crowds of nihon-jin lined up to wave good-bye to those going to work camps, to Schreiber and to beet fields, ghost towns and other places. They waved to us and we waved to them, whoever they were. Some we knew, some we didn't, but weren't we all in the same boat—forced to move out of the restricted area? I hated the thought of leaving Eiko behind, so I blew her a gentle kiss.[1]

---

[1] From a notebook, written in pencil, in the private manuscript collection of Dr. Wesley Fujiwara.

1

I. The Uprooting, 1942

As Muriel Kitagawa boarded the train with her children and her husband Ed, and saw the faces of relatives, friends, and strangers lining the tracks, she was witnessing her community caught up in a catastrophic event. She, too, was just one of some 21,000 men, women and children of Japanese ancestry—17,000 of whom were naturalized or Canadian-born citizens—uprooted from their west coast homes during the turbulent months of January to October, 1942. Lives were utterly disrupted, families and friends torn apart, properties and belongings confiscated, and liberties suspended.

Fear of the unknown pervaded their being: apprehension of a voyage thousands of miles across the country, with four young children to care for, the two youngest ones, twins born only five months before—what would become of the Kitagawas?

By May 1942, Vancouver had become a chaotic scene of confused individuals shipped in large groups from scattered towns along the coast, from Vancouver Island, and from nearby Steveston and the Fraser Valley. Suddenly unemployed, dispossessed and displaced, in a dazed condition, they scrambled for any form of security as protection from the disorder threatening their every move. The Kitagawas were surprised and relieved to receive, at the last minute, special permits to move to Toronto, only the second family to resettle there by the beginning of June 1942.

For a Nisei[2] such as Muriel, who had never before had occasion to doubt her intimate roots in her native land, Canada, and who believed in the sanctity of democratic principles, this moment of separation cut deeply into her consciousness. Six months after the bombing of Pearl Harbor, December 7, 1941, her Japanese Canadian community on the west coast of Canada had been dismantled—permanently, as it would turn out.

What was considered impossible in a democratic country such as Canada had occurred with a swiftness that stunned people like Muriel. In the early weeks of the war, despite the blackouts, the roundup of their fishing boats and the sudden unemployment of some 1800 fishermen, and despite the suspicion of non-Japanese Canadians and

---

[2]The term Nisei, Japanese for "second generation," refers to Canadian-born Japanese Canadians. They are the children of the Issei, the "first generation" of Japanese Canadians who emigrated from Japan. The children of the Nisei are called the Sansei, the "third generation."

police scrutiny there had never been any question that they would support Canada's war effort in whatever way they could. They trusted their country to respect their rights as citizens. As long as the federal government protected them from racial discrimination, they were prepared to endure the animosity directed at them by misguided racists.

The Kitagawas lived on East Pender Street in Vancouver, near Hastings Park, and their community watched and listened with rising concern as demands rose from politicians and other pressure groups for the expulsion of Japanese Canadians en masse from the province. They read and worried over a report in their community newspaper, the *New Canadian*, on December 20, 1941 about the new Pacific Coast Security League, a group spearheaded by Alderman Halford Wilson, well known in the late 1930s as the most notorious and vociferous anti-Japanese Canadian politician in the city. And they were not surprised to hear on January 5, 1942, that Wilson had again proposed to destroy the economic stability of their community by limiting trade licences. There was quiet relief when City Council rejected his resolution because policy on Japanese Canadians was a federal matter; the decision reflected proper government procedure in their eyes. Most had grown up with such a strong faith in democratic values, they had no reason to believe that Ottawa would ever comply with strident local demands coming from anti-Japanese Canadian individuals and groups. The *New Canadian* was voicing a common perception when readers were told that the rumoured "proposal that all Japanese be removed somewhere east of the rockies is regarded simply as 'silly'," and that the "idea of camps equivalent to internment camps is also branded in the same light."[3]

This attitude explains the mood of co-operation in the face of Order-in-Council P.C. 365 (Fig. 1), passed on January 16, which called for the removal of male Japanese Nationals, 18-45 years of age, from a designated "Protected Area" 100 miles from the coast. The measure was the result of the publicized "Conference on the Japanese Problem in B.C." held in Ottawa, January 8-9. Canadian-born Nisei were certainly disturbed by the decision, but they were prepared to accept it as a temporary security measure. The editor of the *New Canadian* reminded his readers on January 14 that "the government has

---

[3]*New Canadian (NC)*, 5 January 1942: p. 2.

TO MALE ENEMY ALIENS
<u>NOTICE</u>

Under date of February 2nd, 1942, the Honourable the Minister of National Defence with the concurrence of the Minister of Justice gave public notice defining an area of British Columbia, as described below, to be a protected area after the 31st day of January, 1942; that is to say, that area of the Province of British Columbia, including all islands, west of a line described hereunder:-

Commencing at boundary point No. 7 on the International Boundary between the Dominion of Canada and Alaska, thence following the line of the "Cascade Mountains" as defined by paragraph 2 of Section 24 of the Interpretation Act of British Columbia, being Chapter 1 of the Revised Statutes of 1936, to the Northwest corner of Lot 13-10, Range 5, Coast Land Districts, thence due East to a point due North of the Northwest corner of Lot 373, Range 5, Coast Land District, thence due South to said Northwest corner of Lot 373 being a point on the aforementioned line of the "Cascade Mountains", (being the area surrounding the village municipality of Terrace); thence following said line of the "Cascade Mountains" to the Western Boundary of Township 5, Range 26, West of the 6th Meridian, thence following the Northerly, Easterly and Southerly Boundaries of said Township 5, to the Southwest corner thereof, being a point on the line of the "Cascade Mountains" (being the area surrounding the village municipality of Hope); thence following the "Cascade Mountains" to the Southerly boundary of the Province.

Pursuant to the provisions of Regulation 4 of the Defence of Canada Regulations, the Minister of Justice has, on the 5th day of February, 1942, ordered that:-

1. All male Enemy Aliens of the ages of 18 years to 45 years, inclusive, shall leave the protected area hereinbefore referred to on or before the 1st day of April, 1942;

2. That, subject to the provisions of paragraph No. 1 of this Order, no Enemy Alien shall, after the date of this order, enter, leave or return to such protected area except with the permission of the Commissioner of the Royal Canadian Mounted Police Force, or an Officer of that Force designated by the Commissioner to act for him in this respect;

3. That no Enemy Alien shall have in his possession or use, while in such protected area, any camera, radio transmitter, radio shortwave receiving set, firearm, ammunition, or explosive.

OTTAWA, February 7, 1942.

S.T. WOOD (Commissioner)
Royal Canadian Mounted Police
TO BE POSTED IN A CONSPICUOUS PLACE

Figure 1: Order-in-Council P.C. 365 (16 January 1942) called for the removal of male Japanese Nationals living within 100 miles of the B.C. coast.

stressed that principles of justice and fair-treatment must be maintained."[4] Four days later he admitted that some innocent people would be hurt, but at least "a distinction is to be drawn between those who are aliens and those who are citizens."[5]

This editorial view of the *New Canadian* was reinforced by government assurances from Ottawa that Japanese Canadians would be "justly treated" and that the "full force of the law will be invoked to prevent anti-Japanese demonstrations and to protect Canadian residents of Japanese race." Steps were even being taken to "organize a Civilian Corps of Canadian Japanese to be used on projects of value to the national cause, in order to utilize the services of the various groups of Canadian Japanese who have indicated their desire to serve."[6] It was in such a context that a reported Ottawa dispatch to one of the Vancouver daily newspapers "declaring that all British Columbia's Japanese population would be moved from the coast" was considered false, merely "a 'kite in the wind', written to support the policy of the paper."[7]

On February 4, the *New Canadian* headline announced that the first ninety Japanese Nationals were to leave on February 9 by CPR to Chapleau, Ontario to work in lumber camps and sawmills. A farewell dinner was held at the Fuji Chop Suey on Powell Street. An estimated 2500 men were to be removed by the April 1 deadline.

The first premonition of disaster came when the ninety Nationals could not leave as planned, their departure delayed indefinitely because protests over their imminent arrival had suddenly and unexpectedly flared up in Ontario. The plan was soon abandoned, and new arrangements were hastily made to send the men to road camps west of Jasper near the B.C./Alberta border. It was then, in the latter half of February, that the tide seemed to turn dramatically. Vancouver City Council changed its earlier non-interventionist policy and passed a resolution asking Ottawa to remove all Japanese Canadians, as well as the Japanese Nationals, from the coast. And soon after the first 100 male Nationals left for road camps at Lucerne and Rainbow, the *New Canadian* reported that the Citizens' Defense Committee, a group of twenty prominent Vancouverites (Austin Taylor among

---

[4]"Keep Cool and Stay Calm," *NC*, 14 January 1942.
[5]"The Government's Decision," *NC*, 16 January 1942.
[6]Press release, January 14, 1942, quoted in Forrest E. La Violette, *The Canadian Japanese and World War II* (Toronto: University of Toronto Press, 1948), pp. 47-48.
[7]"Fabrication," *NC*, 21 January 1942.

them), was being formed to support the removal of all Japanese Canadians as well. They were backed by the Vancouver Rotary Club, the Vancouver Labour Council and the Canadian Congress of Labour. This was a shock, especially in the context of recent events in the U.S.: on February 19, President Franklin D. Roosevelt had signed Executive Order 9066, prohibiting the 120,000 American citizens of Japanese ancestry from living on the west coast of the United States of America, the order which led to their subsequent incarceration in barbed-wire camps.

The passage, in Ottawa, of Order-in-Council P.C. 1486 (Fig. 2) on February 24, issued as an amendment to Order-in-Council P.C. 365, shook the very foundation of the Japanese Canadian community and left it reeling from a deep sense of betrayal. Through a ministerial directive from the Minister of Justice, Louis St. Laurent, the distinction between Nationals and citizens—a distinction Japanese Canadians clung to for support—was erased, and forthwith "all Persons of the Japanese Race" were subject to expulsion from the 100-mile "Protected Area." Through the unlimited powers of the War Measures Act, the RCMP were authorized to enter and search houses of Japanese Canadians without warrants. All cameras, radios and firearms were confiscated, motor vehicles had to be turned in, and a dusk-to-dawn curfew was imposed (Fig. 3). "When the sun goes down," the *New Canadian* reported, "it takes with it light and freedom, and makes a criminal of any person who dares venture out of his home onto the street. And when night comes on, it brings to thousands of Canadian citizens, the feeling that their citizenship is of little value."[8]

Order-in-Council P.C. 1486 had legalized the assumption—anathema to Nisei like the Kitagawas—that racial origin alone, and not individual merit, determines one's loyalty. A deep disillusionment filtered into the community's consciousness. The *New Canadian* editorial of March 3, summarizing the government's increasingly unjust treatment of Japanese Canadians, was written in a tone of frustration and bitterness that would soon permeate the community:

The first steps taken—immobilization of fishing boats, special registration, parole permits, and detention of certain

---

[8]"The Curfew Hits an Unhappy People in Spirit and Body," *NC*, 3 March 1942: p. 1.

NOTICE

TO ALL PERSONS OF JAPANESE RACIAL ORIGIN

Having reference to the Protected Area of British Columbia as described in an Extra of the Canada Gazette, No. 174 dated Ottawa, Monday, February 2, 1942:-

1. EVERY PERSON OF THE JAPANESE RACE, WHILE WITHIN THE PROTECTED AREA AFORESAID, SHALL HEREAFTER BE AT HIS USUAL PLACE OF RESIDENCE EACH DAY BEFORE SUNSET AND SHALL REMAIN THEREIN UNTIL SUNRISE ON THE FOLLOWING DAY, AND NO SUCH PERSON SHALL GO OUT OF HIS USUAL PLACE OF RESIDENCE AFORESAID UPON THE STREETS OR OTHERWISE DURING THE HOURS BETWEEN SUNSET AND SUNRISE;

2. NO PERSON OF THE JAPANESE RACE SHALL HAVE IN HIS POSSESSION OR USE IN SUCH PROTECTED AREA ANY MOTOR VEHICLE, CAMERA, RADIO TRANSMITTER, RADIO RECEIVING SET, FIREARM, AMMUNITION OR EXPLOSIVE;

3. IT SHALL BE THE DUTY OF EVERY PERSON OF THE JAPANESE RACE HAVING IN HIS POSSESSION OR UPON HIS PREMISES ANY ARTICLE MENTIONED IN THE NEXT PRECEDING PARAGRAPH, FORTHWITH TO CAUSE SUCH ARTICLE TO BE DELIVERED UP TO ANY JUSTICE OF THE PEACE RESIDING IN OR NEAR THE LOCALITY WHERE ANY SUCH ARTICLE IS HAD IN POSSESSION, OR TO AN OFFICER OR CONSTABLE OF THE POLICE FORCE OF THE PROVINCE OR CITY IN OR NEAR SUCH LOCALITY OR TO AN OFFICER OR CONSTABLE OF THE ROYAL CANADIAN MOUNTED POLICE.

4. ANY JUSTICE OF THE PEACE OR OFFICER OR CONSTABLE RECEIVING ANY ARTICLE MENTIONED IN PARAGRAPH 2 OF THIS ORDER SHALL GIVE TO THE PERSON DELIVERING THE SAME A RECEIPT THEREFOR AND SHALL REPORT THE FACT TO THE COMMISSIONER OF THE ROYAL CANADIAN MOUNTED POLICE, AND SHALL RETAIN OR OTHERWISE DISPOSE OF ANY SUCH ARTICLE AS DIRECTED BY THE SAID COMMISSIONER.

5. ANY PEACE OFFICER OR ANY OFFICER OR CONSTABLE OF THE ROYAL CANADIAN MOUNTED POLICE HAVING POWER TO ACT AS SUCH PEACE OFFICER OR OFFICER OR CONSTABLE IN THE SAID PROTECTED AREA, IS AUTHORIZED TO SEARCH WITHOUT WARRANT THE PREMISES OR ANY PLACE OCCUPIED OR BELIEVED TO BE OCCUPIED BY ANY PERSON OF THE JAPANESE RACE REASONABLY SUSPECTED OF HAVING IN HIS POSSESSION OR UPON HIS PREMISES ANY ARTICLE MENTIONED IN PARAGRAPH 2 OF THIS ORDER, AND TO SEIZE ANY SUCH ARTICLE FOUND ON SUCH PREMISES;

6. EVERY PERSON OF THE JAPANESE RACE SHALL LEAVE THE PROTECTED AREA AFORESAID FORTHWITH;

7. NO PERSON OF THE JAPANESE RACE SHALL ENTER SUCH PROTECTED AREA EXCEPT UNDER PERMIT ISSUED BY THE ROYAL CANADIAN MOUNTED POLICE;

8. IN THIS ORDER, "PERSONS OF THE JAPANESE RACE" MEANS, AS WELL AS ANY PERSON WHOLLY OF THE JAPANESE RACE, A PERSON NOT WHOLLY OF THE JAPANESE RACE IF HIS FATHER OR MOTHER IS OF THE JAPANESE RACE AND IF THE COMMISSIONER OF THE ROYAL CANADIAN MOUNTED POLICE BY NOTICE IN WRITING HAS REQUIRED OR REQUIRES HIM TO REGISTER PURSUANT TO ORDER-IN-COUNCIL P.C. 9760 OF DECEMBER 16th, 1941.

DATED AT OTTAWA THIS 26th DAY OF FEBRUARY, 1942.

Louis S. St. Laurent,
Minister of Justice

To be posted in a Conspicuous Place

Figure 2: Order-in-Council P.C. 1486 (24 February 1942) ordered the removal of all "persons of Japanese racial origin" and authorized the RCMP to search without warrant, enforce a dusk-to-dawn curfew, and confiscate automobiles, radios, cameras, and firearms.

7

EXTRA!

The New Canadian
THE VOICE OF THE SECOND GENERATION

Vol. V, No. 24 [A]   VANCOUVER, B. C.   THURS., FEB. 26, 1942

號外

Ottawa Orders Dusk To Dawn Curfew

Not Yet Confirmed Here

Order to Remain in Homes To Be Worked Out Soon

VANCOUVER, Feb. 26.—The Canadian Press this afternoon carried an Ottawa dispatch saying that all Japanese living within the British Columbia Protected Area must remain in their homes between sunset and sunrise, under an order approved by the Dominion Government today.

While additional details remain to be worked out, officials of the Department of Justice said, the order is expected to go into effect almost immediately.

The order applies only to all persons of the Japanese race living in the protected area, first and second generation, along the British Columbia coast and the islands. They must return to their usual places of residence before dark, according to the order.

It would not go into effect until official notice of it is posted, however. R.C.M.P. officials said today they had received no information on the new order.

The curfew, it is said, is designed to restrict movements of all persons of Japanese origin until they are moved inland.

MOVE ALL JAPANESE ULTIMATE GOVT. PLAN

OTTAWA.—Naturalized and Canadian-born Japanese will be removed from the British Columbia protected area as well as Japanese nationals, Labor Minister Humphrey Mitchell told a press conference Wednesday night.

Ultimatly, the minister said, the government intended to move every person of Japanese origin, male and female, and of all ages from the protected area.

Workers In Construction Corps To Receive Dollar Per Day

OTTAWA.—Formation of a Japanese Canadian construction corps for employment in war-time projects "within or without" Canada was announced Wednesday by Prime Minister King.

Basic pay of the corps will be $1 per day with dependent allowances at the rate of 50 per cent allowed to armed forces with a bonus at the end of the war of $2 for every month served. Enlistment in the corps is for the duration.

The New Canadian

396 Powell Street

Vancouver, B. C.   PAcific 8431

A paper published by and for second generation Japanese in Canada, and devoted to their welfare as citizens of Canada.

40c month; 6 mos: $2.25 in advance; One year: $4.00 in advance
Published tri-weekly at the Taiyo Printing Company

Figure 3: Announcement of the curfew in the *New Canadian*, 26 February 1942.

8

individuals—were accepted, on the whole, as obviously
necessary in war-time.

More drastic steps emerging from the Ottawa conference
in January—the removal of alien nationals and the banning
of short-wave radios and cameras—were likewise accepted.
In spite of the fact that almost a quarter of its gainfully
employed were affected by the removal order, the whole
community was prepared to recognize that government
authorities were forced to draw some line between citizens
and non-citizens in guarding against the most probable
source of danger.

But tremendous public pressure—arising in the first place
from very sorry sources indeed—was brought to bear upon
the government. In quick order, a whole series of
repressive measures, unlike anything before in the history
of the nation, have been authorized. In effect, the new
orders uproot completely without regard some 23,000
men, women and children; brand every person of Japanese
origin as disloyal and traitorous; and reduce to nothing the
concept and value of Canadian citizenship.[9]

"Yes, Muriel wrote in the *New Canadian*, "we are bitter, with
a bitterness we can never forget, which will mark us for the rest of
our lives . . . ."[10]

Clearly, through the eyes of Japanese Canadians, the government
had given in to racist pressure in branding them all "enemy aliens"—
and the branding would mean that they would be subject to suspicion and threats, treated as potential saboteurs, wherever they went.
It was astonishing but true that the government was legitimizing
discrimination on the basis of race, and thereby sanctioning hostile
attitudes toward a group of identifiable Canadian citizens: Japanese
Canadians. Muriel's outrage and horror flooded into a letter written
to her brother Wes on March 4, 1942:

Okay we move. But where? Signs up on all highways
. . . JAPS KEEP OUT. Curfew. "My father is dying. May
I have permission to go to his bedside?" "NO!" Like moles

---

[9]"Grounds for Questioning," *NC*, 3 March 1942.
[10]"A Record of Dignity," *NC*, 5 March 1942: p. 2. [Editor's note: the full text
of this statement appears as an Epigraph to this book.]

we burrow within after dark, and only dare to peek out
of the window or else be thrown into the hoosegow with
long term sentences and hard labour. Confiscation of
radios, cameras, cars and trucks. Shutdown of all business.
No one will buy. No agency yet set up to evaluate. When
you get a notice to report to RCMP for orders to move,
you report or be interned. "Who will guard my wife and
daughters?" Strong arm reply. Lord, if this was Germany
you can expect such things as the normal way, but this is
Canada, a Democracy! And the Nisei, repudiated by the
only land they know, no redress anywhere.

On March 4, the same day that Muriel sent this letter to Wes, the
federal government passed Order-in-Council P.C. 1665, to establish
the B.C. Security Commission, the body empowered "to plan, supervise and direct the evacuation from the protected areas of British
Columbia of all persons of the Japanese race." The Commission was
granted far-reaching powers: total control over the movement of any
Japanese Canadian both "within and without the protected area,"
including the authority "to order the detention of any such person."
P.C. 1665 also contained the provision, as "a protective measure
only," for properties to be placed *in trust* with the Custodian of
Enemy Alien Property[11](Fig. 4).
  On April 6, the new Commission, chaired by Austin Taylor, a Vancouver businessman, F.J. Mead, Assistant Commissioner of the RCMP,
and John Shirras, Assistant Commissioner of the B.C. Provincial
Police, announced the removal plan in the *New Canadian*. According to their rationalization, "persons of the Japanese race" removed
from the "protected area" needed employment in order to survive,
and therefore some road Project Camps were being established.[12]
But since the "camps are being put into operation for the sole purpose of providing employment," the wages of the men sent there
would be scaled down "to fit the problem with which the Government was faced." The hourly rate was set at 25¢ per hour, out of
which married men would "be required to assign to their wives the
sum of Twenty Dollars ($20.00) per month." They would also

  [11]Order-in-Council P.C. 1665, quoted in Ken Adachi, *The Enemy That Never Was*
(Toronto: McClelland and Stewart, 1976), p. 426.
  [12]"Roads, Ont. Mills, Beet Fields, Interior Towns," *NC*, 6 April 1942: p. 3; all
of the following quotes, unless otherwise indicated, are from this article.

NOTICE TO PERSONS OF THE JAPANESE RACE

OFFICE OF THE CUSTODIAN

The Custodian desires to bring to the attention of persons of the Japanese race the following provisions of Order in Council Number P. C. 1665 dated the 4th day of March, 1942:

"As a protective measure only, all property situated in any protected area of British Columbia belonging to any person of the Japanese race resident in such area (excepting fishing vessels subject to Order in Council P. C. 288 of the 13th of January, 1942, and deposits of money, shares of stock, debentures, bonds or other securities), delivered up to any person pursuant to the Order of the Minister of Justice dated February 26, 1942, or which is turned over to the Custodian by the owner, or which the owner, on being evacuated, is unable to take with him, shall be vested in and subject to the control and management of the Custodian as defined in the Regulations respecting Trading with the Enemy, 1939; provided, however, that no commission shall be charged by the Custodian in respect of such control and management.

"Subject as hereinafter provided, and for the purposes of the control and management of such property, rights and interest by the Custodian, the Regulations respecting Trading with the Enemy, 1939, shall apply mutatis mutandis to the same extent as if such property, rights and interests belonged to any enemy within the meaning of the said Regulations.

"The property, rights and interests so vested in and subject to the control and management of the Custodian, or the proceeds thereof shall be dealt with in such manner as the Governor in Council may direct."

The above provisions do not apply to fishing vessels, deposits of money, shares of stock, debentures, bonds or other securities, or property required to be delivered to any person by the owner pursuant to the Order of the Minister of Justice dated February 26, 1942, but enable persons of the Japanese race to deliver to the Custodian, before they are evacuated from a protected area, such other property as they have not disposed of and are unable to take with them.

All such other property not disposed of or delivered to the Custodian, prior to evacuation automatically comes under the control of the Custodian upon the evacuation of the owner but persons of the Japanese race are urged to report their property immediately instead of waiting until their evacuation as this will enable the Custodian to take prompt action to protect and administer the same.

Forms for setting forth the particulars of such property may be obtained on written application to the undersigned and should be completed as fully as possible by owners of property and mailed to the undersigned without delay.

Dated at the City of Vancouver this tenth day of March, 1942.

G. W. McPHERSON
Authorized Deputy of the Custodian,
1404 Royal Bank Building,
Vancouver, B.C.

Figure 4: This Notice, published in the *New Canadian*, urged Japanese Canadians to register their properties with the Custodian, so that he could "protect and administer" these properties during their absence.

be charged 25¢ for each meal in the camp. The government would subsidize families separated from the men an additional $5 per month for the first child, and $4 per month for each additional child.

As for the families of these men, the government would place them in Hastings Park, a clearing house for the men leaving for the camps, and for the women, children, and elderly who were their dependents. At Hastings Park a boarding fee not exceeding $10 would be charged for the wives, a fee which had to come out of their allowance of $20 from camp and the government subsidy for children. The Commission announced that it still had not finalized details for housing these people during the absence of the men, but that plans were under way to resettle them in the B.C. interior. Although they did not name the towns, the Commission reported that it now had "the necessary authority from the Government to move the people into these areas."

At the time of this announcement, Japanese Nationals had already been sent to road camps near the B.C./Alberta border, because of the earlier order to remove male "enemy aliens." The Commission, however, had now decided to send Nisei men to other provinces, initially to Ontario. This decision was taken, as they explained, simply "because the Provinces expressed a wish to have Canadian Japanese [and not Japanese Nationals], and we endeavoured to comply with their wishes." These men would "be paid the current rate of wages for the district." Some Nisei were going to be sent to Schreiber, Ontario, a clearing pool for employment in various lumber and road camps throughout Ontario.

It had also been determined, "through lengthy negotiations," that families "used to farming and the handling of root crops" would be sent to Manitoba and Alberta for work on sugar beet farms. The Commission "is glad to be able to send large groups" to these farms "for the reason that it means that the family unit will not have to be broken up, which is something the Commission regrets very much in the case of those who have to go to work camps."

Such, then, in its baldest form, was the removal plan presented to Japanese Canadians like Muriel and Ed Kitagawa. Although the scheme seemed to contain some element of choice, however slight, in reality the removal policy was governed by expediency alone. The Commission had a number of options, so they need only manoeuvre or force individuals in one direction or another. Male Nationals in the camps near the B.C./Alberta border, as "enemy aliens," had no choice, nor did their families already confined in Hastings Park. The naturalized and Canadian-born men in the first families to be rounded up were resentful about being ordered to Ontario, forced to separate from their families. As citizens they could see no reason why their choice was restricted and that their families, along with the families of the Nationals, had to go to the Interior detention camps in B.C.—as it turned out, to "ghost towns" such as Greenwood, Kaslo, Sandon, and New Denver. And families from the large farming and fishing communities in the Fraser Valley and Steveston were approached and enticed to go in groups to the sugar beet farms in Alberta and Manitoba. They were drawn in by the provision that families could remain together in this way. Though the Commission may have rationalized that these families chose the method of removal, their fear of family separation made the move almost inevitable. Then there was Hastings Park itself, the government's clearing station, which was "converted from animal to human shelter in only seven days."[13] Former livestock buildings to house human beings, a wretched stench, barbaric living conditions—here the uprooted men, women, children, and the elderly were registered and cooped up, some for months. The men waited for orders to be removed to a road or lumber camp, while their families languished in segregated quarters waiting for the interior towns to be prepared for habitation.

Still, some more fortunate individuals managed to escape the Commission's harsh removal plan by securing permission to relocate in family units on a "self-supporting" basis. These were people who could show that they had the financial resources to re-establish themselves outside the "protected area," and who managed to make special arrangements with the B.C. Security Commission to lease houses and farms in certain areas in B.C. The Commission, however, did not publicly offer *this* choice in their announcement. The families sent to the sugar beet farms in Alberta and Manitoba were not offered this option, nor were the others who were forced to travel across Canada to Ontario. Many in the "self-supporting" group were accorded this privilege on the basis of obvious wealth, but some were included because of their personal influence with the Commission, and many because of their connection with Etsuji Morii, an Issei member of the Japanese Canadian community who enjoyed prefer-

---

[13]Ann Gomer Sunahara, *The Politics of Racism: The Uprooting of Japanese Canadians During the Second World War* (Toronto: James Lorimer, 1981), p. 55.

ential treatment by the RCMP and the B.C. Security Commission. Morii was allowed to investigate a number of sites where the more financially secure Japanese Canadians could move. He himself chose to relocate with his friends in Minto City, an abandoned mining town. Other so-called "self-supporting" sites in B.C. were McGillivray Falls, Bridge River-Lillooet, and Christina Lake. "These fortunate 1400," Ann Sunahara says, referring to those who left the "protected area" on their own resources, "...avoided most of the restrictions imposed on the rest and lived under minimal supervision at the resorts and on the farms they had leased with the government's permission."[14]

There is no doubt that the "self-supporters," by financing their resettlement, saved the government money while they simultaneously contributed to the B.C. Security Commission's work. But in allowing certain individuals preferential treatment, the Commission sanctioned a double standard. Many Japanese Canadians would soon wonder why some individuals, merely on the supposed basis of money, were permitted to live more or less on their own, or with minimal policing. If the government was removing all Japanese Canadians as a "security measure," then how could some in the community suffer less restrictions than the rest? Why weren't all Japanese Canadians given the choice of relocating on their own? Why were the vast majority pressured or coerced to go where the Commission ordered them to go? The inconsistency of the government's actions, and the apparent privileges accorded a few, led many Japanese Canadians to believe that the government's policies were based, not upon the protection of Canada, but simply upon political expediency.

The same inconsistency of policy was applied to some 1300 others, who managed to secure "special permits" to leave the "protected area" for guaranteed employment, or to a place where relatives or friends would assume responsibility for their livelihood. This was the situation for the Kitagawas, who were allowed to move as a family to Toronto (Fig. 5). What about the security risk with all these people? The arbitrary and unequal treatment by the B.C. Security Commission added to the cynicism and bitterness experienced by Japanese Canadians during—and long after—the uprooting. In truth, the double standard proved to them that their community was never really considered a threat to national security.

Nevertheless, the uprooting was successfully carried out by the

---

[14]Sunahara, p. 78.

14

British Columbia Security Commission

VANCOUVER, B. C.

May 26 1942

COMMISSION PERMIT No 01158

JAPANESE REGISTRATION No. 10406

This Permit authorises Mrs. Isukiye KITAGAWA #10406, and her

four children (under 16), 2751 East Pender street,

Vancouver, B. C.

to travel in accordance with the provisions of Orders-in-Council Nos. P.C. 1665 and
365.

to TORONTO, ONTARIO, to live at the home of Mr. and Mrs. Finlay, Toronto,

~~and residents~~ 24 Wellesley Street. They must travel by rail, leaving Vancouver

by June 1st, and must not re-enter the Restricted Area. This Commission assumes

no responsibility for the cost of education of children of school-age.

(Signed) ....

For British Columbia Security Commission.

This Permit not valid unless signed by one of the following authorised signatories:

AUSTIN C. TAYLOR............Chairman
F. J. MEAD............................Member
JOHN SHIRRAS....................Member
GRANT MacNEIL...................Secretary

British Columbia Security Commission.

Figure 5: The permit authorizing Muriel and her children to move to Toronto.

15

Commission. Through the frantic days and weeks from February to May, the Powell Street area, or "Little Tokyo," was like a disaster area as shops closed down and residents disappeared. Hastily uprooted people from Vancouver, the coastal towns, and Vancouver Island poured into the area and were herded into the primitive confines of Hastings Park. With no one to speak on their behalf, with no right of appeal, and with no protection from the abuse of the War Measures Act, the Kitagawas and other "persons of Japanese race" became voiceless exiles in their own country. Worse still, with their citizenship erased, they were powerless—caught up in a government machinery ripe for further betrayals.

Perhaps the most blatant of these betrayals, following the initial loss of rights as citizens, was the confiscation and liquidation of Japanese-Canadian properties and belongings without the consent of the owners. The outline of the April 6 plan of the B.C. Security Commission concluded with what was understood as an assurance from Austin Taylor that properties would be protected and held in trust by the Custodian. In the *New Canadian*, the Japanese Canadian community read the following statement of official policy:

> A Custodian of (Alien) Property has been appointed by the Government and charged with the protection of all property placed voluntary [sic] under his control. This is not confiscation and the Custodian will administer the property in the interests of the people which should prevent them from disposing of their assets at a sacrifice or in an unfavourable market. We mention this because there seems to be a lack of understanding of the Custodian's position.
>
> We repeat that property delivered to the Custodian will be administered in the interests of the Japanese evacuated, taking into consideration debts he owes in the Protected area, and such property will not be disposed of at a sacrifice to pay such debts.
>
> We feel that it is in the interest of those evacuated to place their property under the Custodian's control, and if this is not done before leaving the Protected area, the Custodian cannot protect the property during the absence of any person evacuated.[15]

---

[15]*NC*, 6 April 1942.

Muriel and Ed Kitagawa managed to rent their home before leaving for Toronto, only to be told a year later that the Custodian had been given the power to sell it against their will. Muriel's family counted on this rent to support themselves in Toronto, and besides, they could not understand how owning a house could be a threat to military security. Their request for a change in policy was answered with a bland remark from the Custodian's office that policy was made in Ottawa and unalterable, so the Kitagawa house would be sold. Period. In response to this form-letter dismissal, Muriel unleashed her pent-up anger in a condemnation of a government that had so abused the rights of its citizens that its policies and actions were a complete mockery of all democratic principles held sacred in this country. In her letter to the Custodian, she spoke for many Japanese Canadians who were equally mistreated through unjust policies administered indifferently by government officials:

> Who would have thought that one day I would be unable to stand up for my country's government, out of sheer shame and disillusion, against the slurs of the scornful? The bitterness, the anguish is complete. You, who deal in lifeless figures, files, and statistics could never measure the depth of hurt and outrage dealt out to those of us who love this land. It is because we *are* Canadians, that we protest the violation of our birthright. If we were not we would not care one jot or tittle whatever you did, for then we could veil our eyes in contempt. You . . . and by "you" I designate all those in authority who have piled indignity upon indignity on us . . . have sought to sully and strain our loyalty but, I'm telling you, you can't do it. You can't undermine our faith in the principles of equal rights and justice for all, with "malice towards none, and charity for all."[16]

When the Kitagawas boarded the train for Toronto on June 1, the forced removal of Japanese Canadians was in full swing. Within a few more months, the B.C. Security Commission would have fulfilled its mandate (Fig. 6). By October 1942, some 12,000 Japanese Canadians were incarcerated in B.C. detention camps and ghost towns.

---

[16]"A Series of Three Letters on the Property Issue," in La Violette, *The Canadian Japanese and World War II*, pp. 303-304.

FINAL EVACUATION REGISTRATION
Of All Persons Of Japanese Origin

TAKE NOTICE that all persons of the Japanese race remaining in Greater Vancouver, including Burnaby, B. C., must report to the British Columbia Security Commission Representative at 314 Powell Street, Vancouver, B. C., between now and October 15th at 10 a.m. for the purpose of completing evacuation papers.

THIS IS THE FINAL EVACUATION REGIS-TRATION TO COMPLETE THE SHIPMENT OF ALL JAPANESE FROM THIS AREA.

TAKE NOTICE that 10 a.m. on Thursday, October 15th, 1942, is the FINAL DATE FOR REGISTRATION and anyone failing to register by that time will be liable to prosecution under P. C. 1665.

BRITISH COLUMBIA SECURITY COMMISSION
AUSTIN C. TAYLOR
Chairman.

Vancouver, B. C.
9th October, 1942.

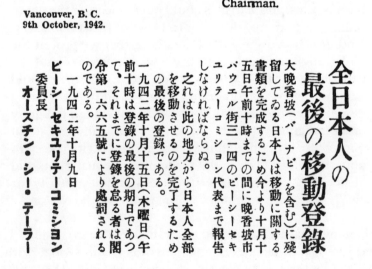

全日本人の
最後の移動登録

大晩香坡（バーナビーを含む）に殘留してゐる日本人は移動に關する書類を完成するため今より十月十五日午前十時までの間に晩香坡市バウエル街三一四のビーシーセキユリテーコミシヨン代表まで報告しなければならぬ。

之れは此の地方から日本人全部を移動させるのを完了するための最後の登録である。

一九四二年十月十五日（木曜日）午前十時は登録の最後の期日であつて、それまでに登録を怠る者は閣令第一六五號により處罰されるのである。

一九四二年十月九日
ビーシーセキユリテーコミシヨン
委員長
オースチン・シー・テーラー

Figure 6: A notice appearing in the *New Canadian* on 10 October 1942.

Another 4000 had been shipped to sugar beet farms in Alberta and Manitoba. 1000 men were still detained in road camps on the B.C./Alberta border and 700 were behind barbed-wire in prisoner-of-war camps in Ontario. Including those in self-supporting sites and those living on special permits, in all, some 21,000 individuals of Japanese ancestry had been uprooted.

Stripped of rights, uprooted, branded "enemy aliens" and potential saboteurs, Nisei like Muriel Kitagawa found their faith severely strained. Their one touchstone, their Canadian citizenship, had become meaningless. The dream of the franchise, the prime motivating force in their lives during the 1930s, was ending in a frightening dead-end. The thoughtless rejection by the Custodian of Enemy Alien Property of Muriel's plea for sympathy and fairness was a final humiliation, though even here the loyalty to democracy defied a temptation to despair. "You can't undermine our faith in the principles of equal rights and justice for all . . .," Muriel answered the Custodian. Her faith lay in her *native* land against the arbitrary actions of the bureaucrats who were attempting to erase her birthright and identity.

For Muriel Kitagawa, the writer, the journey to Toronto prompted her to think and write about her Nisei past. The abrogation of her rights in 1942 was infuriating, but the disappointment in her country struck much deeper. All the hopes and aspirations of her generation, all the struggles they had waged to break down the discriminatory barriers excluding them from full participation in the life of their society—these appeared to be lost in the maelstrom caused by the very forces of racism they had been trying to eradicate. Her Nisei generation had endured a whole spectrum of social, political and legal restrictions because of their ancestry. Now, with the uprooting, they were thrown into another crisis, even more trying. "This is the time," Muriel wrote in "A Record of Dignity," "to tighten our belts, to gird our courage, to condition ourselves to every kind of privation and endure . . . endure . . . and still endure."[17]

---

[17]*NC*, 5 March 1942: p. 2.

II. The Life

Tsukiye Muriel Kitagawa was born in Vancouver on April 3, 1912, the first child of Tsuru (maiden name Toyofuku) and Asajiro Fujiwara, who were living at the time on Triumph Street.

Her father, Asajiro Fujiwara, born in Fukuoka in 1884, had come to Canada at the age of fourteen with his widowed mother Sano Fujiwara, landing in Victoria in 1898. Six years later, in 1904, Sano was to meet and marry Kisuke Mikuni, one of the early Japanese pioneers who had garnered a small fortune by securing the CNR contract for rocks to build the pier in Vancouver Harbour. That same year, she temporarily returned to Japan with her son Asajiro, coming back to Canada on her husband's death in May 1909.

While in Japan, Asajiro was to meet Tsuru Toyofuku in Kurume, the town of her birth, on the island of Kyushu. Tsuru was a high-spirited young girl whose restless temperament would be passed on to her first child, Muriel. At the age of twelve, betrothed to an adopted son of a relative, she found herself much more interested in sports, especially tennis, than in refining herself in the conventional "feminine" patterns of dress and behaviour. When pressured by her adopted mother to get painted and dressed up to be shown off as a prospective bride, Tsuru rebelled and succeeded in convincing her mother Sue Sada to cancel the arranged marriage. The foreign land of Canada, far from her family ties, appealed to her pioneering spirit and instantly attracted her to Asajiro Fujiwara when he came to visit, looking so different in his "western" suit. They were soon engaged, and a few months later, in September 1907, Asajiro brought her back to Canada.[18]

Muriel was the first of five children. Two years after her birth, Tetsumori Douglas was born, followed the next year by Kiyoe Kathleen. The young Fujiwara family restlessly shifted from place to place as Asajiro tried in a variety of ways, all of them unsuccessful, to secure a steady source of income.[19] By the time Muriel was six, they had moved to Sidney on Vancouver Island where, as she says in a private autobiographical sketch, her father was employed in a mill while her mother earned what she could as a dressmaker. Her

---

[18]Information on Tsuru Toyofuku Fujiwara's background was taken from notes written by Muriel in the private manuscript collection of Dr. Wesley Fujiwara; further details were provided by Kay Fujiwara Sano.

[19]Interview, Kay Fujiwara Sano.

second brother Mitsumori Wesley was born there in 1919. Muriel remembered that time as one in which her family "lived in a small village facing the sea":

> We were so poor then, it did not seem possible to become any poorer and still retain our self-respect and independence. We managed somehow, thanks to Mother's thrift.
> We lived behind a shop upon the Main Street, right next door to a general store on one side, the weekly *Times* on the other. During the day I could hear the merry ringing of the cash register, and the funny thumping sound from the other side which did job printing as well as publish a paper.[20]

The Fujiwaras lived in Sidney for only a year, and then moved to New Westminster where Muriel, in her blossoming consciousness, first sensed the acrimony of racial discrimination. She was seven or eight when she first became aware of the "two Worlds . . . separate, irreconcilable . . . the world of the Japanese, the world of the Hakujin (the whites)." Wandering the streets of this riverside town, she came face to face with her own invisibility as an individual, feeling that she existed merely "as a specimen of the yellow peril. It awed me, and I resented it. But what could I do about it? There just wasn't a thing I could do then. I lived in the orbit of the small Japanese community, and knew no other after school life." She had no problem getting along with other children in school, but outside of school her fellow students "took it for granted that parties were not for one of my colour . . . not with them anyway."[21]

In 1922, family problems led to a temporary separation of Muriel's parents. With the threat of severe economic hardship hanging over her, Muriel's mother was forced to work as a live-in housekeeper in Vancouver, while three of her children, Muriel, Kathleen, and Wesley, were sent to Victoria to the Oriental Home, a home for Asian children who were either homeless or whose parents were not financially able to care for them. The three were to remain in Victoria for a year, and then were to live separately for another year in the

---

[20]Unpublished Autobiography in the private manuscript collection of Dr. Wesley Fujiwara.
[21]Unpublished Autobiography.

various homes of friends. The whole family reunited in 1924 when Muriel's father decided to study dentistry. Arranging for financial assistance from his mother Sano, Muriel's father enrolled in North Pacific College in Oregon.

The following five years were to be years of considerable poverty for Tsuru and her four children. They moved back to New Westminster to live in a rickety wooden house on Ewen Street on Lulu Island—a large building housing a number of Japanese Canadians. Ed Ouchi, who would later become one of Muriel's friends in the Nisei community, lived there and attended the Duke of Connaught High School with Muriel. Those were the years when Tsuru earned a living by making gloves at home, the image etched in Muriel's memory "of my mother bending over her sewing machine, the needle whirring over the cotton work-gloves she made to sell that we might eat."[22]

At high school, outside the close-knit enclosure of her home life, Muriel was an enthusiastic learner and an excellent student, especially in languages, English and history. Her delight in these subjects, she recalled,

> used to astonish the teachers, and I could not understand why it should. I just naturally liked those subjects the best, just as other students liked the Sciences better. By the time I got to my third year my marks in English were higher than the others in my class, and the Principal even carried around my exam paper to show to other teachers that a little Jap girl took the best marks . . . in English, mind you! Of course I was proud of my good marks, but I still didn't see why they should be so surprised. I liked the subject![23]

In fact, English literature had become, in those formative years, much more than a "school subject" for Muriel. It was during a literature class that she first experienced a language that suddenly, consciously, gave voice to her love for her country. This moment of revelation, recalled again and again in later years, was sparked by three lines of Sir Walter Scott's poem, "The Lay of the Last Minstrel," that the class had been asked to memorize:

---

[22]"Looking Back," from the Unpublished Autobiography.
[23]Unpublished Autobiography.

Breathes there the man with soul so dead,
Who never to himself hath said:
"This is my own, my native land!"

This experience had been the key, the beginning, which was to give an articulate shape to Muriel's life for the next three decades. Her English teacher, Mr. Lock, was one of those rare individuals who both understood and encouraged her literary instincts, and her emerging talent as a writer.

Muriel came second in the competition for the Governor-General's Award when she graduated from high school in 1929. That same year her father returned from Oregon with his dentist's degree. Her third brother, Alan Nobumori, the fifth and last child in the family, would be born a year later.

Despite her isolation, and a growing sense of separation from her Caucasian friends throughout her school years, Muriel refused to give in to self-pity and a threatening despair. In the 1930s, she finally met others who also consciously inhabited the divided world of the Canadian-born Nisei. They too had been educated to believe in a Canadian democracy, yet they were also painfully aware that this same democracy excluded them, both tacitly and formally, on the basis of their ancestry.

•

After graduation in 1929 from the Duke of Connaught High School, Muriel attended the University of British Columbia, withdrawing for economic reasons a year later. But there and in Vancouver where she settled, she met many like-minded Nisei who saw the need for some kind of united action. Here they were, in B.C., disenfranchised provincially and federally because they, of Asian ancestry, were legally excluded from the provincial voters' list. That restriction, in turn, led to numerous other exclusions. As Japanese Canadians they could not become pharmacists, chartered accountants, and lawyers. Nor could they work for the government or hold public office. Even in instances when they were not kept out of a profession, engineering for example, the racist climate of their society made it extremely difficult, if not impossible, to find employment at any professional level. In the early 1930s, they were growing restless within these restrictions and wanted the freedom to enter the mainstream of

Canadian life as full-fledged citizens with the right to vote and the right to work in the profession of their choice. And they talked endlessly about means by which they could instigate this liberating process and so solve the Nisei "mondai" (problem).

One study carried out in Muriel's community at this time provides an insight into the growing pains experienced by Nisei who were educated in Canadian schools to think *as Canadians*, but who found themselves wedged between two worlds: that of their Issei parents nurtured in Japanese ways, and the Caucasian world in which they themselves had been educated, but where racist attitudes were accepted. Rigenda Sumida, a Japan-born student at the University of British Columbia, had undertaken an ambitious Master of Arts thesis in Economics. His study, *The Japanese in British Columbia*, attempted to record as meticulously as possible the history and the views of his community, from its beginnings in Canada to the present. In the second part of his study, Sumida turned to the situation of the Canadian-born generation, the Nisei, who were just coming of age.[24] Based on extensive surveys, interviews, and lengthy discussions with Nisei—Sumida thanks Muriel for helping organize such talk sessions—he concluded that racial discrimination and its effects constituted the most powerful force with which the Nisei generation had to contend.[25]

Of course, the exclusions resulting from these discriminatory policies and attitudes equally affected the Issei parents of the Nisei, but they were immigrants who, for the most part, accepted these conditions as a fact of their new life in Canada. Their native-born children, however, were educated in Canadian schools and trained to value and believe in democratic principles: the rights of citizenship,

---

[24]In 1931, as Sumida points out, using a 1934 report of the Japanese Consulate in Vancouver, there were 11,081 Nisei, of which only 1158, or approximately 12%, were over 20 years of age. Some 3000 had not begun school yet; 4000 were in public school; and 500 were in high school (Rigenda Sumida, *The Japanese in Canada*, Unpublished M.A. Thesis, University of British Columbia, 1935, pp. 418-421).

[25]Roy Ito in *We Went to War* (Stittsville, Ontario: Canada's Wings, 1984) discusses Sumida and his study (pp. 81ff). Tom Shoyama, employed to assist Sumida, moved into the rooming house on Powell Street owned by Rigenda and his brother Hyosaku. As Ito explains: "It was Shoyama's responsibility to improve the English, draw the charts, and assist with the interpretation of the mass of data gathered by Sumida and members of the Japanese Students Club at the university" (p. 85). In gathering data for his massive study, Sumida had 2106 Nisei interviewed and surveyed through volunteers.

and equality for all regardless of ancestry. In fact, as Sumida discovered, the Nisei ignorance of their parents' Japanese past, and their "westernized" perceptions, created a conflict between the generations. "In my opinion . . .," one Issei parent was quoted as saying, "the Second Generation have no manners and are very conceited. They think they know everything so they try to run the house. Maybe this talk about equality, liberty, freedom has made them lose all respect for their elders, humbleness, and a sense of obedience. In any case, they are a lot different from the Japan-born and educcated."[26] On the other hand, from *their* perspective, one shaped by their education and their day-to-day contact with the Canadian way of life, the Nisei children of the Issei began to think of their immigrant parents as old-fashioned, close-minded, and too Japanese in their attitudes, and they concluded that these patterns of behaviour on the part of their parents were inhibiting their own assimilation into the mainstream of Canadian society.

It was here, out of this difference in perspective, that a psychological dilemma grew to become a dominant concern—at times even an obsession—in the Nisei generation coming of age in the 1930s. They were conscious of being straddled between two opposing worlds, equally imposing: nurtured in the "eastern" values of their immigrant parents, yet pressured by their social environment to adopt "western" modes of thought and action; unable by birth to identify with the past of their parents, yet equally unable, because of racial discrimination, to identify with their native land. No wonder many Nisei concluded that they were trapped by their historical circumstances. As Sumida explained:

> At present, while they are faced with the normal problems
> of adolescence, they are also caught between cross-fixes:
> they are criticised by the First Generation for displaying
> mental characteristics of the Canadian people; they are sub-
> ject to attack from the White people because they retain
> physical characteristics of their parents. Some of the First
> Generation urge them to definitely abandon the Japanese
> culture in order that they may assimilate more fully; some
> of the White people advise them to retain much of the
> Japanese culture and mental characteristics in order that

---

[26]Sumida, p. 426.

25

they might contribute them to Canada. Little wonder that they are in a constant state of bewilderment, unable to decide which course to follow.[27]

What, then, was to be the solution to this problem?

The idealism of young Nisei like Muriel first achieved a focus in the Young People's Society (YPS) of the United Church. In this society, individuals like Ed Ouchi, Dr. Edward Banno, and Hide Hyodo Shimizu could see their generation as a bridge between the culture of their parents and that of their native land, and they wanted to be recognized as full-fledged Canadians with all the rights of citizenship. In his brief editorial to the society's journal, *Young People*, Ed Ouchi spoke of the Nisei as "pioneers," in the sense that they are the "transitional stage between our parents, who are purely Japanese in traditional culture, and the next generation after us, who will be in all things Canadians."[28] Soon, communication through the written word became an important vehicle with which to educate both the Nisei community and other Canadians. In 1932, Muriel would begin to contribute to this emerging public discourse by enthusiastically throwing her support behind the monthly publication *The New Age*, with Hozumi Yonemura as editor, the first newspaper to advance the Nisei perspective and to provide an outlet for their expressive thought and literary writing (Fig. 7). "This journal," the first editorial stated, "starts its humble career with the two-fold object of serving the best interests of the second generation Japanese in Canada and of serving the Canadian public by making it accessible for them to understand the emotions, thoughts and ideals of the Canadian-born Japanese."[29]

The founding of *The New Age* in 1932 coincided with the formation of the first Japanese Canadian Citizens' Association (JCCA) in the same year. The second issue of the paper in April 1932, printed the Constitution of this fledgling organization and listed its first Directors: Dr. H.S. Saita, President; Dr. M. Uchida, First Vice-President; and Miss M. Tamura, Second Vice-President. Eizaburo (Ed) Kitagawa, soon to become Muriel's husband, was listed as Treasurer, and Muriel (as Miss Fujiwara) was a member of the Fellowship Committee. By

---

[27]Sumida, p. 427.

[28]E.T. Ouchi, "Canada," *The Young People*, vol. 2, No. 2 (May 1931): p. 2.

[29]*The New Age*, 12 March 1932; copies of this newspaper were provided by Ed Kitagawa from his personal archive.

THE NEW AGE

Vol I. No. 1   Published Twice Every Month   Vancouver, B. C.   March 12, 1932.   Price Per Year in advance $2.00

MESSAGE TO CANADIAN-BORN JAPANESE

By H. F. ANGUS, M.A., B.C.L.,
Head of the Department of Economics and Sociology, The University of B. C.

PROF. H. F. ANGUS

...under our flags, which are all the same, we have a common nationality, for we are all Canadians and expect that our descendants will be Canadians. What matters most is not mere nationality, which can be adopted or rejected very easily, but the devotion to our country which underlies our nationality and gives it a meaning—the fact that we are proud of our Canadian nationality and attached to it. Nationality and those sentiments which accompany it should outweigh difference of race.

SECOND GENERATION RALLY

Prof. E. Odlum to Speak—Music by Local Artists

The first rally of the second generation Japanese in Vancouver and vicinity will be held in the Japanese Hall, 475 Alexander Street, on Sunday, the 13th, at 2 p.m. The object of this rally is to form an association composed of younger generation of Japanese in British Columbia. All persons born or educated here are urged to attend.

As the principal speaker of the day, Prof. Edward Odlum will speak on the second generation problem. Prof. Odlum, who has been a resident of Japan for a number of years, is a well known author and lecturer.

Such well known artists as Miss A. Saita, Geo. Nakashima, Peter Masuda, S. Nakamura and Y. Katsuyama and several others will lend their talents to the entertainment.

The final item in the programme is the adoption of the constitution and the signing up of members. The older generation are also invited to attend as guests. Dr. H. S. Saita will be the chairman of the meeting.

PRAISES JAPANESE SPORTSMANSHIP

Reg. Woodward Gives His Impressions of Japan to the Holly Club

"We encountered in Japan the highest standard of sportsmanship which we had ever seen," said Reg. Woodward, secretary of the Dominion Rugby Union, in speaking to the members of the Holly Club at the Japanese Anglican Mission, Third Avenue, last Friday evening.

Mr. Woodward, who is a deputy harbour master of this city, accompanied, in the capacity of a manager, the Canadian rugby team that recently visited Japan. He declared that Japanese players committed not a single act contrary to the best traditions...

GREETINGS FROM CONSUL HACHIYA

HON. T. HACHIYA

My congratulations to the publisher of "The New Age"! The initial publication of this journal is a very happy event, as it promises a wealth of interest to those who have been following, or wish to follow... ...their lack of knowledge of the Japanese language have hitherto found themselves seriously handicapped in that they have not been able to read the newspapers published in that language.

It seems almost superfluous to reiterate here what has so often been said, that true understanding of peoples is the most essential factor in the promotion of goodwill amongst the nations concerned, but when we realize that such understanding can be...

Figure 7: Front page of the first issue of *The New Age*, 12 March 1932, the first English language Japanese Canadian newspaper.

issue three in June 1932, Muriel T. Fujiwara was named on the masthead as Senior Editor, and her brief editorial note called on "all young Japanese Canadians" to co-operate with the newly formed JCCA. In issue seven in December 1932, she published two prose poems, "A Fantasy on Snow" and "The Cathedral in the Air," over the name "Dana," a *nom de plume* she would later reserve for her poems in the future newspaper *The New Canadian*.

The New Age folded after a year, a disappointment for a budding writer, but Muriel's young life by then was assuming a shape of its own. That same year she was to marry Ed Kitagawa, the hero of the dazzling Asahi baseball team.[30] With a highly respected job in charge of the Japanese section at the Bank of Montreal, Ed was one of the most eligible bachelors in the community. Their wedding on May 20, 1933 at the Japanese United Church, with the Rev. Y. Akagawa officiating, was described in the Bank's newsletter:

> Dr. H.M. Nomura of Vancouver acted as "Go-between" or "Matchmaker". The church was beautifully decorated for the occasion and some two hundred guests were present at the ceremony, including the Manager and Staff of Main and Hastings Streets Branch. Later a reception was held in the church school room at which brief speeches were made in English and Japanese.[31]

In 1933, Muriel was twenty-one years old, an adult Nisei who had weathered the stormy years of her childhood and who could now look forward to the stability and security of marriage. But those early years still lingered in her memory—and would surface again in her later writing.

•

---

[30]Of this team, which started in 1912, Toyo Takata in *Nikkei Legacy* (Toronto: NC Press, 1983) writes: "Their daredevil brand of baseball made the Asahis the most popular team on the B.C. Lower Mainland, with a legion of non-Japanese fans" (p. 45). Ed Kitagawa played for the Asahis from 1917 to 1931, during which he was captain from 1925 to 1929 and manager during the 1930-31 season. He retired in 1932, the year before he married Muriel.

---

[31]*Staff Magazine*, Bank of Montreal, vol. 5, No. 4 (August 1933): p. 28; provided by Ed Kitagawa.

It was four years after the formation of the Japanese Canadian Citizens' Association (JCCA) that a group of Nisei got together for a more ambitious undertaking: an organization to represent the whole Nisei generation throughout the province. The year was 1936, and the association was called the Japanese Canadian Citizens' League (JCCL). The minutes of the first meeting on February 13, at the Seiko Club in Vancouver, record that the JCCA was dissolved with the following motion: "As a result of the Survey of Japanese Canadians in British Columbia, 1935, need was felt of a federation of all these Second Generation to promote their citizenship and good will between them and other Canadians."[32] Harry Naganobu was elected President, First Vice-President was Dr. Edward Banno, and Second Vice-President was Bert Murakami.

The first order of business for the JCCL was a request from MP Angus MacInnis of the CCF, a friend and supporter of Japanese Canadians, who wanted them to argue their case for franchise to a Special Elections and Franchise Committee in Ottawa. The proposal stirred up considerable opposition and even the threat of violence from the more reactionary elements in the community—specifically from those Issei behind Etsuji Morii, owner of a gambling establishment, the Showa Club, and head of a corps of judo experts. Ed Ouchi, Secretary for the JCCL at the time, was challenged by a Morii supporter at a meeting: "Are you going to send your delegates even if you see bloodshed?" "Those were strong words," he recalled, but his answer had been simple: "Yes, we'll send the delegates no matter what happens." Clearly, the JCCL was determined to get to Ottawa, threats or no threats.[33] Muriel, young as she was, could hardly believe the uproar. "There was an exciting aura of daring in this venture," she recalled. "The rumour went so far as to hint that a gangster was coming up from San Francisco to prevent the delegation from going to Ottawa."[34] The opponents of the delegation argued that such a move would instigate antagonism from the Caucasian community. The JCCL, on the other hand, argued that Japanese Canadians had a responsibility to make their government aware of their right to the franchise as citizens. A number of heated public meetings occurred,

---

[32] Public Archives of Canada (PAC), Japanese Canadian Citizens' Association Papers, MG28 V7, vol. 1, file 1-1, *Minutes*, Japanese Canadian Citizens' League (JCCL).

[33] Interview, Ed Ouchi; for a detailed account of the delegation, see Adachi, pp. 160ff.

[34] Unpublished Autobiography.

but eventually the community came forward with the necessary financial support and the delegation boarded the train for the trek across the country to Ottawa.

Miss Hide Hyodo, a teacher in Richmond (the only Nisei teacher in B.C.) was chosen, along with Minoru Kobayashi from Steveston, Dr. Edward Banno, a prominent Nisei dentist in Vancouver, and Dr. S.I. Hayakawa, a specialist in semantics and a Professor of English at Madison, Wisconsin, and a former native of Vancouver. Dr. Hayakawa was the designated leader of the delegation. Although they created quite a stir in Ottawa—officials were amazed at their command of the English language, thinking they would need translators!—the longed-for franchise did not miraculously come about because of their historic effort. Nevertheless, the fact that the community had at least presented its case to the government formally, and had presented it effectively, showed that the Nisei generation was finally coming of age. It would only be a matter of time before they would win the franchise. More work now had to be done to educate their fellow citizens, to make them realize that racial discrimination was incompatible with democratic principles.

"The delegation to Ottawa climaxed our early efforts towards getting the franchise in B.C.," Muriel noted. The event was an exciting beginning, and for her own part she privately envisioned the responsibility that was on the shoulders of older Nisei like herself to organize the young people in her community. She wanted to develop in them

> the meaning of what constituted good Canadian citizenship, and what the Japanese Canadian youth must do to help their older brothers and sisters in the pioneering for full franchise rights so that they in turn could help their younger brothers and sisters, or their nephews and nieces, to enjoy to the full equal citizenship with the rest of Canada.

In this context, she also thought seriously of the role of young Nisei women; they "should be given a fuller understanding of their duties as the future mothers of new Canadian citizens, so that they can foster such homes as are compatible with our ideal Canadian home which combines in harmony the conveniences and good manners of the west with the respect for the older folk and the family

30

interdependencies of the east, the freedom of the west with the consideration of the east."[35]

Out of this new optimism—this new-found sense that Japanese Canadians had finally begun to work in a formal way toward achieving the democratic goal of full franchise for their community—came, in 1938, the genesis of the *New Canadian*, the Nisei publication calling itself the "Voice of the Nisei" (Fig. 8). A bona fide newspaper, published semi-monthly and distributed widely in the community— and in English—was a tremendously exciting venture for young writers like Muriel. What better way for Nisei to further the struggle for equality than to have a public vehicle to present their views and to nurture their own writers. The experiment began with a trial issue, printed as a supplement to the *Tairiku*, a Japanese-language newspaper in the community. The *New Canadian* was deemed a success and regular publication began in February 1939. The nucleus of the founding group consisted of Shinobu Higashi as Editor (who left to work for a newspaper in China soon after), Tom Shoyama, Ed Ouchi, Irene Uchida, Yoshimitsu Higashi, and Seiji Onizuka.

The *New Canadian* allowed Muriel to begin writing in earnest. Throughout 1939 and 1940, it was this community newspaper that provided her with an outlet for numerous essays on topics and issues of personal concern. Readers became familiar with the lively voice of "T.M.K." who had strong, and usually unconventional, views on everything from arranged marriages to the liberation of Nisei women. "T.M.K." represented the voice of a new community struggling to break away from older immigrant values transported from Japan and transplanted in Canada. But the growth of this new community was to be stunted: "While their sons and daughters became westernized and talked a different language," Muriel wrote in Toronto, thinking back to *those days*,

> the Issei kept the reins over matters of marriage and birth
> and death, of filial piety, and submergence of the individual
> into the pattern of the family. Out of this grew the seeds
> of Nisei revolt, until war came to tear out the roots of our
> lives, and we were washed down helter skelter on the roaring flood.[36]

---

[35]All quotes from the Unpublished Autobiography.
[36]"Growing Up as Nisei," from the Unpublished Autobiography.

Voice of
the Nisei

THE NEW CANADIAN

Review of
Nisei Doings

Vol. 1 No. 1   ****   Vancouver, British Columbia, Thursday, November 24, 1938   ****   Special Issue

Second Generation Employment Is Theme Of Annual National Confab

"There is a need for dispersion eastward, and above all, for individual enterprise and initiative, for stout hearts and loving ones, too" —these words spoken by Thomas Shoyama, main speaker, struck the note pervading the general session of the Third Annual Convention of the Japanese Canadian Citizens' League, held at the Nippon Club last Sunday afternoon with Sam Okamoto in the chair.

Some hundred odd Japanese Canadians crowded into the session chamber to discuss the grave problem of employment facing the Nisei of today in Canada.

"Nisei Employment," Thomas Shoyama offered a brief outline of the position of the second generation in the economic life of Canada. He dwelt on the increasing volume of anti-Japanese agitation and the effect of the discriminations on the average Japanese youth.

Dr. E. C. Banno, popular Nisei dentist, then outlined the future of the Japanese in the various professions. "It is hard for a Canadian to enter into a profession. It is much harder for a second generation. He must therefore, possess a greater degree of those characteristic essential for success in any other line."

No Nisei Lawyers

The Nisei, he pointed out, is not able to become a lawyer, a pharmacist or a chartered accountant because of his race. These discriminations arose out of a fear that Nisei practitioners would monopolize the whole Japanese clientele. "There are many doctors and dentists among the Canadian population who have a great number of Japanese coming to them," he said.

After a brief discussion, Mr. Kabu, secretary of the Canadian Japanese Association of Steveston, stated that the second generation, outside of those with fishing and licenses, could not look forward to finding a means of living in the fishing industry. The only unrestricted line was the catching of greyfish, which is made into fertilizer.

Harry Naganobu gave a picture of farming conditions in B. C. He pointed out that agriculture in the days of our

— Photo by Cakuyku Studies.

THOMAS K. SHOYAMA

who spoke to the general session on the topic, "General Survey of the Nisei Employment Problem."

Gakuyukai Boasts Largest Number

The Gakuyukai, established in 1916, claims the honor of being the oldest and larg

Editorial

Again the daily press breaks out with write-ups regarding Alderman Wilson's efforts to effect an amendment to Vancouver's special municipal charter. Alderman Wilson aims through this amendment at the exclusion of Japanese from certain trades, and their limitation in others.

His drive is against the Oriental. Yet he fails to see the complex character of this group. The Japanese national is here in Canada, under the stipulations of a "most favored nation's" treaty, signed between Japan and Great Britain in 1911, and ratified by Canada in 1913, giving to him the right to settle and pursue a livelihood without hinderance.

The Japanese some 7,000 in number, are under the protection of the Japanese government. Once the amendment is passed, they can appeal to the representatives of the Japanese government, and can win ultimate exemption from its restrictions, on the ground that the legislation is ultra vires.

But the position of the second generation and naturalized Japanese is radically different. As nationals of this country they have no body to which they can appeal for redress of grievances. The situation is indeed ironical. British subjects are less privileged than the nationals of a foreign country in a British Dominion.

Alderman Wilson is obviously not aware of all these implications. Neither does he realize that the present number of Orientals in the petty business is the result of migration from other restricted occupations. As long as he is hitting at the Orientals he is satisfied.

The question arises, what does he intend to do with the children resulting from marriages between Orientals and Europeans? Every year, according to the returns of the Federal Department of Vital Statistics, there are approximately 50 annual births from mixed marriages. Is he going to class these people as Orientals or as Europeans?

Every thinking individual should realize the grave consequences that might arise from the 'muddling through' policies of such irresponsible men.—S. H.

Naganobu New President

The National Council of the Japanese Canadian Citizens' League, composed of the National executive and delegates of the various chapters throughout the province, met Sunday morning at Nippon Club to deliberate on the past year's activities and to formulate the policies of the organization for the coming year, under the chairmanship of Harry Naganobu.

due to a large surplus for the preceding year and that there was an actual deficit of $150. In spite of the difficult cancel by the creation of the Alberta charter, the National Council passed a budget of $500 for the coming year.

E. Yamaoka was elected Chairman of the Legal Research Committee and was empowered to study the various suggested

Shinobu Higashi Adjudged Winner Of First J.C.C.L. Oratorical Meet

By KAZUMA UYENO

"We award the cup to Mr. Higashi." These words pronounced by Professor J. Friend Day, marked the climax of the first oratorical contest in English held last Saturday evening by the Japanese Canadian Citizens' League for the second-generation Japanese Canadians.

The chairman for the evening, E. Nobuichi Yamaoka, opened the meeting with a few words of appreciation to Dr. N. F. Black, advisor to the contest committee; to Honorable H. Nemichi, E. Kagetsu, and Y. Kawata, the donors of championship cups, and to the judges, Dr. Black, Professor Day and Spencer Baynes of the Y.M.C.A.

M. Kabu, then outlined the aims of the newly inaugurated contest: To train capable vindicators of the second generation position and to arouse interest in the problems of the nisei. Mr. Kabu expressed a hope that with the enthusiastic support of the public this affair might continue and become the "major annual event of the younger generation."

Shinobu Higashi, first speaker, spoke on "The Great Adventure." Sam Okamoto of Victoria, followed with an address on "Youth and Education." "The Problems and Duties of the Second Generation" was the topic of the third speaker, S. E. Yoshida of Chemainus. He countered and elaborated the three-fold problem and the two-fold duty of the Nisei.

Lily Washimoto Stars

After a musical intermission, during which Lily Washimoto, accompanied at the piano by Phyllis Dilworth, entertained the audience with two delightful songs, North Fujita of Vancouver, continued the contest with her talk on "Are You An Encourage?"

The last speaker of the evening, T. Yomeda of Victoria, outlined the "Essentials of Citizenship." Laboring under the disturbing "choo-chooing" of a locomotive moving back and forth on the railway yards behind the Japanese Hall, Tarry Yoneda described the four requirements of citizenship which must be fulfilled before the Nisei's 'inherent longing to be called a citizen' can be satisfied.

— Courtesy Uhytzer

SHINOBU F. HIGASHI

who spoke on the subject, "A Great Adventure" at the J.C.C.L. National Oratorical Contest.

Niseis Make Name In Musical World

In no other field have the second generation covered themselves with more laurels than that of music. It has often been said that the Japanese excel

III. The Times

The World War II story of the incarceration of innocent Canadians whose only crime was their Japanese ancestry has been well-told by historians of the subject. The first book-length account, *The Japanese Canadian and World War II*, by sociologist Forrest E. La Violette was published in 1948. The official history of Japanese Canadians, *The Enemy That Never Was* by Ken Adachi, was published in 1976. Adachi focused his attention on the wartime injustices. Soon after the publication of his book, Ann Sunahara completed her investigations into the wartime incarceration through the government's own documents, which had finally been opened to the public after a thirty-year ban on access. The results of her research, published in 1981 in *The Politics of Racism*, substantiated what Japanese Canadians had known all along through personal experience. "The documents," Sunahara announced, "demonstrate that each order-in-council under the War Measures Act that affected Japanese Canadians—uprooting, confinement, dispossession, deportation and dispersal—was motivated by political considerations rooted in racist traditions accepted, and indeed encouraged by persons within the government of the day. The documents also show that at no point in the entire seven years of their exile were Japanese Canadians ever a threat to national security."[37] Other historians will no doubt approach this area of Canadian history from other perspectives, as Roy Ito has recently done in *We Went to War*, an account of the Japanese Canadian contribution to the Armed Forces of Canada in both World World I and World War II.

In contrast to those historical studies, the "Letters to Wes" and the other writings of Muriel Kitagawa included in this volume are unique and rare. They are dramatic, impassioned documents from the time in which the living words, the descriptions and statements, were set down—sometimes frantically—in the heat of the turmoil. The driving force of Muriel's thinking as a Japanese Canadian writer was her desire to keep the record straight: her community was an innocent group of individuals who became the victims of racist policies and actions.

The "Letters to Wes," the heart of *This is My Own*, were written in response to requests from Muriel's brother Wes, a medical student

---

[37]Sunahara, p. 3.

33

in Toronto, for exact and detailed reports on the events occurring in Vancouver. Confined to her home because of her pregnancy and the birth of her twins, Muriel's instinct as a writer prompted her to write more than comprehensive letters only to inform Wes—she also sought to record the personal and social impact of the uprooting for future reference. Her words come directly out of the events she lived, as she struggled for her family's survival throughout the ordeal.

As documents of the time, the letters reveal a two-fold drama. Muriel's personal crisis, on the one hand, is folded into the internal strife that flared up in her community, on the other, as the government's inflexible policies caused splits and dissensions. The factions that grew in the community in the spring of 1942 appear and disappear in the letters, as Muriel hears about the disturbances and tries to explain the Vancouver scene to Wes, though naturally her support always goes to her friends, Tom Shoyama and Kunio Shimizu, and their efforts. To understand this wider political context of the letters, some background material on the tensions in Muriel's community is necessary.

•

Soon after Order-in-Council P.C. 1486 was passed on February 24 to authorize the mass removal of Japanese Canadians, the newly established B.C. Security Commission appointed Etsuji Morii (the very same Etsuji Morii who had opposed and then threatened the 1936 delegation to Ottawa) as head of the Japanese Liaison Committee which was to represent the Japanese Canadian community. The appointment, recommended by the RCMP on the basis of previous dealings with Morii, was a serious misreading of the community's internal social structure. A letter by F.J. Mead, the RCMP representative on the B.C. Security Commission, demonstrates this error of judgment. As early as 1940 Mead trusted Morii's own explanation that he managed to control many organizations in his Japanese Canadian community because "he continuously adopts a neutral attitude where any differences of opinion between Japanese are the cause of trouble, and he has their confidence on this account."[38]

Mead failed to understand that Morii, though powerful and even

---

[38]PAC, Department of National Defence Papers, RG24, vol. 2730, file HQS-5199x, F.J. Mead, Assistant Commissioner, RCMP, to S.T. Wood, Commissioner, RCMP, 21 August 1940.

feared by some, was not respected in the community. He ran a gambling house on Powell Street, intimidated people through his judo associates, and was thought to be connected with the Black Dragon Society, a Japanese nationalist underworld organization. To many law-abiding Japanese Canadians, it seemed incredible that the government would appoint such an individual—in their eyes, a gangster—and ignore their legitimate representatives: business and church leaders, teachers, and others who were trusted by the community. Rightfully or not, Morii soon came to be viewed by Japanese Canadians as an RCMP informant who used his privileged position to further the power and status of his friends at the expense of the community's welfare. The Nisei especially saw Morii as anti-democratic, hence as anti-Canadian, hardly a suitable individual to negotiate with the government on their behalf. Muriel voiced a common attitude concerning Morii when she wrote to Wes, explaining: "When the evacuation first started, Morii (you know that racketeer, big boss on Powell?) was king pin. He and his henchmen virtually became dictators and were a law to the poor Japs" (March 30, 1942).

Formal opposition to Morii's position developed when members of the Japanese Canadian Citizens' League (JCCL) scheduled an emergency meeting on March 22 and requested Nisei organizations to send three delegates each. Representatives from fifty-one groups met, and elected a thirty-member Japanese Canadian Citizens' Council (JCCC) with the objective of co-operating with the B.C. Security Commission. The JCCC intended to provide assistance in social services such as education, health, and relief for the growing number of Japanese Canadians confined in Hastings Park. In this way they thought the Nisei could monitor and perhaps even influence government policy. Muriel was originally on the Council, but her home life prevented her from taking an active part. However, her friends, Tom Shoyama and Kunio Shimizu, the Secretary of the organization, worked at the centre.

Further criticism of Morii came from members of his own Issei generation. They formed the Naturalized Canadian Japanese Association (NCJA), also known as the Kikajin-kai, representing some thirty-eight community organizations, including the longstanding Canadian Japanese Association (CJA). Bunji Hisaoka, CJA President, became their leader. Like the JCCC, they were alarmed at Morii's influence with the RCMP and with the B.C. Security Commission.

The first joint venture of these two new groups (setting aside Issei and Nisei differences to work against a common foe) was a letter to the B.C. Security Commission objecting to Morii as a representative of their community. The letter also contained a plan of the NCJA for removing Japanese Canadians to a designated area, for instance, to crown land, where houses could be built for a self-contained and self-supporting community. The estimated cost was quoted at $1,884,009.[39]

This letter was submitted to the B.C. Security Commission on April 1, and the plan was immediately rejected because it was deemed too costly; moreover, Chairman Austin Taylor explained that no area available would allow Japanese Canadians to move in as a group. On April 4, the NCJA submitted a second plan, this one requesting that the estimated 5577 women, children under 16, elderly men and invalids, who had no place to go, be settled in the "ghost towns" first, before the men were asked to leave for the road camps. These men could then assist in reconstructing the towns. Along with this proposal was sent a statement that Morii's "past behaviour in committing numerous acts of violence make it impossible our accepting him as the acting guardian of our families during the period of separation, or his having any control or direction in the affairs and welfare of our families in any Japanese community."[40]

The second plan was also rejected, but at least Morii's power had begun to wane. On April 9, the B.C. Security Commission announced that no group would be considered "official," and that they would meet with other groups. Tom Shoyama, Kunio Shimizu, and Chitose Uchida were added to the Japanese Liaison Committee as Nisei representatives of the JCCC, so there now appeared to be sufficient checks on Morii's influence.

As this one crisis subsided, however, another division tore the community apart: Nisei men were increasingly resisting the breakup of families. The first stage of a refusal to obey the B.C. Security Commission on this issue had already been evident on March 25 when the first group of Nisei men were ordered to Schreiber, Ontario. Over 100 of them defied the orders; 86 were later caught at the Tairiku Hall in the Powell Street area, and 17 were rounded up in Vancouver. They were detained in the Immigration Building, and those who persisted in their refusal to obey were interned in prisoner-of-war camps

---

[39]PAC, Japanese Canadian Citizens' Association (JCCA) Papers, MG28 V7, vol. 1, file 1-2, Japanese Canadian Citizens' Council (JCCC), *Minutes*, 25 March 1942.
[40]*Minutes*, JCCC, 3 April 1942.

in Ontario at Petawawa and Angler. As the threat of mass defiance mounted, the JCCC actively supported a group of 103 Nisei who had agreed to go to Schreiber. A petition to the community, dated March 29 (Fig. 9), resolved that:

> The Japanese Canadian Citizens' Council commends the decision of the men as a service to the whole community, and earnestly urges that each member of the group carry out his pledge to report to the Hastings Park Clearing Station from 3:30 to 4:00 p.m., March 29.

The resolution also urged the community to "stand behind these men in carrying out this service and their pledged word."[41]

A serious split in the JCCC flared up at the beginning of April. Council members Fujikazu Tanaka and Robert Y. Shimoda began promoting resistance to the breakup of families, a move that undermined the JCCC's co-operative stance with the B.C. Security Commission. Tanaka and Shimoda were asked to resign, and this severance opened the way for a major division. By April 15, the newly-formed Nisei Mass Evacuation Group, spearheaded by Tanaka and Shimoda, issued an open letter to the B.C. Security Commission (Fig. 10) opposing the unnecessary separation of families. "As you clearly understand . . .," the petition read,

> we have said "YES" to all your previous orders however unreasonable they might have seemed. But, we are firm in saying "NO" to your last order which calls for break-up of our families.
> When we say "NO" at this point, we request you to remember that we are British subjects by birth, that we are no less loyal to Canada than any other Canadian, that we have done nothing to deserve the break-up of our families, that we are law abiding Canadian citizens, and that we are willing to accept suspension of our civil rights—rights to retain our homes and businesses, boats, cars, radios and cameras. Incidentally, we are entitled as native sons to all civil rights of an ordinary Canadian within the limitations of Canada's war effort. In spite of that we

---

[41]*Minutes*, JCCC, 29 March 1942.

37

March 29, 1942.

Dear Friend:

At a general meeting of the Japanese Canadian Citizens' Council held Sunday morning, the following resolution was adopted by the Council:

WHEREAS 103 Nisei have received assurances from the B. C. Security Commission that the welfare of their families will be safeguarded by the Commission;

AND WHEREAS these Nisei have solemnly pledged their word to the Commission that for the sake of the whole Japanese community they will proceed to Schreiber, Ontario.

therefore be it resolved that:

The Japanese Canadian Citizens' Council commends the decision of the men as a service to the whole community, and earnestly urges that each member of the group carry out his pledge to report to the Hastings Park Clearing Station from 3:30 to 4:00 p.m., March 29;

and further be it resolved that:

The Japanese Canadian Citizens' Council earnestly urges that the whole Japanese community stand behind these men in carrying out this service and their pledged word.

Yours Sincerely,

JAPANESE CANADIAN CITIZENS' COUNCIL

K. Shimizu

per Kunio Shimizu
(General Secretary)

Figure 9: The petition issued by the Japanese Canadian Citizens' Council to members of the community, urging them to support the Nisei who had agreed to leave for Schreiber, Ontario.

Austin C. Taylor, Esq., The Chairman,
B. C. Securities Commission,
Marine Building,
Vancouver, B. C.

Honourable Sir:

We Canadians have reached a point where we must stop and think deeply regarding our evacuation. For that purpose we have carefully reviewed the development of events which has brought us to this point where we are ordered to part with our families, perhaps never to meet them again for a long time to come. We enclose a summary of our above-mentioned review.

As you clearly understand and as it is fully mentioned in our review, we have said "YES" to all your previous orders however unreasonable they might have seemed. But, we are firm in saying "NO" to your last order which calls for break-up of our families.

When we say "NO" at this point, we request you to remember that we are British subjects by birth, that we are no less loyal to Canada than any other Canadian, that we have done nothing to deserve the break-up of our families, that we are law abiding Canadian citizens, and that we are willing to accept suspension of our civil rights - rights to retain our homes and businesses, boats, cars, radios and cameras. Incidentally, we are entitled as native sons to all civil rights of an ordinary Canadian within the limitations of Canada's war effort. In spite of that we have given up everything. In view of this sacrifice we feel that our request for mass evacuation in family groups will not seem unreasonable to you.

Please also remember that we are not refusing to go. Indeed if it is for our country's sake, we shall evacuate to whatever place Canada commands. Yes, it was in that spirit that we obeyed all your previous orders.

Another point which we request you to remember is that separation of our families would not contribute anything towards Canada's war effort, whereas a soldier's separation from his family does result in a definite contribution.

Considering the above facts, we think it totally unnecessary that our last remaining freedom should be taken from us - the freedom to live with our families. We were taught in our Canadian schools that we should always cherish freedom and do our utmost for the protection of women and children. We can now fully appreciate what they meant. We were also taught in our church that the unity of family is sacred and must be regarded as God-given human right and should be cherished as life itself.

We understand that it is the intention of the B. C. Securities Commission to avert all unnecessary hardship and ill-feeling in dealing with this problem, and we should like to bring to your attention the fact that by allowing us to be evacuated in family groups you would do this, and further, you would gain co-operation from us in carrying out your orders.

For these reasons we request your kindness in granting our humble request for the mass evacuation in family groups. We do so because we have confidence that British fair play and justice, even in war-time, will manifest itself and grant us our most human and reasonable request.

Respectfully yours,

NISEI MASS EVACUATION GROUP

Representatives:

Figure 10: An open letter to the B.C. Security Commission from the Nisei Mass Evacuation Group, opposing the breakup of families.

THE SURVEY OF DEVELOPMENT OF EVENTS RE EVACUATION OF CANADIANS OF JAPANESE ORIGIN

1. On December 7th, 1941, a most unfortunate international circumstance comes as a fact which was later to affect all persons of Japanese origin in B. C.

2. The government orders and public actions swiftly heightened to make it increasingly difficult for all persons of Japanese origin to maintain wartime normality of living: loss of business' and jobs, confiscation of boats, cars, radios and cameras, and imposition of curfew law. Ultimately circumstances threatened the family unity itself.

3. The government orders all male enemy aliens of military age to evacuate from the defense area by April 1st. On February 23rd, Morii persuaded the first group of Japanese nationals to evacuate to designated work camp, on pretext of sacrificing them for the future security of the Japanese race residing within the defense area without consulting them.

4. The government orders all able-bodied males of Japanese origin to evacuate to designated points and jobs.

5. At this point, the niseis hold a meeting of representatives from 52 over-lapping organizations, electing an emergency nisei council which was generally to cope with circumstances arising out of male evacuation. The method of election was thus: the chairman selected a nominating committee of five, which in turn nominated 30 members; finally the chairman recommended and the representatives agreed to accept the 30 nominees to-gether with the nominating committee, thus making a council of 35.

6. The J.C.C.Council tried to better the evacuating conditions of all males of the Japanese origin and also to prevent the ultimate separation of families but reported that to be inevitable. Therefore the general policy of co-operation with the authorities was adopted. On March 23rd, the first group of approximately 150, mostly 'teen-aged boys, received orders classifying them as "Enemy Aliens" to evacuate to designated destinations. At this point not all nationals and no naturalized Canadians had as yet been evacuated. The niseis refused to follow order under the classification of "Enemy Aliens", and moreover as British subjects they considered the removal order as void. However, after detention and various method of persuasion, the authorities were able to evacuate approximately 100 niseis.

7. A group supported by the nisei majority feeling that evacuation en masse, in family groups, was the last human right lawfully due to any one, intervened. After deliberation, the J.C.C.Council accepted their demand to again confer with the Securities Commission.

8. The J.C.C.Council endorsed a concrete plan worked out by the Naturalized Canadians and submitted to the Securities Commission for consideration. The basis of the plan was thus: a piece of land outside of the defense area, materials at the cost of $1,800,000., labour to be supplied by the evacuees.

9. The Securities Commission refused to accept the plan on the grounds that there is no land available. The J.C.C.Council and the Naturalized Canadians accordingly accepted the Commission's reply as final.

10. The second plan of mass evacuation of women and children to be followed by males to other designated points was put forth for consideration to the Commission by both groups. But the latter condition of this plan was rejected. The J.C.C.Council and the Naturalized Canadians accepted the revised plan. At the mass meeting on April 7th the combined groups publicly informed the audience that they would co-operate hereafter in adherence with the orders of the Commission. The meeting was predominated by a feeling of public refusal to comply with the revised plan. This attitude of the public climaxed in the detention of approximately 60 Canadians.

Figure 10 (continued)

have given up everything. In view of this sacrifice we feel that our request for mass evacuation in family groups will not seem unreasonable to you.[42]

As Nisei resistance continued to grow, some 140 went underground in Vancouver, while others openly demanded internment as a show of protest. Even the RCMP began to fear that outright defiance threatened to disrupt the removal plan of the B.C. Security Commission. In a letter dated April 9 to the RCMP Commissioner in Ottawa, C.H. Hill, Assistant Commissioner, expressed his concern about the growing number of Nisei who were refusing to comply with B.C. Security Commission orders. He advised "that unless some drastic action were taken in respect of these people the situation would deteriorate and, possibly, get completely out of hand."[43] The blame for the resistance began to shift to the JCCC, and despite their efforts to work in co-operation with the B.C. Security Commission, they soon came to be seen as "trouble makers."[44]

As May began, a number of important community leaders were systematically ordered to move. Then, on May 10, the JCCC was stunned to hear that their Secretary Kunio Shimizu, a key member because of his equal fluency in Japanese and English, had received his notice. The deferment he had just received had been reversed for no given reason. However, the JCCC *Minutes* of May 11 reported that

> Shoyama . . . saw a list of Isseis who were blacklisted by the RCMP as undesirables and would be shipped off to camp in a few days. Some of the men, in fact most of them on the list were known to be men of high moral integrity and clear-thinking leaders, that it was ridiculous to have them termed as undesirables and potentially dangerous.

---

[42]PAC, B.C. Security Commission Papers, RG36/37, vol. 3, file 66, Nisei Mass Evacuation Group to Austin Taylor, 15 April 1942. Sunahara points out that ironically the petitions of both the JCCC and NMEG, as later noted by the RCMP, "were typed on the same typewriter" (p. 66).

[43]PAC, Royal Canadian Mounted Police Papers, RG18 F3, vol. 3568, file C3129-1-5, C.H. Hill to RCMP Commissioner, 9 April 1942.

[44]*Minutes*, JCCC, 16 April 1942.

After this meeting, the JCCC members "went down to the CPR station to see off Kunio and the rest of the boys going to Schreiber and other work camps."[45]

Kunio Shimizu's forced departure coincided with the similar removal of other religious and community leaders. A letter in the Public Archives of Canada reveals that this move on the part of the authorities resulted from Shimizu's being wrongfully branded a dissident by the RCMP. On May 8, the day before he received his note to leave, C.H. Hill of the RCMP wrote to the B.C. Security Commission about the pamphlet written and circulated by the Nisei Mass Evacuation Group. Hill says: ". . . we have endeavored to secure evidence against the leaders of this group from Secret Agents and other confidential Japanese contacts. As a result, we have come to the conclusion that the following should be placed in custody . . . ." The list included Shimizu, as well as such prominent individuals as Reverend K. Shimizu, Reverend Y. Akagawa, and Bunji Hisaoka.[46]

•

Despite the assumptions of many Nisei, especially those in the Nisei Mass Evacuation Group, Austin Taylor was not opposed to removal in family units. In a letter dated March 4, the day the B.C. Security Commission was formed, he wrote to Ian Mackenzie, Minister of Pensions and National Health, and Humphrey Mitchell, Minister of Labour, recommending two methods of uprooting Japanese Canadians, neither involving the breakup of families. They could be resettled "in isolated crown grant areas of communities where these families can reestablish themselves on land and in minor and restricted industrial effort." Or, a number of "ghost towns" in the B.C. interior to "accommodate three thousand males or one thousand families" could be rehabilitated through the labour of male Japanese Canadians, sent out first to prepare the housing for their families. Although the former plan would be more expensive, Taylor argues that it "deserves your very serious consideration," because it would assure co-operation from Japanese Canadians and appease protests from B.C. communities. He added that further restrictions on

---

[45]*Minutes*, JCCC, 11 May 1942.
[46]PAC, B.C. Security Commission Papers, RG36/27, vol. 2, file 53, C.H. Hill to B.C. Security Commission, 8 May 1942.

Japanese Canadians will "create an element of distrust and complete lack of confidence which will add tremendously to our present problem."[47] Taylor's recommendations corresponded exactly with the two plans proposed by the Naturalized Canadian Japanese Association, plans which he rejected a month later, in the first week of April. Was this merely a coincidence? Perhaps Taylor had heard about the two plans and wanted to devise a removal scheme that would not cause unnecessary resistance from the Japanese Canadian community. In any case, when he became the Chairman of the B.C. Security Commission, he did not recommend the breakup of families.

In his response to Austin Taylor's letter containing these proposals, Ian Mackenzie, a well-known anti-Japanese Canadian Liberal MP, had advised "that individual movement of Japanese from coast should cease," and "that male Japanese of adult years should be assembled immediately using any available buildings on coast and transferring as soon as practicable to interim points." From these points, they would be distributed "to work camps farm colonies or whatever type of enterprise decided upon."[48] Mackenzie's advice that men be separated from their families became the official policy adopted by the B.C. Security Commission—until the beginning of July, when plans were made for the reunion of families. But by then, the community had been split apart by internal strife.

Muriel's letters, though personal, reflect this turmoil in the community. Her brother Doug, a single male Nisei, was bitter about the treatment of Japanese Canadians, but eventually co-operated with the B.C. Security Commission and went east with others, much to Muriel's relief—"because those who resist are being imprisoned in concentration camps," she told Wes in a letter dated April 29, 1942. All this is seen in the context of her own indecision and insecurity regarding the fate of her family during the weeks she and Ed scrambled to find a way of leaving the "Protected Area" with their four young children. The move to a ghost town would mean a separation from her husband, and she would be left alone to care for them. And the thought of the other alternative, confinement in Hastings Park with her children, was terrifying. Living nearby, she could visit others of her community there with a pass, and witness first-hand the

---

[47]PAC, B.C. Security Commission Papers, RG36/27, vol. 2, file 31, Austin Taylor to Ian Mackenzie and Humphrey Mitchell, 4 March 1942.

[48]PAC, B.C. Security Commission Papers, RG36/27, vol. 2, file 45, Ian Mackenzie to Austin Taylor, 5 March 1942.

barbaric living conditions, the stench of the livestock buildings where the women and children were confined, the primitive washing facilities, the substandard food, and the lack of privacy. The humiliation of being cooped up in such degrading living quarters haunted her. "Going through the place," she wrote to Wes, "I felt so depressed that I wanted to cry. I'm damned well not going there" (April 20, 1942).

•

The Kitagawas were greeted in Toronto by the first of a growing number of Canadians who started to understand their helplessness as "persons of Japanese race." During the summer of 1942, they were to stay at the home of Rev. James Finlay and his family, the minister at Carlton United Church where her brother Wes had found support. Later, they managed to find a house in that "foreign" city and settled in as well as they could.

The Kitagawas were the second Japanese Canadian family to receive special permits to resettle in Toronto. They were followed by other Japanese Canadians who drifted east in 1942 and 1943 with permits for prearranged employment, for the most part in domestic work. Soon there was a need for an organization to assist in relocation and employment. In December 1944, the Japanese Canadian Citizens for Democracy, perceived as a continuation of the defunct Japanese Canadian Citizens' League (JCCL), was formed to protect and further the rights of Japanese Canadians, seek racial equality, and maintain contacts with other Japanese Canadians across Canada.[49] By July 1945, the JCCD had begun to issue a newsletter, *Nisei Affairs* (Fig. 11), to present their views and comments on public issues. The prominent subject of the first number was the recent "repatriation" survey conducted by the government. Muriel contributed regularly to *Nisei Affairs*, for a time acting as its Managing Editor. Although she and others were to discover that the initial violation of their citizenship rights had opened the floodgates for further violations—mass uprooting, dispossession, forced dispersal, and expulsion from Canada—in Toronto they were prepared to defend their innocence and affirm their loyalty to their *native* land. Muriel's

---

[49]The objectives in the JCCD Constitution are quoted by George Tanaka in his article, "The Story of the JCCD," *NC*, 21 December 1946: p. 2.

Figure 11: Front cover of a 1947 issue of *Nisei Affairs*, the publication of the Japanese Canadian Citizens for Democracy. The JCCD formed in December 1944 in Toronto to protect the rights of Japanese Canadian citizens. For a time, Muriel was Managing Editor of the magazine.

writing to 1948 reflected the aspirations she shared with her community.

•

In January 1943, the Custodian of Enemy Alien Property was given legal sanction to dispose of properties held in trust for Japanese Canadians without the consent of the owners, thereby ensuring that Japanese Canadians would no longer have homes and businesses to which they could return. Then, in the spring of 1945, to prohibit them from resuming their lives in B.C. after the war, the government instituted a second uprooting, once more stirring up massive anxiety and uncertainty in a community already traumatized by three years of internment. How ironic, Nisei like Muriel would think, that only a year before, in August 1944, Prime Minister Mackenzie King had declared in the House of Commons: "It is a fact no person of Japanese race born in Canada has been charged with any act of sabotage or disloyalty during the years of war."[50] The government of Canada acknowledged their innocence, yet could set up the machinery which could deport them, or otherwise exert unjustified pressure to force their dispersal "east of the Rockies" across Canada. This was the next stage, initiated in the spring of 1945.

The essentially racist motive of the government's "dispersal" policy was sharply evident in the same speech in which Prime Minister King pointed to the innocence of Japanese Canadians. King rationalized the policy in the following way:

> The sound policy and the best policy for the Japanese Canadians themselves is to distribute their numbers as widely as possible throughout the country where they will not create feelings of racial hostility.[51]

According to King's twisted reasoning, since the victims of racism are the cause of racism, they should not be allowed to live in proximity to each other; the government, therefore, was forcing Japanese Canadians to distribute themselves east of the Rockies throughout

---

[50]W.L.M. King, *Debates*, House of Commons, 4 August 1944; quoted in Adachi, p. 431.

[51]King, *Debates*, House of Commons; Adachi, p. 433.

Canada for their own good. King was, in reality, advocating a policy of cultural genocide and disguising it as benign paternalism.

The plan for dispersal began with what was euphemistically called a "repatriation" survey. RCMP officers entered the towns where Japanese Canadians had been detained for the past three years and asked them to sign a form declaring whether or not they wished to go to Japan after the war was over (in the spring of 1945 Japan's impending defeat was already in sight). The term "repatriation" was viewed as despicable; the majority of those affected were individuals whose "patria" or country of birth was Canada, so they could not be "repatriated." In fact, the survey harboured the more sinister motive of pressuring many disheartened people to give up their Canadian citizenship and be expelled from their native land. The pressure was reinforced by the announcement of the government's "dispersal" policy (Fig. 13) which simultaneously accompanied the "repatriation" notice (Fig. 12). Japanese Canadians saw both documents in the *New Canadian* on March 17, 1945, side by side on the same page.

Though the government advertised the "repatriation" survey as a voluntary decision on the part of Japanese Canadians, clearly the so-called "choice" offered was weighted in favour of expulsion to Japan. Those signing to go to Japan were allowed to stay in B.C. until they left, and they were offered free passage plus a resettlement allowance. East of the Rockies they were on their own. The government may have explained, to the Canadian public, that Japanese Canadians were free to choose their future, but the notice for dispersal carried a terrifying threat which drastically inhibited actual freedom of choice: those who did not co-operate with the government's directive could be considered disloyal to Canada and therefore subject to deportation later. That was how many Japanese Canadians interpreted the statement that those "who want to remain in Canada should now re-establish themselves East of the Rockies as the best evidence of their intentions to co-operate with the Government policy of dispersal," and the loaded warning that those who do not comply "may seriously prejudice their own future by delay."[52] And their fears were fuelled by an announcement that Prime Minister King was proposing the "establishment of a quasi-judicial commission to examine the background, loyalties and attitudes of all persons of

---

[52]Notice, 12 March 1945, Department of Labour, "To All Persons of Japanese Racial Origin Now Resident in British Columbia," signed by T.B. Pickersgill, Commissioner of Japanese Placement; quoted by Adachi, p. 428.

47

DEPARTMENT OF LABOUR

CANADA

NOTICE

TO ALL PERSONS OF JAPANESE RACIAL ORIGIN
HAVING REFERENCE TO MAKING APPLICATION FOR
VOLUNTARY REPATRIATION TO JAPAN

The Minister of Labour has been authorized by the Government of Canada to make known the following decisions made with respect to persons of Japanese ancestry, now resident in Canada, who make voluntary application to go to Japan after the war, or sooner where this can be arranged:

1. The net proceeds realized from the disposition of their property, real and personal, in Canada, and standing to their credit at time of repatriation, will be secured to them and may be transferred by them to Japan upon repatriation following the close of the war.

2. In the case of persons sent to Japan under any agreement for exchange of Nationals between Canada and Japan before the close of war, under which agreement the amount of personal property and funds carried by the repatriates is limited, the Custodian of Enemy Alien Property will be authorized, on the advice of the Department of External Affairs, to provide such Japanese repatriates with receipts showing the property left behind in Canada, or net proceeds of same if sold, with a view to their being permitted to secure possession of their property or the net proceeds thereof after the end of hostilities.

3. Free passage will be guaranteed by the Canadian Government to all repatriates being sent to Japan, and all their dependents who accompany them, and including free transportation of such of their personal property as they may take with them.

The above assurances will apply to such persons as have already made written application in satisfactory form to the Government of Canada to go to Japan, or who make written application hereafter for that purpose to the Government of Canada within the period of time fixed by the Commissioner of Japanese Placement for the completion and filing of applications.

These assurances do not apply to persons of the Japanese race repatriated on other than a voluntary basis.

Dated at Ottawa this 13th day of February, 1945.

HUMPHREY MITCHELL
Minister of Labour.

The special R.C.M.P. Detachment for taking applications will be at

.... from ....

to .... and will take applications at

.... Every person of Japanese origin 16 years of age and over is required to report to the R.C.M.P. Detachment on one of these dates to signify his or her intention concerning repatriation.

T. B. PICKERSGILL,
COMMISSIONER OF JAPANESE PLACEMENT

Vancouver, B. C.
March 12th, 1945.

Figure 12: The so-called "voluntary" repatriation notice that led to the exile of 4,000 Japanese Canadians to Japan.

48

DEPARTMENT OF LABOUR

CANADA

NOTICE

To All Persons of Japanese Racial Origin
Now Resident in British Columbia

1. Japanese Nationals and others of Japanese racial origin who will be returning to Japan, have been informed by notice issued on the authority of the Honourable Minister of Labour, that provision has been made for their return and for the filing of an application for such return. Conditions in regard to property and transportation have been made public.

2. Japanese Canadians who want to remain in Canada should now re-establish themselves East of the Rockies as the best evidence of their intentions to co-operate with the Government policy of dispersal.

3. Failure to accept employment east of the Rockies may be regarded at a later date as lack of co-operation with the Canadian Government in carrying out its policy of dispersal.

4. Several thousand Japanese have already re-established themselves satisfactorily east of the Rockies.

5. Those who do not take advantage of present opportunities for employment and settlement outside British Columbia at this time, while employment opportunities are favourable, will find conditions of employment and settlement considerably more difficult at a later date and may seriously prejudice their own future by delay.

6. To assist those who want to re-establish themselves in Canada, the Japanese Division Placement Offices and the Employment and Selective Service Offices, with the assistance of local Advisory Committees, are making special efforts this Spring to open up suitable employment opportunities across Canada in various lines of endeavour, and in areas where prospects of suitable employment are best.

7. The Department will also provide free transportation to Eastern Canada for members of a family and their effects, a sustenance allowance to be used while in transit, and a placement allowance based in amount on the size of the family.

T. B. PICKERSGILL,
COMMISSIONER OF JAPANESE PLACEMENT

Vancouver, B. C.
March 12th, 1945.

Figure 13: Announcement of the government's policy to disperse Japanese Canadians east of the Rockies, 12 March 1945.

Japanese race in Canada to ascertain those who are not fit persons to be allowed to remain here."[53] The news of this commission, termed a "Loyalty Tribunal," was sandwiched between the notices for "repatriation" and "dispersal" in the *New Canadian*! Japanese Canadians were trapped by government policy, and the mass fear that swept through the detention camps was instantaneous. In a letter, now in the Public Archives of Canada, which typifies the dilemma, one Nisei spoke for many who felt completely caught between two worlds:

> Isn't it pitiful this situation of us? I mean Nisei! We're a people without a country. We're not wanted here, we're not suited to Japanese customs, gosh what a pickle! If we go east, we're called Japs and shunned—if we go to Japan, they'll consider us something like "hakujin" because we're born and educated out here in America.[54]

John Nihei, an Issei who worked at Tashme, the largest internment centre, just outside of Hope, B.C., knew then that the "repatriation" plan would entice Japanese Canadians—in their psychologically damaged condition—to agree to their expulsion from their own country. He advocated strongly against signing the form, seeing it simply as part of a scheme to banish as many Japanese Canadians from Canada as possible. At a meeting with T.B. Pickersgill, Commissioner of Japanese Placement, the official who had signed the "Dispersal" notice, Nihei told him that the terms offered by the government favoured the move to Japan. He wanted to know the merits of moving east of the Rockies, and he posed five questions:

1. Do we have free choice of living space?
2. Do we have free choice of occupation?
3. Will our children have equal education?
4. Do we have any security after we move into the new place? Suppose I want to go to Toronto, but I haven't the savings and nothing there, then how am I going to keep

---

[53]King, *Debates*, House of Commons, 4 August 1944; Adachi, p. 432.

[54]Censored letters between Japanese Canadians were described and recorded in the "Intercepted Letters" file, now in PAC, Department of Labour Papers, RG27, vols. 1527 and 1528; the quoted passage is taken from one letter (dated April 15, 1945) from hundreds of letters in response to the "repatriation" survey.

my family going? We have been interned for years, so you have to give us some help to establish ourselves.

5. If you send us to the most anti-Japanese locality, and if anything happens to me or my family, who is going to be responsible? The government, or are we just out of luck?

Pickersgill's answer, which Nihei remembered as if it were yesterday, was: "If you have those worries, sign the repatriation form and your worries are all gone."[55] Of course, the government would give no assurances for those going east of the Rockies.

The Japanese Canadians who had been confined in detention centres in the interior of B.C. for three years were spiritually broken and disillusioned, and a shocking 10,000 initially agreed to expulsion to Japan. Many of them signed only in order to stay in B.C., being led to assume by the RCMP officers that they could change their minds later. The "repatriation" survey was not to be taken as a binding legal document. In the meantime, they could at least remain in B.C. either to care for elderly or weak family members, or because they were still afraid of living conditions elsewhere in Canada. Still others signed because they had lost faith in their country. One Nisei wrote to a friend:

> After all the hard times we came through trying for a decent home and then to lose everything. I guess I may as well sign up like the folks. It is no use of us fellows going out of B.C. It will be the same old thing. As soon as you get settled down they don't want you.[56]

Others, like Muriel, were hardly willing to give in to yet another attempt by the government to destroy their loyalty to Canada. Even she, already outside of B.C, was asked to state her intention vis-a-vis expulsion to Japan. She answered T.B. Pickersgill publicly in an open letter, in which she declared: "We chose Canada long before you ever thought to ask us to choose. We chose Canada then, and we choose Canada now, with our eyes wide open to the probable consequences of our choice."[57]

---

[55]Interview, John Nihei; quoted in *Redress for Japanese Canadians: A Community Forum* (Vancouver: Japanese Canadian Citizens' Association Redress Committee, 1984), p. 8.

[56]From an Intercepted Letter, PAC; quoted by Ann Sunahara, p. 123.

[57]"Canada is Our Choice," *NC*, 23 June 1945: p. 2.

Once the threat of deportation became evident, many changed their minds, only to be told by the government that it was too late. However, throughout the fall of 1945 as the government made plans to institute legislation to deport some 10,000 persons of Japanese ancestry, the forces against this manoeuvre suddenly flared up across the country. The work of the Co-operative Committee on Japanese Canadians, a group consisting of the JCCD and some twenty Caucasian organizations, brought to public awareness the injustices being inflicted on Japanese Canadians and managed to arouse widespread public protest against deportation of Canadian citizens who had not committed a crime—nor had they ever been charged with a crime![58] Muriel, too, attacked the deportation in an article, "Deportation is a Violation of Human Rights."[59]

The legality of the Orders-in-Council which were to be used by the government to carry out the deportation were challenged by the Co-operative Committee. Amazingly, the Supreme Court upheld the authority of the government to act in whatever way it deemed necessary under the War Measures Act—even unjust policies could not be questioned by the courts—but the ruling did not include women and children who did not sign for "repatriation." By then, the government's actions were so unpopular that the deportation issue was dropped. Despite this change in policy, in 1946 nearly 4,000 were exiled to war-torn Japan. "The main casualties," as Adachi says, "were the Canadian-born, who comprised over half of the repatriates, 33% of whom were dependent children under 16 years of age."[60]

In the fall of 1946, the JCCD undertook an assessment of economic losses to Japanese Canadians resulting from their uprooting and dispersal during the period from 1942 to 1946. To do so, they surveyed 198 family heads who had resettled in Toronto. In 1947, with the results of their survey in hand, they enlisted the support of the Co-operative Committee to press the government to investigate the variety of losses suffered by Japanese Canadians.[61] The government sought to allay potentially embarrassing public pressure

---

[58]The important work of the Co-operative Committee in defence of Japanese Canadians is described at length in Edith Fowke's *They Made Democracy Work: The Story of the Co-operative Committee on Japanese Canadians* (Toronto: Garden City Press, n.d.).

[59]*NC*, 3 November 1946: p. 2.

[60]Adachi, p. 318.

[61]Sunahara summarizes the estimate of losses for the 198 families surveyed: "The overall losses were staggering. The estimated losses on sold property approached

on this question by establishing, in July, a Royal Commission under B.C. Justice Henry Bird. In response, the JCCD saw the need to form a national association for Japanese Canadians across Canada to participate in the Commission. At a conference in Toronto in September 1947, the JCCD was therefore dissolved and the National Japanese Canadian Citizens' Association (NJCCA), the first national organization for Japanese Canadians, was constituted. Work began immediately with the Co-operative Committee to prepare the claimants for the hearings.

The Bird Commission, as it was called, was given such narrow terms of reference that Japanese Canadians were extremely disappointed with its results. Bird was allowed to evaluate only those losses resulting from the difference between fair market value and sale price—and the onus was on the claimant to demonstrate fair market value. Income losses and other losses resulting from the forced uprooting would not be considered, and Bird had no authority whatsoever to question government policy on Japanese Canadians. The narrow terms of reference, when placed in relation to the horrendous social and political upheaval which had been suffered—not to mention the humiliation and degradation caused by the gross violation of basic rights—made the Bird Commission itself appear just one more betrayal.[62] Reading about the Commission's limitations, Muriel would write:

> Were I the victim of the conquering madmen from Berlin, my hate of oppression would give me strength to fight for liberty; but to be bound and gagged in legal verbiage by the "honourable" men, the "respectable" men who govern us in democratic freedom is to struggle in despair of bitter taste.[63]

The Bird Commission, then, was viewed by Japanese Canadians as merely a political gesture on the part of the government, not as a means of dealing fairly with the injustices inflicted on them.

$800,000, while an additional $300,000 worth of property remained unaccounted for, or had been lost, stolen or destroyed. When combined with the estimated lost revenue and wages, and sundry other losses, gross losses for the 198 families surveyed approached $4 million for the five years between 1942 and 1946" (p. 152).

[62]For further discussions of the Bird Commission, see Adachi, pp. 325ff, and Sunahara, pp. 152ff.

[63]"Who Was the Custodian?" *NC*, 16 August 1947: p. 2.

•

Japanese Canadians would finally receive the right to the federal vote on June 15, 1948. They would receive the right to the vote in B.C. on March 7, 1949. On March 31, 1949, the last of the wartime restrictions was lifted. By April 1, 1949, *four years after the war was over*, they were at last free to return to the west coast if they so desired. But when Justice Bird submitted his report in 1950 with recommendations for such minimal compensation that it seemed a mockery of actual losses, Japanese Canadians had been betrayed too many times. Their former lives on the west coast had been destroyed, and their savings and whatever money they had received from the liquidation of their homes and belongings had been used up. Government policy had even dictated that they should pay for their own internment—a barbaric policy which could not be questioned by Justice Bird. With no hope of justice from the government of the day, most turned only to the future and the need to rebuild their lives in scattered places across Canada. Muriel, too, from 1949 on turned her attention away from the wartime years, though the injustices, unresolved, would continue to linger. Her statement in an unpublished manuscript of that time reaches across to another generation:

> Time heals the details, but time cannot heal the fundamental wrong. My children will not remember the first violence of feeling, the intense bitterness I felt, but they will know that a house was lost through injustice. As long as restitution is not made, that knowledge will last throughout the generations to come . . . that a house, a home, was lost through injustice.[64]

•

The letters and writings of Muriel Kitagawa remain as fresh as ever. No other Nisei writer has captured the texture of the wartime years, the hopes and fears, the despairs, the struggles, and the courage and determination to survive, so that her generation could "forge a record of dignity and endurance to leave as a proud heritage for our sons

---

[64]"I Stand Here Tonight," PAC, Muriel Kitagawa Papers, MG31 E26.

54

and daughters to come." With her words, Muriel has forged a record of her times—which is, by virtue of her writing, bound up in our times. I can think of no finer heritage than this gift of words. They retain the immediacy of a community's history.

Postscript

Muriel Kitagawa died on March 27, 1974, a week before her birthday on April 3. She would have turned 62 years old. A year later, the thirty-year ban on access to the government's wartime documents was lifted, allowing historian Ann Sunahara to re-examine the treatment of Japanese Canadians in the light of brand new evidence.

Muriel's writings during the 1940s constitute a record of the direct impact of the government's wartime measures on the Japanese Canadian community—a community torn apart, dispossessed, dispersed, and victimized for being "of the Japanese race." She was one of many individuals who attempted to defend their loyalty to their native land time and again, knowing full well that the mass removal of their community from B.C. was the result of racial prejudice. But they discovered, time and again, that the power of the War Measures Act was too formidable. No matter where they turned or what they said, the government had but to pass another order-in-council to abrogate their freedoms and to prevent them from asserting their rights.

With the wartime documents of the government finally accessible, the extent of the abuses inflicted on individual Japanese Canadians can finally become a matter of public record. Had Muriel lived to see the evidence presented in Ann Sunahara's book, *The Politics of Racism*, irrefutable documentary evidence to show that the uprooting of Japanese Canadians was a political measure, not a security measure, she would have been relieved. Certainly people looked upon the treatment of Japanese Canadians as shameful, but the opinion persisted throughout the 1950s and 1960s that the government's policies and actions were understandable, given the hysteria of the times. On the contrary, the documents clearly show that certain politicians and public leaders, well known for their racist animosity towards Japanese Canadians, manipulated the potentially volatile wartime atmosphere on the west coast to have their way with these "people of Japanese race."

Available documents reveal that the leading military advisors of the government, at the crucial Conference on the Japanese Problem, held in Ottawa on January 8-9, 1942, were opposed to the uprooting. It is an unfortunate fact of history for Japanese Canadians that Ian Alistair Mackenzie, MP for Vancouver Centre, should be the only Liberal from B.C. in Prime Minister Mackenzie King's cabinet at the time. King therefore accepted him as the "authority" on the "Japanese problem," as well as his personal advisor on policy. Japanese Canadians, like Muriel and Ed Kitagawa, knew Ian Mackenzie in the late 1930s for his obsessive desire to drive their community out of B.C., a motive that formed a major part of his political platform. In his nomination speech in September 1944, Mackenzie declared: "Let our slogan be for British Columbia: 'No Japs from the Rockies to the seas.' "[65]

It was Ian Mackenzie who chaired the Conference on the Japanese Problem in B.C., called to discuss the wartime fate of Japanese Canadians. The minutes of that meeting reveal a sharp division of views on the question of interning Japanese Nationals as a defence measure. The majority position came from representatives of the Armed Forces and the RCMP, in other words, from the government's leading advisors on national security. They opposed the measure and "assured the Conference that the requirements of national defence and security can be met by the measures already taken or recommended, and do not warrant such action." And the following warning was added: "The acceptance of this proposal would be a contradiction of Canadian and Allied professions of justice and humanity."[66] Some representatives argued that Japanese Canadians could assist in the war effort:

> Mr. Couper of the Department of Labour and other members of the Conference from Ottawa emphasized that if Canada was to make the utmost possible contribution to victory in the war it was necessary to make the most effective use of the abilities of all residents of Canada

---

[65]Quoted in *Democracy Betrayed: The Case for Redress* (Winnipeg: National Association of Japanese Canadians, 1984), p. 13.

[66]PAC, Ian Mackenzie Papers, MG27IIIB5, vol. 32, file x-81, *Report*, Conference on the Japanese Problem in B.C., 8-9 January 1942.

including persons of Japanese racial origin. They based their contention on the impending labour shortage in Canada and argued that racial discrimination was not only unjust but inefficient and thus affected detrimentally Canada's war effort.[67]

The minority position came from the B.C. delegates who were supported by Ian Mackenzie, and these included George S. Pearson, Minister of Labour in the B.C. government; F.S. Hume, the Mayor of New Westminster and Chairman of the Standing Committee on Oriental Problems in B.C.; Lt. Col. MacGregor MacIntosh and A.W. Sparling, members of that committee; and finally, T.W.S. Parsons, the B.C. Police Commissioner. These men from B.C. urged the internment of Japanese Nationals to avert the threat of civil violence—whites in B.C., they claimed, would riot in the streets if this action were not taken—and to avert any possible subversive moves by the Japanese living on the coast. The racism amongst this group was so strong that Escott Reid, a diplomat from the Department of External Affairs, would later recall:

> They [the delegates from B.C.] spoke of the Japanese Canadians in a way that Nazis would have spoken about Jewish-Canadians. When they spoke, I felt in that room the physical presence of evil.[68]

On January 10, when Mackenzie wrote his confidential report on the conference to Prime Minister Mackenzie King, he down-played the position of the military advisors and threw his support behind the B.C. delegates. He even included in his report a biased letter from R.O. Alexander, Pacific Command, who urged the removal to "prevent inter-racial riots and bloodshed."[69]

Mackenzie's recommendation that Japanese male Nationals be forcibly removed from the west coast was accepted as government

---

[67]PAC, Department of External Affairs Papers, RG25 G2, Acc. 83-84/259, Box 199, File 3464-B-40C, Part 1, *Minutes*, Conference on the Japanese Problem in B.C., 8-9 January 1942.

[68]Escott Reid, "The Conscience of a Diplomat: A Personal Testament," *Queen's Quarterly*, 74 (Winter 1967): pp. 6-8; quoted in *Democracy Betrayed*, p. 13.

[69]PAC, Ian Mackenzie Papers, MG27IIIB5, vol. 32, file x-81, *Report*, Conference on the Japanese Problem in B.C., 8-9 January 1942.

policy, and on January 14, Order-in-Council P.C. 365 was passed to carry out this action. By April 1, all male Japanese nationals 18-45 years of age were to be moved 100 miles from the coast, away from the designated "protected area." A month later, this order was enlarged to include all "persons of Japanese race," regardless of citizenship.

No sooner had the uprooting begun when government officials like Ian Mackenzie initiated steps to dispossess Japanese Canadians in order to expel them from B.C. As early as April 14, only six weeks after the B.C. Security Commission had been established to carry out the order for mass uprooting—and when Japanese Canadians believed that the Custodian of Enemy Alien Property was holding their land and possessions in trust—Mackenzie was already setting in motion his plan to confiscate and sell farms in the Fraser Valley. Ostensibly, he wanted to purchase the farms for returning World War II veterans, but the move would also accomplish his political motive: the destruction of the social and economic base of the Japanese Canadian community. He planned to work through the Veterans' Land Act, but since this Act would not become law until August, he needed the compliance of T.A. Crerar, Minister of Mines and Resources and Administrator of the Soldier Settlement Act, to acquire the farms through the Soldier Settlement Act. In a letter to Crerar, Mackenzie revealed that the instigated takeover had already begun (Fig. 14):

> The Custodian's representative in Vancouver is already in touch with a committee of white farmers and cannery men who know the properties intimately and who have already brought in a number of white farmers to take over some of the properties. They are of the opinion that they could obtain a suitable number of tenants to maintain these properties, pending their disposal to soldier settlers.[70]

Crerar then authorized Gordon Murchison, Director of the Soldier Settlement Board, to determine the feasibility of Mackenzie's plan and to evaluate the farms. In the meantime, Order-in-Council P.C. 5523 was passed on June 29 to freeze the sale of farms without Murchison's permission. This would prevent Japanese Canadians

---

[70]PAC, Ian Mackenzie Papers, MG27IIIB5, vol. 25, 70-25D, Ian Mackenzie to T.A. Crerar, 14 April 1942.

Ottawa, April 14, 1942.

My dear Colleague:

In connection with the evacuation of
the Japanese from the protected area on the Pacific
Coast, several hundred Japanese berry farmers are
being compelled to abandon their properties. For
the most part, these are well developed properties
with good dwellings on them. They are providing a
living, in each case, for a Japanese family.

The berry industry is an important
part of British Columbia's agricultural life.
During the war, in particular, large quantities
of jam and processed berries have been required for
Great Britain.

The abandonment of these farms raises a
problem of the conservation of the continuity of production
in the berry industry.

The British Columbia Security Commission
has no authority to deal with the properties, excepting
such items as motor vehicles and radios which are
ordered confiscated. The Custodian of Enemy Alien
Property has no authority to touch these properties
unless and until they have been actually abandoned.
In practice, the Japanese are endeavouring to lease and
sell, often at sacrifice prices. The canneries and
market agencies are greatly concerned, lest there be
little or no crop on the Japanese farms this year,
which will seriously disturb the whole economy of the
Fraser Valley.

The Honourable T.A. Crerar, M.P.,
    Minister of Mines and Resources,
        OTTAWA.

Figure 14: Only six weeks after the Japanese Canadian community had been assured
of the Custodian's intent to protect their properties, Ian Mackenzie, Liberal MP for
Vancouver Centre and a prime force behind the dispossession of Japanese Canadians, wrote this letter to a fellow MP, recommending the appropriation of Japanese
Canadian owned farms in the Fraser Valley.

I am impressed with the thought that these excellent small farms would be most suitable establishments for soldier settlers under the pending Veterans' Land Act. This Act will confer upon the Director, when he is appointed, the right to buy farms and hold them for prospective settlers. He has authority to enter into agreements for leasing such properties, in order that they may be conserved and developed during any interregnum between their purchase and the arrival of a prospective soldier settler.

Unfortunately there is no prospect of the Veterans' Land Act becoming law in time for the Director appointed thereunder to deal with these properties. It seems unfortunate, however, that the opportunity should be missed.

I should appreciate your considering the advisability of an Order in Council under the War Measures Act, authorizing the administrator of the Soldier Settlement Act, or some other appropriate official, to step in at once and buy any of these Japanese farms that commend themselves as suitable for soldier settlers. They can be administered meantime exactly as the Director under the Veterans' Land Act would administer them and can be turned over to him when he is appointed. The submission to Council can follow the language of the Veterans' Land Bill with respect to the powers which it would be necessary to confer upon the official selected for this purpose.

The Custodian's representative in Vancouver is already in touch with a committee of white farmers and cannery men who know the properties intimately and who have already brought in a number of white farmers to take over some of the properties. They are of the opinion that they could obtain a suitable number of tenants to maintain these properties, pending their disposal to soldier settlers.

....

Figure 14 (continued)

The vital consideration in this proposal is
that we act immediately; otherwise the properties
will have been disposed of in various unsatisfactory
ways and the opportunity to develop sound soldier
settlement in that area will be lost.

I should be glad to be associated with you in
a joint submission to Council, and I may say that we
have in the Department, in connection with our A.R.P.
organization, Mr. H.G. Eakins, who is one of the two
or three best informed men in British Columbia with
respect to the berry industry.

Yours sincerely,

(I. A. MACKENZIE)

Figure 14 (continued)

from either selling their farms or leasing them during their absence.

Ian Mackenzie would be successful in acquiring the Japanese Canadian farms. In a letter to Crerar on December 7, 1942, agreeing to the takeover of properties through the Director of Soldier Settlement, Mackenzie justified his actions:

> I believe that from these lands formerly occupied by the Japanese, we can establish some very fine holdings for the soldiers of the present war.
>
> I also believe that we can lease them, if necessary, until the soldiers are able to occupy them. I also believe that we should not permit these Japanese to take re-possession of their lands. That is the view of British Columbia and will certainly find expression when the war is over.[71]

For racist politicians like Mackenzie, the uprooting of Japanese Canadians from the west coast was *the* opportunity to confiscate and liquidate their properties—to eradicate their presence in B.C. By January 1943, he would be even more pleased with Order-in-Council P.C. 469 which gave the Custodian of Enemy Alien Property the power to sell all property and belongings of Japanese Canadians without the consent of the owners.

Once dispossessed and expelled from the west coast, Japanese Canadians endured a seven-year period of injustice that would continue four years beyond the end of the war, until April 1, 1949.

•

On November 21, 1984, the Japanese Canadian community, using the wealth of evidence from the Public Archives of Canada, presented the government with *Democracy Betrayed: The Case for Redress*, a brief documenting the injustices suffered by Japanese Canadians during and after World War II. It was submitted by the National Association of Japanese Canadians (NAJC), formerly known as the National Japanese Canadian Citizens' Association (NJCCA), the first national organization established in Toronto in 1947. The "Call for Redress" in its conclusion asks that justice finally be done for

---

[71]PAC, Ian Mackenzie Papers, MG27IIIB5, vol. 25, File 70-25C, Ian Mackenzie to T.A. Crerar, 7 December 1942.

those Canadians like Muriel and Ed Kitagawa whose rights were so grossly violated:

CALL FOR REDRESS

Contrary to officially stated reasons in 1942, the forced removal and incarceration of Japanese Canadians during World War II had no basis in military necessity. In reality, the government's policies of uprooting, detention, confiscation of property, expulsion and deportation were motivated by political considerations based upon racist traditions accepted and encouraged by politicians within the government of the day. Those policies were racist in character and resulted in the abrogation of the human and civil rights of Japanese Canadians between 1941 and 1949. Although the repressive measures against Japanese Canadians were most actively promoted by politicians from British Columbia, the silent compliance of the federal cabinet was crucial to the implementation of those measures.

The principles of democracy were betrayed when the government, instead of invoking the full force of the law to protect Japanese Canadians against racist agitation, incarcerated the **victims** of race prejudice and, without consent, liquidated properties and belongings to compel the victims to pay for their own internment. The people of Canada were abused when they were unfairly led to believe that Japanese Canadians threatened the nation's security. By its actions, the Government of Canada betrayed not only Canadians of Japanese ancestry, but also the men and women it was sending to Europe and Asia to fight and die in the cause of justice and equality for all.

As a visible minority that has experienced legalized repression under the War Measures Act, we urge the Government of Canada to take such steps as are necessary to ensure that Canadians are never again subjected to such injustices. In particular, we urge that the fundamental human rights and freedoms set forth in the **Canadian Charter of Rights and Freedoms** be considered sacrosanct, non-negotiable and beyond the reach of any arbitrary legislation such as the War Measures Act.

In consequence of the abrogation of the rights and freedoms of Japanese Canadians during and after World War II, the National Association of Japanese Canadians calls on the Government of Canada to acknowledge its responsibility to compensate Japanese Canadians for injustices suffered and seeks a commitment from the Government of Canada to enter into negotiations towards a just and honourable settlement of this claim.

I

Letters to Wes

The sequence of letters from Muriel Kitagawa to her brother Wes Fujiwara begins on December 13, 1941, a week after Pearl Harbor. Wes, then 21 years old, has just begun his studies as a medical student at the University of Toronto. Muriel is 29 years old. She has been married to Ed Kitagawa for seven years, and they have two children, Shirley Emiko, aged 7 and Carol Meiko, aged 4. By this time, Muriel is confined to her house in the last weeks of a difficult pregnancy, and her condition, as she says to Wes, prevents her from taking a leading part in preparations for Christmas. Her father is Dr. Asajiro Fujiwara, a Vancouver dentist, and she has two other brothers, Alan (called Nobi), 11 years old and living with Dr. Fujiwara, and Doug, 27 years old. Doug's uncertain status and future as a single, male Nisei is a constant source of apprehension in the letters. Muriel's younger sister Kay, 26 years old, and her mother Tsuru Fujiwara are in Japan, prevented by government regulation to return to Canada. Friends mentioned include Kunio Shimizu and Tom Shoyama, editor of the New Canadian, *the only newspaper in the Japanese Canadian community permitted to continue publishing. Both Tom and Kunio are prominent members of the community through their involvement over the years in the Nisei organization, the Japanese Canadian Citizens' League (JCCL). Eiko Henmi Etheridge is a friend and fellow writer for the* New Canadian, *who wrote as "Peg" and "Cinderella" (or "Cindy") in her articles. Fumi Shoyama Katsuyama, Tom's sister, is also a close friend. Uncle Fred Toyofuku, the younger brother of Tsuru Fujiwara, and his wife Sei and daughter Janet are also mentioned in the letters.*

Muriel writes to Wes from her home at 2751 E. Pender in Vancouver. Some of Wes' letters, a selection written during May, are included to provide continuity and to illuminate the Toronto milieu awaiting the Kitagawas. Telegrams sent by Muriel in the final weeks before her departure are incorporated in the editorial notes accompanying the letters.

Editorial additions are enclosed in square brackets.

December 13, 1941.

Dear Wes:

Just got your second air-mail letter, and instructed Eddie to send you a wire. Keep your chin up. We've got to endure this with all the courage we have.

Dad is getting along in his usual way, and Doug is OK. So far we have had no word of any bad news in the family, so don't worry.

Doesn't the fact that you are Canadian-born do you any good in getting a job? Dad's been in this country for over 40 years. That's more than a lot of Occidentals can say.[1]

Just get through your exams and we'll parley after.

Love from all of us, and don't get discouraged.

Mur.

Expect big parcel soon.
Just some "eats."

December 18, 1941.

Dear Wes:

Just to let you know, plans have changed a bit and I won't be able to send you a package. Baking is too much for me, and if I'm going to buy things I might as well save the postage and add that to the amount, so we are sending you some money. I know this sounds all cold and un-Christmas-sy—but you'll forgive me this once? Except

---

[1]Wes had applied for a post office job for the Christmas holidays, and the form required information on the citizenship of his father. Since his father was a National, Wes did not qualify. Being Canadian-born did not matter.

for the kids we aren't doing much. I've only 3 weeks to go, and can just sit and sigh. Will write in detail soon.

Love,
Mur.

December 21, 1941.

Dear Wes:

I hope first of all that you have as merry a Christmas as you can, and that you will splurge with this money on a real dinner with the trimmings. Of all times for me to be helpless. We have already felt the effects of my not being able to lead the house into the festivities. Everything is upside down, and I just have to go without some of the 'musts' of other years. Eiko is going to cook for the family, and since there is no Christmas Ball this year, I think she will have plenty of time to wash dinner dishes too . . . with Fumi to help. There were so many things I wanted to do for you, but it is just a physical impossibility. I will make up for it as soon as I can. My problem now is to hang on till the 25th, so I won't miss the kids' getting up and finding things. This year is for the kids mainly. We got Shirley a huge doll buggy with a big baby doll inside. In fact, Eddie just shut his eyes and splurged on it. For Meiko, who is not yet so demanding, we got a smaller size doll and a stove and paper cut-outs etc. Already they are counting the days and nights. Even Meiko is exact in her figures. Yesterday Shirley's Sunday school had a Christmas concert and I let Meiko go with her as part of the audience, since I couldn't go. And what do you know, they thrust poor Meiko on the stage in her everyday dress to sing "Away in a Manger" with the other 4-year-olds. Was she surprised . . . and I'm afraid somewhat tearful. Anyway they both came home with a candy-filled stocking and a pair of hair barrettes for a present and they've hung them on the tree. The tree too they decorated themselves, with Daddy of course, and I didn't have to do a thing. Not that I could. Things are a bit makeshift, but they don't seem to miss anything yet. For the first time Shirley is going shopping on her own account. I feel that if she wants to give gifts to her friends she should do the picking herself, within financial limits of course, and that the money part should be within her possibilities, so that she will not get too extravagant ideas. She bought her own Christmas cards too. Yes sir, she is growing all right.

I had brown hooded coats made for them, and when they go out together they look like a pair of gnomes. How Meiko loves her new coat! The chinchilla is so tight for her now, and she is so fashion-conscious she hates wearing it. She is a vain little rascal.

So far as the new war affects us, I really haven't much to say. It is too early to estimate the effects. On the whole we are taking it in our stride. We are so used to wars and alarums, and we have been tempered for the anti-feelings these long years. It has only intensified into overt acts of unthinking hoodlumism like throwing flaming torches into rooming houses and bricks through plate glass . . . only in the West End so far. What that goes to prove I don't know. We've had blackouts the first few nights but they have been lifted. Bad for the kids, because it frightens them so. Of course we have to be ready just in case and I sure hope there won't be any emergency . . . not with the kids around. All three Japanese papers have been closed down. We never needed so many anyway. It is good for the *New Canadian* though, as it can now go ahead with full responsibility, though at first it is bound *to* be hard on the inexperienced staff.[2] All Japanese schools have been closed too, and are the kids glad![3] Of course I have never intended my kids to go anyway so it doesn't affect us in the least. I am glad in a way that they have been closed

---

[2]The three Japanese-language newspapers, the *Tairiku* (*Continental Times*), *Canada Shimpo,* and the *Minshu* (*People's Daily*), were closed as a security measure with the agreement of the owners. The *New Canadian*, the "voice" of the English-speaking Nisei since 1938, was the only community newspaper allowed to continue operating as an information outlet. Tom Shoyama, its young editor, recognized the gravity of this responsibility in his first editorial after Pearl Harbor by advising his readers to exercise control of their actions, to control their tempers, and to co-operate with the government's security measures ("Let's Watch Our Step," *New Canadian*, 12 December 1941).

[3]A report on the closure of the Japanese newspapers and the shutdown of the fifty-nine language schools in B.C. revealed that the Issei were lost without their newspapers and that the young Nisei were pleased that they no longer had to attend Japanese school after regular hours in the Canadian public school. Reactions from Nisei were quoted: " 'More time to play,' one sang gleefully. 'I hate Japanese school,' another one spat. 'Phooey,' a tough young man shouted, 'blackout is more fun than school any day' " ("Loss of Language Papers Severe Blow But Kids Rejoice in School Closure," *New Canadian*, 12 December 1941).

down. I hope for good. But it is hard on the teachers who depended on them for a living.

There have been the usual anti-letters-to-the-editor in the papers. Some of them are rank nonsense, and some of the writers think like that anyhow, whatever the provocation. The majority of the people are decent and fair-minded and they say so in letters and editorials.[4] The RCMP is our friend too, for they, more than anyone else, know how blameless and helpless we are, and they have already in one instance prevented tragedy when the City Fathers proposed cancelling all business licences, to say that we did not rate such harsh treatment. Now the North Vancouver Board of Trade goes on record to demand that all our autos be confiscated, but I hardly think that could be practical. What then would our doctors and businessmen do? Also, it is hard to take everything away from 22,000 people without the rest of B.C. feeling some of the bad effects. The dog salmon industry is already short-handed because the Japanese cannot fish any more. How they will make up the lack in the next season I don't know, though the 'white' fishermen seem to be confident, if they could use the fishing boats now tied up somewhere in New Westminster.

There was one letter in the *Province* protesting this confiscation of the right to earn a living from 1880 people . . . said it wasn't democracy.[5] Yes sir, when a people get panicky, democracy and humanity and Christian principles go by the board. Rather inconsistent, but human nature I guess. Some silly mothers even go so far as to say, what right have the black-haired kids to go to school with their own precious? One schoolteacher had the courage to say to one of the 'white' pupils who wanted all Japs to be kicked out of school—how they reflect their parents' attitude!—that there were no Japs, and in any case they were far better Canadians than the

---

[4]Soon after Pearl Harbor, two Vancouver dailies, the *Province* and the *News-Herald* advised their readers not to confuse Japanese Canadians with the Japanese in Japan. *News-Herald* columnist Jack Scott, in an article reprinted in the *New Canadian* on December 12, asked his readers not to blame Japanese Canadians for the Pacific War. *Province* readers were told in "Show Them Consideration," an editorial of December 8, 1941: "Our quarrel is with Japan, not with Japanese nationals here or people of Japanese blood. To these, in the very difficult situation they are compelled to face, is due every consideration." On December 19, *Province* readers were again assured that the "authorities have the situation well in hand" (p. 4).

[5]Some 1200 fishing boats impounded and held in New Westminster left the fishermen suddenly unemployed. The letter in protest which Muriel refers to was printed in the *Province*, 20 December 1942.

protester. Strange how these protesters are much more vehement against the Canadian-born Japanese than they are against German-born Germans, who might have a real loyalty to *their* land of birth, as we have for Canada. I guess it is just because we look different. Anyway it all boils down to racial antagonism which the democracies are fighting. Who said it was Woman . . . or the Moon that was inconstant? Oh well, it is only the occasional one here and there. I personally have had no change in my relationship with my neighbours, or my Egg-man, who told me not to worry. Most of the hakujin[6] deplore the war but do not change to their known Japanese friends. It is the small businesses that are most affected . . . like the dressmakers, the corner store, etc., because the clientele are rather shy of patronising in public such places, whatever their private thoughts may be. Powell Street is affected too, in that they have a slightly increased volume of sales to people who usually go to Woodwards etc. But so many have been fired from jobs that belts are tightening everywhere. I don't know yet how all this is going to affect Dad. Most of his patients are fishermen or farmers. So far the farmers haven't been touched.

Last Sunday, the national President of the IODE [Imperial Order of the Daughters of the Empire], who must live far from contact from the Nisei because she didn't seem to know the first thing about us, made a deliberate attempt to create fear and ill-will among her dominion-wide members by telling them that we were all spies and saboteurs, and that in 1931 there were 55,000 of us and that that number has doubled in the last ten years. Not only a biological absurdity, but the records of the RCMP give the lie to such round numbers. The trouble is that lots of women would like to believe their president rather than actual figures. Seems to me illogical that women who are the conservers and builders of the human race should be the ones to go all out for savagery and destruction and ill-will among fellow-humans. They are the ones who are expected to keep the peace with their neighbours in their particular block, but when it comes to blackballing some unfortunate people, they are the first to cast the stone. In times like this I always think of that line:

> If there be any among you that is without sin, let him cast
> the first stone.

---

[6]Japanese for "Caucasians," literally "white men."

Or words to that effect. And certainly we Nisei are neither harlots nor criminals. We're just people.

But more to the point, how are you getting along there? Is the feeling worse in Toronto where they don't know the Nisei as B.C. does? How does the war affect you personally? Can you get a loan to get through next year and the year after? After all, you are Canadian-born, and the Army needs MD's. How has it affected your living conditions at the Lethbridges? Or your acquaintance with Dent and others? Has it affected the wearing of your uniform?[7] Your standing in class and lab? Have you heard from George Shimo? Please let me know fully. So far Doug hasn't let me know by word or line how he is, but he's never one to write, and he's carefree. I think he is all right. If he doesn't lose his job through this, I'll ask him to send you what he can every month. Dad and Nobi are getting along but I think Nobi's kind of sad that he won't see Mom again, and he does miss a home life. But I can't do a thing to help as Dad rejects every offer. I guess that when gas rationing starts Dad won't be able to use that darned car so often in its really affronting sleekness. He has to report every month to the RCMP, just because when he first came to B.C., which was over forty years ago, and plenty of time to naturalize, he didn't look far enough ahead to know how it would have helped his children.[8] That! for people who live only day to day. Politics never meant a thing to him, and doesn't yet. So long as he can eat and swank in his car he lets important things slide.

We're getting immune to the hitherto unused term 'Japs' on the radio and on the headlines of the papers. So long as they designate the enemy, and not us, it doesn't matter much. The Chinese here were indecently jubilant . . . paraded and cheered in their quarters when the war was announced. They are rather childish that way. Of course, now they hope that both the U.S. and Canada will fork over a lot more help than they have so far. I think they are naive. War nowadays is too complicated and can't be compared simply to a street-fight. I am glad however that the Russian army is licking something out of Hitler's troops. The sooner Hitler stops his enslaving

---

[7] Wes was staying at the home of the Lethbridges, a family that ran a rooming house for students. Dent—Wes could not recall his first name—lived there too. Muriel is also asking her brother about his status as a cadet (Interview, Wesley Fujiwara).

[8] The *New Canadian*, 12 December 1941, reported that Japanese Nationals, labelled "aliens," and those naturalized since 1923 were required to register by 7 February 1942, and sign a declaration "pledging themselves to report periodically, to obey the law in all respects, and to guard against any subversive activity."

of conquered people . . . you know, ship-loading them into Poland or into Germany proper to work for nothing in the fields and factories far from home and children; his way of stealing food from the conquered peoples; his system of captive labour; shooting hundreds in reprisal for one . . . then the sooner will the little peoples have a chance at life again.

Ugh! I hate wars, and I've had one already, though I wasn't old enough to know anything then. Now I'm going through a worse one. War, active war, is easier to bear with courage than this surging up of mass hatred against us simply because we are of Japanese origin. I hope fervently that it will not affect the lives of Shirley and Meiko and the unborn son, as the doctor believes. After all, my kids, as only proper being my kids, are so thoroughly Canadian they would never understand being persecuted by people they regard as one of themselves. Already Meiko came crying home once because some kid on the block whose father is anti, said something. Yet I try to rationalize things for them, so that they won't be inundated by self-consciousness. Children are so innocent, but they are savages too, and reflect faithfully their parents' attitudes. That was the one thing my doctor was worried about. Otherwise he, with most of the others, tells us not to worry. We're Canadians and can expect decent treatment from decent people.

Remember when Shirley was little she was more shy of Japanese strangers than she was of the hakujin? She used to stare goggle-eyed at them. Because they, even now, rarely see Japanese people out here, and the ones they see they are so used to that they don't even see the difference in colour. One day they asked me whether they were Japanese or Chinese or English or Scotch or what in the world? It made me laugh. I told them they were Canadians, and that is what they sincerely believe. They are a couple of the most reasonable kids you ever saw, barring Meiko's lapses into 'yancha.'[9] We haven't picked a name for the newcomer yet, but if it is a boy he will be Jon, without the 'h.' I'd like a girl to be named Jennifer, if the opposition won't be too loud. Can't think of a Japanese name at all. I like Phillip, too. Jon is short for Jonathan, you know. While I'm not fussy about the longer one, I do like Jon. What do you think?

Gosh! I never knitted so much in all my life! Guess what: I made three sweaters for Shirley, two for Meiko, one heavy golf cardigan

---

[9]Japanese for "naughty" or "mischievous."

74

for Eddie, one for Nobi, one for you, those two toques and two pairs mitts, a scarf for Eddie . . . this last is a secret yet . . . three jackets (infant), two pants (also infant), two bonnets (ditto), four socks (ditto), one vest (ditto), all in this last couple of months. I'm slightly surprised myself.

Don't let things get you down. You've got to get through. You are far from home, but you know we are backing you up, and we'll never let you down. You are a decent Canadian-born citizen and can depend on it that decent people will always be decent. Let us not think of the dark side, but hope for the best.

We are giving the kids a real Christmas as usual. So have yourself one too. I have written a special column for the Christmas issue of the NC [*New Canadian*]. If it comes out, read it well. I also hope they will print the slightly inebriated verse about the milkman.[10] We can do with some laughs.

Cheerio and thumbs up! A merry Christmas and a happier New Year to you and all of us.

Love,
Mur.

December 30, 1941.

Dear Wes:

Never was I so glad to get your gift and the little note that went with it telling me what a good Christmas you had. Not knowing a thing about Toronto and your Varsity customs I was kind of worried. Now I can say that my Christmas was more than satisfactory. At the dinner here, we drank a toast to you . . . Tom, Kunio, Eiko, Fumi, Eddie, Dad, Nobi, the kids and myself, and Doug. We had a hilarious time, with Tom absolutely relaxed from office worries. He finally got so hoarse he couldn't talk another word. Eiko had such a time too. It's the one time when she really relaxes, and she does

---

[10]Muriel is referring to her article "Christmas for the Children" (*New Canadian*, 25 December 1941: p. 5). The "inebriated verse" is her poem "The Milkman on His Rounds," in the same issue (p. 10).

so, knowing that we understand. Kunio stayed sober . . . he always does from preference and high blood pressure, and I from necessity, but that did not prevent us from having us a time.

Did you have a good time in Brantford?[11] I wish we had sent more, as I'm afraid it wasn't near enough. Oh but I'm glad that you have such nice friends. You know when the days passed without a letter from you I was awfully worried. I had terrible visions of you spending a lonely Christmas day. You don't know how relieved I am that you were busy having a good time. Tell me all about it. I want to know everything you did, and what your friend is like, and what his home is like.

Thanks for that etching.[12] There is always something about an etching that fascinates me, because of what the artist does, I suppose. He doesn't paint or sketch does he? Working on fine plate seems such exquisite work. Sort of a cross between miniature painting and goldsmith-work. Someday I must visit Hart House. The more I hear of it the more I am curious about it. Baked ice-cream! What absolute swank! With candles on it! Oh dear me . . .

Here's what we did:

On the day before, I got everything ready . . . this year it was mostly out of cans and bottles. I just could not afford to do things and end up prematurely in the delivery-room. Anyhow, the turkey was hand-stuffed as usual . . . Dad praised it, glory be! . . . and I emptied the ice-box so I could get it in. Remember the very last Christmas we as a family had together about three years ago? Remember the turkey I roasted and took over then? That bird had an unfortunate accident, though no one knew about it at all that day or for months later when I told Eddie. You see, it was such a tremendous bird and the ice-box was so full of other things that I left it in the pantry, just covered up from the mice, trusting to the cold outside to keep it from going bad. Well, the next day I got up at 6 a.m. and when I went to the pantry one sniff was enough to drive me crazy. No one was up yet; I worked like mad with soda trying to get rid of the terrible odour, but no good. I was frantic. Then I thought of the garlic in the cooler. I peeled a whole one and rubbed and rubbed it into the skin of the bird. I rubbed in enough to smell up the whole house,

---

[11] Wes was invited by Jim Carson, his lab partner at the University of Toronto, to the Carson home in Brantford, Ontario (Interview, Wesley Fujiwara).

[12] Every year Hart House invited out-of-town students for a special Christmas dinner with a present. That year Wes received an etching of the Hart House quadrangle, which he sent to Muriel (Interview, Wesley Fujiwara).

but it just faded the stink a little. Then I melted a quarter pound of butter and worked some flour, salt and pepper into it and covered the whole bird. Then I hurriedly thrust it into the oven before anyone had a chance to come and smell it. If I remember correctly, Dad said that it was delicious. Eddie, too, told me privately that it had the best taste of any turkey yet. Thank goodness for that garlic. That's why this time I kept the turkey in the ice-box, even if I had to leave the other things out. It was good and tender, and did we slaughter it. But even at that, it lasted right to Monday.

It was a sort of catch-as-catch-can dinner. Eiko and Fumi were running around with unaccustomed housewifeliness, while the men slobbered into their napkins, and chewed on celery, and picked at the ends of the bird as it rested on the kitchen table. We did not take the bird to the dining room as there was no room. We carved in the kitchen, and every now and then Tom or Kunio or Fumi or Eiko would take a strip of skin or flesh and assuage their hunger while the plates in the dining room were being filled. We sang as we ate. Tom made innumerable speeches, dotted plentifully with excerpts from the latest *New Canadian*. I wish you had been here. Doug stayed just long enough to eat and then he went to another dinner party. He was homesick for fresh meat, having lived on tinned food so long. From what he tells the meat was sure a treat for him. The dessert just wilted in the ice-box; no one had the energy to eat any more of anything. Dad downed two glasses of beer and sang a solo off-key. Nobi was so happy he almost cried when he had to go home, because he had just recovered from stomach trouble. We had movies, Nobi's new ones that are a step better than the last one. But mostly we just sat and sang after we washed the dishes . . . that is Tom washed, all the time giving us a talk on the origin of washing dishes. He got so dreadfully mixed up that it is a wonder he did not break a dish. Or that Eiko and Fumi didn't drop any in the process of wiping. They were just helpless with laughing. Me too. I ached all over with laughing. I just sat like a Buddha and watched. It was such fun, I forgot that there were two in the family who were not having Christmas as we in Canada have it. But it does no good to think of it anyway. Mom, if she lives through this, will be a white-haired old lady before we see her. As for Kath, she may be a war-widow, and we may have more nieces and nephews.

Doug may be enlisting because his job is insecure . . . it being in a purely export industry. However, if he does join the Army, and he has applied just in case, he says he will give you his pay. He and Sam [Uyede] went to the Recruiting officer here but were referred to Ottawa. They could go to Alberta to join. George Hori was interned. Don't know why yet, as they never tell these things. Apparently he was born in Chosen [Korea], and is not a Hori, but was adopted. He hadn't registered early this year. But mostly the hakujin are fair and friendly. They have written to the daily papers to protest the undemocratic way the fishermen have been treated . . . especially the way those boats have been handled. Swamped in the water etc., the savings of a lifetime under water for lack of careful handling. Others cry out and want every one of us . . . 'man, woman, and child' thrust into camps. They, the vindictive ones, all say we took the bread out of their mouths by working so hard and uncomplainingly. Anyone who works well and hard deserves to eat. There are so many who want to eat without working.

There's plenty of us going to starve for lack of work now. People who have served their employers faithfully for twenty years have been fired without notice, and their sons too. No one to feed them at all. The Welfare appropriated an extra $200 for this need.

(Doug just came in and told me he had been again to the Recruiting Office but they were too busy so he left.)

The one thing we feel is that we have been betrayed. No one here ever expected all the alarums and noise would actually boil down to war. Eddie says that if there ever is an air-raid here, and if this house should be bombed, he's going to get so mad he's going up to fight them himself and tell a thing or two. That's what Kunio says too. He says that this is our home and no one is going to bomb it and get away with it. After all the hard work and love we put into this place, when this is the only home we know, when all our loved ones are around us . . . boy! let one of them be hurt, say we! Kunio was so mad he wanted to join the air force right away. That's the way most of us feel. But there's Mom stuck over there . . . she's most likely worrying about us being bombed. Lord what an awful mess. I hope America hurries up with those defence industries. I knitted a pair of Red Cross socks in two days, a record for me. Now I haven't a scrap of wool in the house so have to get a new batch. I'm going to knit you a jumbo sweater. I've just measured Doug and added a few inches here and there, where I thought you were longer than him. I've added three inches to his arm length. Don't know when I can get it done, but if I knit steadily I should be able to send it to you while Toronto is still freezing. You see, I won't be able to knit in the hospital, or for a week or so afterwards.

Well, I just can't stay up at this machine another moment, so will write again. I'm trying to hang on till past New Year as Eddie is awfully busy at the Bank and cannot get off till maybe the 5th or so. We can't get a maid for love or money. Some kind of shortage, and I'm fussy.

Love,
Mur.

The kids and us all wish you a Happy New Year.

(I steamed open the envelope to get this in.)

December 31, 1941.

Dear Wes:

Well, this is the last day of this miserable year. What a year it has been—starting with my being shrimp-poisoned, Mom going etc., etc., etc. I for one shall be glad to see the last of it. It's been too full of sick days to suit me.

I got your long letter this morning and was reading it when Doug came for lunch again.

Got a great kick out of your description of the Carsons "en famille." Sounded like a lot of fun. I'm awfully glad they are so friendly in Toronto. Reverses my fears.

As you say, the Nisei on the whole are a lackadaisical bunch of nincompoops with no idea at all how to go about things—they are still infants yet so far as the world is concerned and can't be condemned much. They're still pretty much spoon-fed. They go on having good times or else they shrink into caves. Absolute indifference or super-super-self-consciousness. Just now a few hotheads want to grab every vestige of power from the first generation when we youngsters have neither the age, experience or money stability to back up our words. Granted that the elders have been about as stubborn as mules about a lot of things—the kids sure take after them.

79

Training, or the lack of it, is very evident. This is the time we need wise leadership—not firebrands. There's going to be abuse of power—plenty. Little Napoleons and all that sort of thing. It's very touchy.

Good lord! Why say "Jon" is unspellable—it's my idea of a compromise with Eddie. I don't care for this "Johann"-sounding name, but Eddie likes it so we compromise by leaving out the 'h' which isn't sounded anyway. As for "Jennifer," well that's different. The other two kids have odd names for "nihonjin"[13] and I've got to keep it up. Besides, every other name I like has been taken up by my friends and I don't want any mixups. Plain "Jenny" is fine for everyday use. Besides, "Jennifer" is a fine old English name. Anyway, ain't I the odd one with an odd name?—every one of us have "different" names. Who has heard of a Doug, or a Wes, or an Alan, or a Kathleen amongst the Nisei? They're mostly Freds and Toms and Eds etc. Too many of them. They have made too common some fine names I love. You ought to be glad I don't like appendages like "Wellington," "Sterling," "Winston," "Charleen," "Yvonne" etc. Too fancy. I like plain Jon, short for Jonathan, meaning "Gift of God." I like the quaintness of Jennifer, its old fashioned "braids and pinafore" air. So there!

Say! I thought you *were* getting the NC? Well I phoned up Yoshi[14] and he says you'll be getting it from the Xmas issue and your subscription has been extended. Too bad you didn't get them before. It publishes twice a week now to make up for the lack of any other paper.

Well, I'm due at the hospital any day. I've had a bad time—won't be able to do it again I don't think. I've never been so helpless, so sick, so tired. I haven't gone down the front steps for 6 weeks now and feel like a caged bear

I look forward to the day when you'll again drape yourself over the chesterfield with a handful of raisins or whatever you unearth in the pantry.

Thumbs up! Chin up! and cheerio!

Lovingly as always,
Mur.

---

[13]Japanese for a "Japanese person."
[14]Yoshimitsu Higashi, brother of the first editor of the *New Canadian*, Shinobu Higashi, worked as Business Manager of the newspaper.

Dear Wes:

You'll be properly flabbergasted, I hope, when you get this. It's twins!!!! Born on the 7th.

    Boy – 7 lbs. 15 1/2 ounces, 11:00
    Girl – 6 lbs. 12 ounces, 11:04

And did it cause a sensation. Wowie! Eddie has quite recovered from the shock. I gave up "Jennifer" for the girl but still cling to "Jon" even if I have to have the rest of it.

Had a bit of trouble after, but they say "no wonder" —

                             Love,
                             Mur.

January 21, 1942
In bed at home.

Dear Wes:

I gathered from your last letter that the fact that I have twin babes left you in somewhat of "a dither." It has created something of a furor here, and people have quite overlooked the fact that two other Nisei families have had infants at about the same time. Such is the world.

Well, to go into detail.

Since October I had been unable to locomote, so either stayed in bed, or sat propped up in the "wing" chair with my knitting. Seriously, I thought I would bust. The skin and tissues of my abdomen had stretched so much that there was a real danger of them tearing—so thin they were! (As a matter of fact, after I had the babies, I chanced to glance at my tummy when I was horrified to see long thin streaks

81

of coagulated blood. Apparently I was beginning to tear.) Around Christmas I couldn't bear the weight any more, so I begged the doctor to let me have it over with, but he said it was too dangerous both for the babe and for me. On Jan. 6, my patience snapped. I told him I was going to the hospital and that he would just have to do something. On the 7th (Wednesday) he gave me instructions (castor oil etc. etc.—ugh!) and that evening at 7 p.m. I went. It had started showing that very day. For the next 5 days I was one mass of cramps, backache, stomach-ache, and general discomfort—and was dosed constantly with Frosst 292, sleeping pills, and laxative oils. Then slowly things began to mend, and on the 9th and 10th days after, I was feeling rather good, so the doctor let me come home on the condition that I have a trained nurse stay with me for a week. Jon is a little hog and Ellen is as sweet as an elfin fairy. I think both names suit them remarkably well. Jon is a good 2 lbs heavier than Ellen, and looks very, very pudgy, while Ellen is light and all eyes and a wide mouth. She is slightly spoiled already. She was so popular at the Hospital she got carried around extra and now knows when she's picked up. We've been figuring out ways and means of parking them into what space we have. We're not getting the attic finished yet— prices have gone up and fixings have disappeared from the market.

About this "moving" business. I'm afraid it will affect Dad and Doug: Dad because he's not naturalized, and Doug because he will be unemployed pretty soon, if not already so. No clear details yet. I still really can't say how it is going to affect this particular family. If Dad goes we'll have to take in Nobi—feed, clothe, and educate him on the little we have if Dad makes no money, or if Doug doesn't send any when he is entered into this "Civilian Corps."[15] I really don't know whether to be glad or sorry, and Mom and Kath aren't here to add to the burdens or to relieve me of them. I have tentative plans made just in case.

Since they are moving the unemployed Nisei first, I don't think Ed will be affected. After all, they could hardly expect him to leave a good job for road work when he has a big family to feed. I have my fingers crossed—all ten of them. Of course, since I have been house-bound from October I haven't felt the full force of the changes since Dec. 7th.

---

[15]On January 14, the *New Canadian* reported that male Japanese nationals would be removed from the west coast and that plans were underway to form a Civilian Corps of Japanese Canadians for Canadian-born Nisei to work on various projects.

[Alderman Halford] Wilson and his bunch are making political hay out of this. He does so with bland half-truths and falsehoods and hypocrisies enough to turn your stomach. So does the *Sun* paper.[16] They are deliberately inflaming the mob instinct and inciting the irresponsible elements to a bloody riot—the kind they had in 1907, the one in which Wilson's father had a dirty hand.[17] Once the flames catch, Powell Street will be in for a bad, bad time, not mentioning the scattered but large number of families in certain suburban districts. How that Wilson can square his conscience, eat three meals in peace, with his brand of patriotism that stinks to hell—I don't know.

The *Province* and *News-Herald* have been editorially condemning Wilson and his bunch and appealing to B.C. at large to give the local Japs a chance. Acts of vandalism make the headlines, and there has been one murder. Yoshiyuki Uno was shot to death by a 17 or 19 yr old bandit.[18]

Gosh Wes, sometimes I wish you were here with us if only for moral support. The twins are sure going to kick someday when they find out that they missed your brand of nursemaiding. This year we are planting a lot of vegetables and less flowers. The front lawn will be dug up for potatoes. It seems a pity after all the work you put into it, but as we are told that spending brings on inflation, we try not to, of course. These last few days, money slips through my fingers like water. I've had to double my order for diapers, bottles, gowns, panties, sheets for the crib etc. and we have to buy another crib. It's been a holocaust really. The department stores and the drug stores both hail the twins as a slight "boom."

You can see by the writing that I am in bed. Hope you can make out what I wrote. If ever I need help Wes, I'll holler for you—if you're

---

[16]As one example, the *Sun* editorial of January 2 pressed for the removal of all men of Japanese ancestry, assuming without qualifications that they would betray Canada; readers were told that if Japan were to attack "we may expect Japanese civilians to do all in their power to assist the attacker."

[17]Muriel is referring to the 1907 Powell Street riot, when anti-Japanese feelings reached a fever pitch and groups of Caucasians entered the Japanese area breaking windows and clashing with its residents. Discussing Wilson's relentless animosity towards Japanese Canadians, Ken Adachi in *The Enemy That Never Was* writes: "The antecedents for his obsession were clear, for he was the son of the Reverend G.H. Wilson, a chief speaker at the anti-Oriental rally of 1907" (p. 186).

[18]Muriel considered the murder of Yoshiyuki Ono the result of anti-Japanese violence, though nothing in the *New Canadian* report proved this fact. Ono was killed at his Fairview home during a robbery by three men who were apprehended and tried for murder ("Many Clues Unearthed in Nisei Death," *New Canadian*, 19 January 1942).

within reach and not in the Army. With four kids and Nobi, I will need a couple of stout masculine helpers.

So just keep your shirt on and hope for the best. Someday I'll show you some clippings I've kept to prove that there are a lot of decent people in this mad world.

Study hard, and try not to quit. What of the 150 others if the loan doesn't come through? Do they quit too?[19] Please let me know further developments.

My regards to Roger Obata if you see him. I haven't seen him for so many years now.

Chin up and cheerio!

Love,
Mur.

January 31, 1942.

Dear Wes:

I am up now, but find myself still unsteady and dizzy, and my left leg still drags at times. The twins thrive on canned milk, and yell a lot in relays, sleep at the wrong time, and use up an awful lot of diapers. I have 14 milk bottles lined up in the ice-box. Quite a factory. Jon gains like a heavyweight and Ellen is much lighter. She has a very special charm about her that just gets you. You are apt to coo over her in quite an adoring fashion. And you are just as apt to poke fun at Jon for looking so very puggish. Fumi Shoyama agreed to stay with us. My left leg is somewhat paralyzed in the thigh. There's a patch of deadness between hip and knee. I hope it clears up. I would hate to drag my left foot around.

I guess you want to know the final decision on their names. Golly, they (our friends) have set up a regular "Names" Committee, and it's been a cat and dog fight, until last night when we took the initiative, and filled out the registration forms willy-nilly beyond recall. It's been decided thusly and is most likely being filed at Victoria now.

---

[19]Because of the shortage of doctors, the university decided to cram three years into two by continuing through the summer when the students normally worked to support themselves the following year. Wes managed to stay in university through a personal loan (Interview, Wesley Fujiwara).

Jon Eiji, and *Ellen Chiyeko*.

In my exasperated moments I shall holler "Jon*athan*" as a reminder he'd better be good or else . . .

Kunio has appointed himself as one-man Committee to see that Jon turns out to be the U.S. open golf champ. Tom questions his ability and I believe they still argue about it. Eiko and Fumi have been "thumbs down" on ELLEN, but good gosh, after me making a sacrifice in giving up JENNIFER and just getting used to ELLEN, I was having no new name to get used to all over again. Even Doc Banno[20] phoned up to put his foot down on JENNY. My! My! You should have heard some of the fancy names that were offered to me on a plate!

They look vastly different and have their own characteristics. Getting kind of spoilt too. Shirley and Carol (she insists we call her "Carol") can't keep from cuddling them.

Fumi isn't with me any more. She sure was a life-saver, so efficient and neat I didn't have to repeat anything twice.

I hear Eiji Yatabe is headed for Toronto. Quite a few Nisei are headed there. How's chances of my being welcomed there—in case. There's some talk here of a near possibility of a bomb-attack on our west coast. Honest-to-gosh! I don't think there are near enough defence forces here. I wish Ottawa would hurry up and do something and we'd feel a lot safer then. People east are so "bomb remote" they don't realize our danger.

I've often wondered about the right thing to do—whether to evacuate or not? Should I stick here and share what thousands of others will suffer, the kids, too; or should I go somewhere that is reasonably "safe" for the kids. Some people send their kids to a "crèche" but I like to know how my kids are myself. I'd like them to know a mother when they need her most, when all around them are bogies of fear and hate and they need someone to comfort them. What do you think? Do you think it would be selfish of me to move someplace remote from bombs? Do you think I ought to stick around here and let the kids take their chance the same as others? I think this is a problem that has tried the hearts and souls of mothers in England.

---

[20]Doc Banno is Dr. Edward Banno, a prominent Nisei dentist, well known to Muriel during the 1930s through their participation in various community groups, starting back in the late 1920s with the United Church Young People's Society. He was a founding member of the Japanese Canadian Citizens' League (JCCL), and was part of of the four member delegation to Ottawa in 1936 to seek the franchise for Japanese Canadians.

Got a letter from the Sugawaras.[21] They're OK yet. As long as the Gov't doesn't expect Eddie to give up a perfectly satisfactory job to "volunteer" in a road gang, he's OK in his job. I don't like the implication of that word "volunteer." It sounds very much like: "Volunteer, or else. . . . " Dad is still commuting to his office, but I haven't the foggiest idea how he is or how he fares, or what he thinks, or what he tells Nobi. Since Dad is nearer 60 than 40, he won't be "moved" for some time. Only able-bodied men will go first. Uncle Fred will go I think and Auntie will run his garden business. He was wishing you were here to take over his clientele—either you or Doug—if you quit school he would prefer you.

We had an earthquake last night—scared the wits out of Eddie. I was in the bathtub and didn't feel anything. I may have and just put it down to my general grogginess.

I am sending you some newspaper clippings. You'll have to sort out the dates. They are the ones I kept while at the hospital.

This is all I can manage as I have to bathe the twins now in hopes they'll sleep through tonight.

Goodnight, Wes.

Love,
Mur.

February 5, 1942.

Dear Wes:

Well, have you read in Toronto papers that 90 Japanese loggers are headed for some godforsaken lumber camp in the North Ontario bush where the Italian loggers are on strike for something or other. It is a modern Siberia in a way, except that the trekkers are volunteers in a way. Things are beginning to happen. All the B.C. coastline west of the Coast Range is taboo for the aliens.[22]

---

[21]Hanako Uyehara Sugawara was a good friend of Muriel's mother, Tsuru. The Uyehara family is mentioned in Toyo Takata's *Nikkei Legacy*, pp. 77-78.

[22]The headline of the *New Canadian*, 4 February 1942, read: "Ninety Nationals Leave Monday for Ontario." These men were destined for lumber camps and sawmills around Chapleau, Ontario. The same issue announced the designated "Protected Zone," 100 miles from the coast, from which Japanese male Nationals were to be removed.

We still don't know what the Nisei will be expected to do.

Love,
Mur.

February 19, 1942.
Dear Wes:

How's things? That was a good letter you wrote to the N.C.[23]

Well, I guess you've read in the papers that there isn't a province in Canada that will take the "Japs," and B.C. just has to have us whether she will or no. Ian Mackenzie has again come out with "Volunteer or else —." Vancouver City Fathers have petitioned Ottawa to put the OK on a ban of trade licences to Japanese here—850 or so. Won't the Relief offices be flooded then! How on earth the Wilsonites[24] expect us to eat, I don't know. They don't care anyway—under their hypocritical Christian faces. It beats me how they can mouthe "Down with Hitler," and at the same time advocate a program against "Japs" (4-letter syllable in place of "Jews"). Now that attack on this coast is becoming more of a concrete threat, feeling is running pretty high—tho' the individuals in most cases are pretty decent. The rabble-rousers and the mob—haven't we learned about "mobs" in Roman days and in Shakespeare's works? —they are the ones to cause all the trouble. Even the Youth Congress has come out with a plea to move us all out someplace, anywhere except on the coast.

Doug was here the other day so I asked him when his work would stop—and darn him, he wanted to know why! After telling me his job was so insecure. Apparently it's OK. Anyway I'm not sure what to believe these days. Dad takes no thought of his eventual transfer

---

[23]Wes' piece, "A Warning to Nisei Going East" (*New Canadian*, 16 February 1942, p. 2), advised those going east that people in Toronto are still unfamiliar with Japanese Canadians, so prejudice as in B.C. does not exist, though the potential is there. To prevent racial animosity from developing against them as a group, Nisei should go as individuals and avoid congregating together.

[24]Supporters of Alderman Halford Wilson.

to a camp. (They're moving the over-45-year-olds after they get the first batch settled.) In fact, if the war comes any closer we'll all be kicked out.

Gosh, but hasn't 1941 been the awfullest year in our life?

Love,
Mur.

February 25, 1942.

Dear Wes:

I'm worried because I haven't heard from you for such a long time. You're not sick are you? Things are changing fast here, and I think Nisei will be moved too. We are looking around for some place to go to, but not knowing any place but Vancouver, find it very difficult to choose. Uncle Fred is going to Westbank, B.C. I think. Eddie says he's going to join the Civilian Labour Corps if all his friends do. I don't know what Doug is going to do. Or Dad.

We were thinking of Kamloops, but maybe that's too close to the boundary of the "protected area." Personally I want to go to Toronto and be near you.

When the Corps is formed Tom and Kunio will be the first to volunteer.

It's awful here—with the agitation mounting higher. Now it isn't just a matter of sabotage or military necessity. It's just rank race persecution.

Please write at once if you can. I have things to tell you.

Love,
Mur.

March 2, 1942.

Dear Wes:

What a heavenly relief to get your letter. I was just about getting frantic with worry over you. That's why I hope you'll forgive me for writing to Jim Carson. Eddie and I thought that was the only way to find out what really was happening to you. Oh Wes, the things that have been happening out here are beyond words, and though at times I thank goodness you're out of it, at other times I think we really need people like you around to keep us from getting too wrought up for our own good.

Eiko and Fumi were here yesterday, crying, nearly hysterical with hurt and outrage and impotence. All student nurses have been fired from the [Vancouver] General.

They took our beautiful radio . . . what does it matter that some-one bought it off us for a song? . . . it's the same thing because we had to do that or suffer the ignominy of having it taken forcibly from us by the RCMP. Not a single being of Japanese race in the protected area will escape. Our cameras, even Nobi's toy one, all are con-fiscated. They can search our homes without warrant.

As if all this trouble wasn't enough, prepare yourself for a shock. We are forced to move out from our homes, Wes, to where we don't know. Eddie was going to join the Civilian Corps but now will not go near it, as it smells of a daemonic, roundabout way of getting rid of us. There is the very suspicious clause 'within and *without*' Canada that has all the fellows leery.[25]

The Bank is awfully worried about me and the twins, and the manager has said he will do what he can for us, but as he has to refer to the main office which in turn has to refer to the Head Office, he can't promise a thing, except a hope that surely the Bank won't let us down after all these years of faithful service.[26] Who knows where we will be now tomorrow next week. It isn't as if we Nisei were aliens, technical or not. It breaks my heart to think of leaving this house and the little things around it that we have gathered through the years, all those numerous gadgets that have no material value but are irreplaceable. My papers, letters, books and things . . . the

---

[25]As Tom Shoyama recalled, the strongest rumour running through the community at this time was that the eastern road and lumber camps did not exist, and that Nisei men would end up in the North Atlantic working on tankers which were targets for German submarines (Interview, Thomas Shoyama).

[26]Ed Kitagawa started working at the bank in 1922.

azalea plants, my white iris, the lilac that is just beginning to flower . . . so many things.

Oh Wes, the Nisei are bitter, too bitter for their own good or for Canada. How can cool heads like Tom's prevail when the general feeling is to stand up and fight.

Do you know what curfew means in actual practice? B.C. is falling all over itself in the scramble to be the first to kick us out from jobs and homes. So many night-workers have been fired out of hand. Now they sit at home, which is usually just a bed, or some cramped quarters, since they can't go out at night for even a consoling cup of coffee. Mr. Shimizu is working like mad with the Welfare society to look after the women and children that were left when their men were forced to volunteer to go to the work camps. Now those men are only in unheated bunk-cars, no latrines, no water, snow 15' deep, no work to keep warm with, little food if any. They had been shunted off with such inhuman speed that they got there before any facilities were prepared for them. Now men are afraid to go because they think they will be going to certain disaster . . . anyway, too much uncertainty. After all, they have to think of their families. If snow is 15' deep there is no work, and if there is no work there is no pay, and if there is no pay no one eats. The *Province* reports that work on frames with tent-coverings is progressing to house the 2,000 expected. Tent coverings where the snow is so deep! And this is Democracy! You should see the faces here, all pinched, grey, uncertain. If the Bank fails Eddie, do you know what the kids and I have to live on? $39. For everything . . . food, clothing, rent, taxes, upkeep, insurance premiums, emergencies. They will allow for only two kids for the Nisei. $6 per., monthly. It has just boiled down to race persecution, and signs have been posted on all highways . . . . . . JAPS . . . KEEP OUT. Mind you, you can't compare this sort of thing to anything that happens in Germany. That country is an avowed Jew-baiter, totalitarian. Canada is supposed to be a Democracy out to fight against just the sort of thing she's boosting at home.

And also, I'll get that $39 only if Eddie joins the Chain Gang, you know, *forced to volunteer* to let the authorities wash their hands of any responsibilities. All Nisei are liable to imprisonment I suppose if they refuse to volunteer . . . that is the likeliest interpretation of Ian MacKenzie's "volunteer or else." Prisoners in wartime get short shrift . . . and to hell with the wife and kids. Can you wonder that there is a deep bitterness among the Nisei who believe so gullibly in the democratic blah-blah that's been dished out. I am glad Kazuma [Uyeno] is not here.

There are a lot of decent people who feel for us, but they can't do a thing.

And the horrors that some young girls have already faced . . . outraged by men in uniform . . . in the hospital . . . hysterical. Oh we are fair prey for the wolves in democratic clothing. Can you wonder the men are afraid to leave us behind and won't go unless their women go with them? I won't blame you if you can't believe this. It *is* incredible. Wes, you have to be here right in the middle of it to really know.

How can the hakujin face us without a sense of shame for their treachery to the principles they fight for? One man was so damned sorry, he came up to me, hat off, squirming like mad, stuttering how sorry he was. My butcher said he knew he could trust me with a side of meat even if I had no money. These kind people too are betrayed by the Wilsonites . . . God damn his soul! Yet there are other people who, while they wouldn't go so far as to persecute us, are so ignorant, so indifferent they believe we are being very well treated for what we are. The irony of it all is enough to choke me. And we are tightening our belts for the starvation to come. The diseases . . . the crippling . . . the twisting of our souls . . . death would be the easiest to bear.

The Chinese are forced to wear huge buttons and plates and even placards to tell the hakujin the difference between one yellow peril and another. Or else they would be beaten up. It's really ridiculous.

And Wes, we are among the fortunate ones, for above that $39 we may be able to fill it out by renting this house. Now I wish I hadn't given my clothes to Kath. We will need them badly. Uncle has been notified to get ready to move. Dad will be soon too.

There's too much to say and not enough time or words.

Can't send you pictures now unless some hakujin takes the snaps . . . STRENG VERBOTEN[27] to use even little cameras to snap the twins . . . STRENG VERBOTEN is the order of the day.

My apologies to Jim Carson.

Love,
Mur.

---

[27]German for "strictly forbidden."

March 3, 1942.

Dear Wes:

This is just to warn you: Don't you *dare* come back to B.C., no matter what happens, what reports you read in the papers, whatever details I tell you in letters. You stay out of this province. B.C. is hell.

Rather than have you come back here, we'll come to Toronto if we can.

I'll keep you posted by letters, but I repeat, there is nothing for you here. Even if you quit school, stay in Toronto—anywhere East of the Rockies.

Yoshi Higashi went to Camp last night with 7 hours notice.

Eddie will be about the last to go anywhere, whether to another branch bank or elsewhere. If I really need you I'll come to Toronto. *Remember!*

For the love of God, don't you come here. Not you, a single male. You'll be more help to me and to others if you stay where you are—free—even if starving.

Love,
Mur.

March 4, 1942.

Dear Wes:

Just got your air-mail letter. I'll try to tell you as much as I can get down on paper.

We are Israelites on the move. The public is getting bloodthirsty and will have our blood Nazi-fashion. Okay we move. But where? Signs up on all highways . . . JAPS KEEP OUT. Curfew. "My father is dying. May I have permission to go to his bedside?" "NO!" Like moles we burrow within after dark, and only dare to peek out of the window or else be thrown into the hoosegow with long term

92

sentences and hard labour. Confiscation of radios, cameras, cars and trucks. Shutdown of all business. No one will buy. No agency yet set up to evaluate. When you get a notice to report to RCMP for orders to move, you report or be interned. "Who will guard my wife and daughters?" Strong arm reply. Lord, if this was Germany you can expect such things as the normal way, but this is Canada, a Democracy! And the Nisei, repudiated by the only land they know, no redress anywhere. Sure we can move somewhere on our own, but a job? Who will feed the family? Will they hire a Jap? Where can we go that will allow us to come? The only place to go is the Camp the Government will provide when it gets around to it. Ah, but we are bewildered and bitter and uncertain.

As for Eddie and us, the Bank is worried about us. At any rate, there is so much business that he has to clear up for the removees that no hakujin can do, so though we don't know for certain, he may have to stay till the last. We may stay on with him or move first to wherever we have to go, either to Camp or to some other city where there is a Branch big enough to let Ed do routine work behind the counter, but never at the counter as he is doing now. Perhaps we can move together. I don't know. This uncertainty is more nerve-wracking than anything that can happen. I don't know whether to pack all my stuff or sell it. I can take only the irreplaceables. I hope that by the time we go the twins will be big enough to stand the trip in some discomfort. But again I don't know. I may have to cart 12 bottles and 6 dozen diapers. By myself or with Ed, I don't know. Much as I would hate to sell my books I may have to. My wedding presents, all those little things that are more valuable than furniture or $300 radios, what to do with them? If we go to Camp we shall need more blankets, warm clothes, which we haven't got at all . . . winter or summer I wear cotton dresses. In any case, wherever we go will be colder and hotter than Vancouver. We can't even get around to saying good-bye to friends. Our whole way of life is disrupted. My nights are filled with exodus nightmares. My friends are so sorry for me . . . now that I have four kids, twins at that . . . they daren't phone me for fear of hurting me. So I heard. They are so kind. They come and mind them when I want a bit of time for myself. They wash dishes for me too. But now it's every man for himself and devil take the hindmost. Just the same, I am worried about Eiko and Fumi and Uncle and Aunt Toyofuku, Nobi, and the rest of them. When shall we ever meet again if we scatter? *Don't you dare come here!!!* I'll lose you for sure if you do, then where will we be? You sit tight and maybe if Ed isn't transferred, he may find a job where you are, even as a house-servant if he has to. At least we will be together. The Nisei would have been so proud to wear the King's uniform! Even die in it.[28] But not as Helots, tied to the chariot wheels of Democracy. "Labour within or without Canada". . . who knows but the 'without' may be the hot sands of Libya, hauled there as front-line ditch-diggers. And you know that most of the people here call this a 'damned shame,' this treatment especially of the Canadian-born? It's just the few antis who have railroaded Ottawa into this unfairness. Talk about opportunists. Was there ever a better excuse for them to kick us out lock stock and barrel?

I'll try to salvage as many of your books as possible, but honest Wes, I can't promise. You see, we don't know what's going to happen next. Maybe we can move everything . . . maybe we can take nothing. Just depends on whether we go to Camp or to some other city.

So the saga of the Nisei begins. I, too, mean to survive this. This is the furnace where our worth will be tempered to white-hot resilience or not at all.

Pray for us all, you who are in 'safe' areas. For me, whose faith these last few years is sorely tried and wearing thin. Gosh, your first year at school has been a hell of a time. Don't mind my cuss-words . . . we're doing nothing but.

Tommy has bedded down at the NC office since the curfew tolled. We visit in the mornings, and do our housework at night. Every night, when Ed is late getting home and the minute hand gets nearer seven, I sweat blood, wondering whether he'll make it before he's nabbed. He's so busy at the office transferring accounts and helping the Japanese straighten out their affairs, that he stays till the last possible minute. I sweat and sit fuming and helpless. And he can't leave the house before eight either.

---

[28]After Pearl Harbor—and until late 1944—Nisei were not allowed to serve in the armed forces. Opposition came from such powerful political figures as B.C. Premier T.D. Patullo who wrote to Prime Minister Mackenzie King: ". . . if they are called up for service, there will be a demand they be given the franchise, which we in this province can never tolerate" (Public Archives of Canada, William Lyon Mackenzie King Papers, MG26 J1, vol. 331, T.D. Patullo to W.L.M. King, 23 September 1940).

So there you have a blurred picture of what life is like here. I'll keep you posted.

Martial law on the coast in the States. 120,000 Japs on the move inland. But there they don't have to join Gangs, or go to Camps . . . which may be better or worse I don't know. The watchword is "I don't know."

I'm glad you are in Toronto.

Love,
Mur.

March 12, 1942.

Dear Wes:

Enclosed you'll find $50.00 to tide you over some bumps till term's end. I don't know how far you can go on this, but I hope you can finish your full year at least. Let me know how much it takes to finish this term—exclusive of fee—just how much it takes for board, food, sundries. Lectures continue till the end of June, don't they? I would like you to have a complete year, before you start working.

I'm sending a letter through regular mail. Also clippings.

Jon and Ellen are growing fast. They laugh and coo, and enjoy company. If I can get the boy next door to lend me his camera, I could take pictures of the twins to send to you. Life is rather dull without radio or night life.

Don't give up hope. Do you think I could say "How do you do" to Rev. Finlay through you? If so, please do.

Love,
Mur.

March 12, 1942.

Dear Wes:

Just got your letter of the 9th inst. (as the executives say). Don't start looking for house-to-rent yet—very uncertain whether we could go to Toronto at all. Last ruling forbids anyone—even Nisei—to go anywhere in this wide Dominion without a permit from the Minister of Justice St. Laurent, through Austin C. Taylor of the B.C. Security Commission here.[29] We go where they send us.

Honest Wes, I don't know where all to start talking. Things happen so fast, so sudden; so much has happened—that I'm in a daze—(and thankful for it) and nothing affects me much just now except rather detachedly. I mean—everything—I must wake up—yet I know it's real—there's no sadness when friends of longstanding disappear overnight—either to Camp or somewhere in the Interior. No farewells—no promise at all of a future meeting or correspondence—or anything. We just disperse. Uncle Fred's going to Westbank—I hope—to work in a Nursery. Eddie's cousin went to Camp—. We're hit so many ways at one time that if I wasn't past feeling I think I would cry. This curfew business is horrible. At sundown we scuttle into our holes like furtive creatures. We scan the papers to look for the time of next morning's sunrise when we may venture forth. The gov't has requisitioned the Livestock Bldg and the Women's Bldg at Hastings Park to house 2,000 Japs pending removal.[30] Men (white) pictured blithely filling ticks with bales of straw (for mattresses to sleep on the floor I presume) and putting up makeshift partitions for toilets, wash basins, etc. etc. Here the lowly Japs will be bedded down as per livestock in stalls, perhaps open for display to a morbidly curious crowd of "whites," or maybe closed around under police guard, I don't know. The Nisei will be "compelled" (news report) to volunteer in the Labour Gangs. The worse the news from the Eastern Front, the more ghoulish becomes the public. We are the billy-goats and nanny-goats and kids—all the scapegoats to appease a damfoolish few who don't figure that our presence here is

---

[29]Announced in the *New Canadian*, 5 March 1942.

[30]On March 16, the first group of Japanese Canadians from the coastal area entered Hastings Park Manning Pool on the Pacific National Exhibition (PNE) grounds in Vancouver. By March 25, 1593 persons were confined there. "At the peak of its habitation, on September 1, 3,866 persons were living there and over 8,000 passed through the Park at one time or another" (Adachi, *The Enemy That Never Was*, p. 246).

the best security for this Coast. I can't imagine how the government is going to clothe and educate our young when they can't even get started on feeding, or even housing 22,000 removees. Yet the deadline seems to be July 1st or 31st—I forget. Seems to me that either there's no fifth columnist among the Japs or else the secret service men can't find them. If the FBI in the States have rounded up a lot of them, golly, you'd think the RCMP would too, and let the innocent ones alone. I wish to goodness they would catch them all—I don't feel safe if there's any on the loose. But I like to think that there aren't any.[31]

The Manager at the Bank told Eddie he'd do what he can for us, maybe get Eddie transferred to another inland branch or something. Nothing is certain though.

Gosh I miss you. Have lots to say, but don't know how or where to start. Maybe when we're old we can recount these things over a bowl of tea.

Love,
Mur.

March 22, 1942.

Dear Wes:

Well, things are swiftly getting worse out here. If we stick around too long we and the kids are going to be chucked into Hastings Park. The way it is now it is awful. Miss Hyodo[32] is helping the women

---

[31]A letter recently uncovered by Ann Sunahara reveals that the RCMP searched in vain for saboteurs amongst Japanese Canadians. S.T. Wood, Commissioner of the RCMP, writing in August 1942 to William Stephenson, the Canadian Coordinator of British Intelligence in New York City, admitted: "We have had no evidence of espionage or sabotage among the Japanese in British Columbia . . . . The fact remains, however, that we have searched without let-up for evidence detrimental to the interests of the State and we feel that our coverage has been good, but to date no such evidence has been uncovered" (Quoted by Ann Sunahara, "Redress and Government Documents," *Redress for Japanese Canadians: A Community Forum* [Vancouver: Vancouver Japanese Canadian Citizens' Association, 1984], p. 14).

[32]Miss Hyodo is Hide Hyodo Shimizu, a highly respected teacher and community leader and a recipient of the Order of Canada. Her friendship with Muriel dates back

there and she says the crowding, the noise, the confusion is chaos. Mothers prostrated in nervous exhaustion, their babies crying helplessly, endlessly. Families torn from their fathers without a farewell—leaving home and belongings behind—all crammed into two buildings like so many pigs. Children taken out of school—no provision made for future education—more and more people pouring into the Park—forbidden outside of the barbed wire gates and fences—the men can't even leave the building—police guard around them—some of them fight their way out to come to town to see what they can do about their families. Babies—1,000 of them on the way to be born—motherless children stranded because their father got taken to camp (the oldest child in 8 is 13).

Miss Hyodo said the women were going to be mental cases. Rev. Kabayama and family got thrown in too. Oh Wes, this is going to be an ugly fight to survive among us. They're making (they say) accommodation for 12-13,000 women and children. In that little Park![33] Bureaucrats find it so simple on paper so they translate it willy-nilly into action, and the muddle resulting is kept "hush-hush" from the public who are already kicking about the "luxury" allowed to Japs.

There is a little Napoleon and his henchmen running things arbitrarily with the OK of the RCMP and now Kunio and Tom are in bad with them.[34] It's a case of "obey or be interned." In short Der

---

to the early 1930s. In the spring of 1943, she and Terry Hikada, the only two Japanese Canadians to be granted teaching certificates in B.C., were appointed Supervisors to train 140 Nisei as primary school teachers in the detention centres in the B.C. Interior (Sunahara, *The Politics of Racism*, p. 97).

[33]Muriel is reacting to what was considered a rumour that the government planned to detain the community in Hastings Park for the duration of the war. However, in a letter dated 14 March 1942 to S.T. Wood, Commissioner of the RCMP in Ottawa, F.J. Mead, a member of the B.C. Security Commission and an Assistant Commissioner for the RCMP, says that "the thought is already in the minds of the Commission as to whether or not it would be advisable to keep the women and children in these buildings for the duration of the war." An estimated 8000 people could be housed in Hastings Park. The reasoning is simply economic: the "ghost towns" would be much more expensive (Public Archives of Canada, Records of the RCMP, RG18, F3, vol. 3567, file C3129-1-4, vol. 1, F.J. Mead to S.T. Wood, 14 March 1942).

[34]The "little Napoleon" is Etsuji Morii, appointed Chairman of the Japanese Liaison Committee by the B.C. Security Commission because of his prewar connections with the RCMP. Shoyama remembered being summoned, with Kunio Shimizu, to meet with RCMP Commissioner Mead after the first group of Nisei who were supposed to go east refused to comply. Mead said he was informed that Shoyama and Shimizu "had been in 'constant communication' with the Japanese Consul ever since

Reichstag has been set up with Nappy as der Fuehrer. There's even a Goering and a Goebbels. Uncle Fred was going to Westbank, but now he can't. He has to go to Camp. If the women and children stay here as is now most likely, they'll be kept like animals in the Pool.[35] In that case Eddie might just have to stay on at the Bank to look after their small accounts. But me and the kids might not get preferred treatment. We might have to go to the Park too. So I've asked Eddie to send us to Toronto if he can get the Bank to guarantee his job and salary. We are then going to rent this house to have that much extra for food for us. I don't know though, if the war goes bad for Canada, would we be safe in the Park—or on our own in Toronto? That's what we try to answer in planning one way or the other. Among our relations, we are the only ones who at present seem to be the luckiest—being Nisei, a good permanent (I hope) job, a home—but then our fate is the most uncertain. Mine is the only place (among our relatives) with small babies needing special care, and I dread the thought of being dumped onto one straw pallet with 4 kids. No privacy—fight for share of food—and all the complex tragedy of being caged.

We can't make any definite plans. If we can go to Toronto, then you must find me a house, perhaps not too far from the Campus so that you can stay with us. If I can feed you, perhaps you can get your degree. I don't know though what we are going to do. Everything is so uncertain.

What do you think? Do you think we might be worse off in Toronto? Of course we couldn't go unless I was sure of a steady income.

I'll close now, and get back to work.

Lovingly,
Mur.

Pearl Harbor. We denied this and asked about his informant and, of course, we speculated about Mr. Morii and his 'henchmen.' The Commissioner, as I recall, did not deny that." Shoyama and Shimizu were pressed to go east voluntarily. Shoyama, as Editor of the *New Canadian*, was permitted to stay, but shortly after, Shimizu was ordered to leave (Interview, Thomas Shoyama).

[35]That is, Hastings Park Manning Pool.

March 25, 1942.

Dear Wes:

I received your letters, and also letters from Mrs. Ray Pannell and Mrs. Grace Mack.[36] Please say "thanks" for me, though I've written to them too.

The Nisei have formed a Japanese Canadian Citizens' Council and I'm on.[37] 30 of us. Tom and Kunio and Chitose Uchida are our reps for the Commission. 100 fellas have to go to Ontario camp. 100 more on Thursday. Awful mess. Bureaucracy, inefficiency, etc. etc. Chaos, bitterness, near riots among internees or should I say confinees at the Park Pool. If, in any event, I can go to Toronto, if the Bank would make some arrangements, the only way I can get a permit to go would be if several people from Toronto wrote to the Commission saying they'd welcome me and take me in etc. etc. In that case I'll write air-mail, so will you please ask someone to write? Not until I say "when," though, as this plan may not go through and I may after all be chucked willy-nilly into the Pool. Old Morii is going to get his. All his crooked henchmen, too. Tell you all about it sometime, while our mail is still uncensored. Try and hang on there until we are settled one way or the other. Will send you eating money, meanwhile.

NC moved HQT to Tairiku.[38] Subsidy by Issei. Council subsidized up to $1000 per month by Issei. Morii blackmailing $60,000 out of suckers.[39] One hell of a mess. Tom and Kunio acknowledged leaders. Wish you were here, but better stay there. You'd only get chucked into camp.

Will write again. Cheerio. How long can you eat on $50? I mean, when will you need another lump? Let me know.

Love,
Mur.

---

[36]Ray Pannell and Grace Mack were members of the Carlton United Church in Toronto who assisted Muriel and her family in getting to Toronto.

[37]For a discussion of the activities of the JCCC, see Introduction, pp. 35ff.

[38]Tairiku Nippo Building, 215 E. Cordova.

[39]Muriel is voicing a common rumour in her community, though the charges were not substantiated later when a government inquiry was formed to investigate them. For further details of the inquiry and Morii's alleged connections with the pro-nationalist, Japanese underworld organization, the Black Dragon Society, see Adachi, pp. 244-246.

March 27, 1942.

Dear Wes:

Enclosing $40.00 to add to that $50.00 you have. Maybe you can eat 3 months yet, whether you go to school or not.

Those boys didn't go to Ontario. Wouldn't. So they were arrested. Both trainloads. Otto Yanagisawa too.

Sab Takahashi was arrested, then learned he was suspected as a "spy." Had a road map. Friend drew it as directions for his benefit in driving to Edmonton.[40] Now he's in the Pool.

Situation getting worse. Now Nisei are treated as "enemy aliens." The Minister of War or Defence or something is flying here to take drastic steps.

I'm in one damned hurry.

Love,
Mur.

March 30, 1942.

Dear Wes:

Got both your letters today. Situation here changes daily till I don't know where to stand. Last reading says I might not be able to set foot out of this town while Ed's at the Bank. Uncle Fred's going tonight, at long last, with Kakichi [Fujiwara], Tateishi, Takashima[41]—about 150 to Jasper. Last night over 100 boys entrained for Schreiber, Ontario. Gosh I don't know where to begin.

Well, the first batch of 100 refused to go. They got arrested and imprisoned in that immigration building. Next bunch refused too.

---

[40]Sab Takahashi was mistakenly arrested on suspicion of intent to sabotage at Trail, B.C. for possessing maps. He had left the University of B.C. to continue his engineering course at the University of Alberta, and the map of the Trail area was drawn by a friend who wanted Sab to drop in on his parents ("Sab Takahashi Case Fully Cleared," *New Canadian*, 28 March 1942).

[41]The Takashimas in Muriel's letters are the family of Shizuye Takashima, author of *Child in Prison Camp* (Montreal: Tundra Books, 1971), an account of her childhood memories of the wartime uprooting. Her mother, Teru Fujiwara Takashima, is the younger sister of Muriel's father Dr. A. Fujiwara.

They were arrested. Then on Saturday they were released on the promise that they would report back to the Pool. There was every indication they wouldn't so the Council (united Nisei) worked like mad to make them keep their word. They went to Ontario. That was a huge hurdle and the Commission cabled Ralston[42] to come and do something. Gosh where'll I start?

Well, it's like this:

When the evacuation first started, Morii (you know that racketeer, big boss on Powell?) was king pin. He and his henchmen virtually became dictators and were a law to the poor Japs. They hustled the single males, ordered them to go to labour camps, and commandeered cash from any who wanted to buy a permit to stay. The RCMP have a couple of men who aren't above having their palms greased—and greased well. They are in cahoots with Morii. It's a case of "or else." The story that goes around, and since the Council discussed it, it is most likely true (victims are also confessing now) that there are about 300 illegal entries still here. These 300 paid thousands and thousands of dollars to be overlooked when the Oriental Commission[43] came to investigate. Morii must have arranged things with someone so that they (the 300) were never found. Now, it's a case of Morii saying: "Give me my way or I'll talk." But it's loaded at both ends. The Mounties tell Morii: "You do this for us or we talk too." It's a case of their propping each other up and sacrificing 23,000 for the 300 and all the dirty work in between. How much can be proved is very very doubtful. The honour of the redcoats can't be "smirched" you know. So the Mounties give Morii orders: "Here's a list of names. Get 100 to the station or else." Indifferent to all individual sufferings and tragedies. The men on that list have had to go. Any who didn't want to, paid hundreds of dollars to Morii and were placed conveniently on a Committee, now numbering nearly 200—a committee being allowed to stay till the last. A lot of "nationals" left on their own, and are now stranded all over the Interior. The husband of Frances [Takimoto Yoshida] is in Kelowna, and Frances can't get to him. Nippon Garage Maikawa is also somewhere unable to budge.

---

[42]J.L. Ralston, Minister of National Defence.

[43]The "Oriental Commission" is most likely a reference to the Board of Review, chaired by Hugh Keenleyside, appointed in 1938 by Mackenzie King to investigate charges of illegal entries on a large scale of Japanese to Canada, though after careful scrutiny the Board could not substantiate the charges (see Adachi, pp. 180-181).

Then Morii's men went too far, and the heretofore quiet Japs started to howl: "Down with Morii," "Kill him," "Burn him up." The reaction against his high-handedness is terrific and Vancouver Japs—nay, B.C. Japs—are split into 2 factions, pro and anti Morii. The "Naturalized" and the Nisei have sunk Issei and Nisei differences and have joined hands against a common foe. Even the Nationals are backing us up against Morii and his clique. Nishiguchi from New Westminster is on our black list. So is Nishio (a National). Heck! I don't know where else to start from.

Then the Hastings Park Pool began to fill. Yanagisawa, Shoji, Sugumoto were the 3 men in charge of the Japs incoming. No system. Haphazard bedlam resulted. Near-riots of confinees yelling: "Tear 'em apart. At them, the skunks!!" (meaning the three, who individually may not be bad men, but together as a committee were the ace of mishandlers). It got so bad that they quit in fear for their skins. We put in our own men then. The three were pro-Morii—picked by him. On Thursday night the confinees came down with terrible stomach pains. Mild ptomaine I gather. Imagine, a wholesale company is contracted to feed the confinees! You know what that means: profiteering. Also there are no partitions of any kind whatsoever there—and the people are treated worse than livestock. No plumbing of any kind. They can't take a bath. They don't even take their clothes off—2 weeks now. Lord! Can you imagine a better breeding ground for typhus? They are cold. Vancouver has a fuel shortage. They are undernourished; they are unwashed. One of the men who came out to buy food told Ed it was pitiful the way kids scrambled for food and the late ones went empty. I'm not going in there, no matter what happens. God damn those dirty politicians that brought this tragedy on us.

Wilson got beaten up. Very hush-hush but is fact. A "white" boarder at the Sadas (without any prompting) said his doctor treated Wilson (apparently not a regular patient) for multiple bruises. A German and a Dago followed him and dragged him out of his "lim" and mopped the road with him. The other day Doug saw him with a police bodyguard.

Ed has to report tomorrow and will most likely be told when to go where. A day's notice at most. Now it'll remain for the Bank to do some fast work and keep him here. Gosh Wes, I don't know what's going to happen. If Ed stays on at the Bank, we have to stay here. If he *has* to go to Ontario, I don't see why we can't too, but then probably we won't be allowed. Then even if he can stay here, there is the possibility that we would be thrown into the Pool anyway. I shall fight to keep out. It's murder—slow murder that's what.

Honest to gosh Wes, sometimes I wake up and think it's all a nightmare. The daily papers have been hush-hush about Nisei being arrested etc. The Youth Congress protested at ill-treatment, but since then, not a word appears in the papers about us here. One baby was born at the Park, premature I think. Poor little waif, born on a straw tick. Who knows what he'll (or she'll) turn out to be?

About those letters: I'll let you know if and when I need them. I don't know but things might change again. The Commission seems to be as ignorant as the rest of us about what's going to happen next. There is some talk of 100 Issei (Nationals, mind you) being left behind to look after the women and kids at the Pool. "Nationals!" Definitely there's dirty business afoot.

Eiko's at the Pool, clerking at the Administration office. I haven't seen hide nor hair of her for over a month now.

Jon is definitely a boy. Blunt featured, fair, husky (13 lbs.) a great eater and cry-baby. He yells. Good-looking, I think. Ellen is definitely a girl. Sweet-faced, elfin features (even to the big ears like Shirley's), and a screecher. She's 9 1/2 lbs. They both "coo" and gurgle now, and very much "down" on cod liver oil. (Have they taste buds so young?) Shirley and Meiko just love the twins and fight to carry them. I have Hiroko Sada working for me now, else I'd never get my things packed. Got my dishes and silver boxed. Gave your books to Pete [Yamada]. Saved the ones you listed. Steve [Yamada] was here yesterday. He's like you in a way.[44]

Gosh but when I got those letters from Mrs. Mack and Mrs. Pannell, we were touched. Mrs. Pannell used to live in Vancouver. I told them a little about how things were here. I phoned Tommy about Mitch and he said, "Yes, I think they will be exploited at the beginning."[45] I guess that's where Doug will be heading too. Maybe you can see him then.

Was my letter incoherent? We all are now. Maybe this one is as clear as mud.

---

[44]Peter and Steve Yamada are cousins of Muriel and Wes. Their mother, Asao Fujiwara Yamada, is Dr. A. Fujiwara's younger sister.

[45]Mitchell ("Mitch") Hepburn, Premier of Ontario, was arranging for a handful of Nisei males to work on his farm.

March 31:
Well, Eddie went to report this morning.

April 1:
Awful things happened one after the other yesterday. Eddie has to go on the 7th, unless the Bank can stop it in time.

Eddie's cousin Tsuji socked a mountie and the whole mob of Japs piled onto the cop. That's how come liquor permits were cancelled. He showed us his bruised knuckles. Of course I don't know how much of his colourful tale to believe, but what we heard was very funny and interesting. I get a great kick out of that guy. I like his rascality much, much better than some stupid harmless people. I always stand up for him. He's always stewed in spirits, where he gets it I don't know, but gosh is he colourful. Bleary-eyed, nodding his head laughing, spieling braggadoccio stories. I love listening. To hear him is to forget my troubles. He sounds as if he's battling the cops single-handed! Lovely man. Even now a chuckle rises. I wish he would come every day.

Doug's going to Ontario in about 10 more days I think. Round about the middle of this month he'll be at Schreiber. So he thinks. Uncle Fred went last night.

Wes, go out to some lonely spot and swear up and down for me. I feel so damned helpless. I can't even cry. I haven't cried yet. I want to but I can't.

Regular mail's too slow.

Will write often, to keep you posted. As soon as we find out definitely what will happen to us, will let you know. Then you can do your part.

Stand by, Wes.

Love,
Mur.

––––––––––––––––––

April 2, 1942.

Dear Wes:
Got your next two letters today. Eddie's sick in bed. The long

105

months of steady hard work, helping me at home, no exercise, no fun, not much sleep, worries, have laid him low with fatigue. Think it is flu too. Anyway he is too tired, too aching of joints to be anything but terribly miserable. Since the evacuation started he has had no letup at all, and the curfew has prevented him from getting his evening exercise, the only thing he can do in the winter. The Bank hasn't let us know yet what we can do. If it doesn't do something in a hurry, Eddie will have to entrain on the 10th.

I'm afraid now that those kept in Hastings Park will be held as hostages or something, perhaps to ensure the good behaviour of the men. Sab's in there. The maps in his possession were drawn by his classmate as directions for him how to get somewhere. He was cleared of all suspicion. He's helping out at the Park Pool now, and I hope to get to see him soon when I get my pass. I think he'll eventually get to Alberta.

Steve's family has a lawyer working for them. This lawyer went to the Security Commission's lawyers to get some action on behalf of the Yamadas. He reported back that these lawyers told him to go easy, to let the matter drift, because they intended to let the Japs suffer as much as possible. I asked Steve if his lawyer was reliable. The answer was "yes." I was horrified. The Commission is responsible to the Federal Gov't through the Minister of Justice St. Laurent. It works in conjunction with the RCMP. The Commission has three members, Austin C. Taylor to represent the Minister of Justice, Commissioner Mead of the RCMP, and John Shirras of the Provincial Police.

I'm going down the points in your letter.

Yup, Vancouver is a paradise to live in. I hate to leave the old burg, but then I never want to see it again for it contains too many bitter memories. The water here is swell, so's the weather. It is spacious, it is friendly. It is home. If I go to Toronto I will need at least 3 moderate sized bedrooms, or 2 large ones. I would prefer a house even if far from town, or in a place near a few stores . . . something like our suburbs. But then this too depends on whether the Bank will transfer us to that place. We may have to go to some town in Alberta or Saskatchewan or Manitoba. But I'm hoping for Toronto. You see, if I go with Eddie we have to go wherever the Bank sends us. Then if Eddie stays here we may be able to do so also, but within the confines of the Pool. I don't know. That's why I can't answer any of your queries yet. But I am making several alternative plans. One of them is the Toronto move. *Nothing is definite yet.* It makes me weep with gratitude to think that your friends are ready to rally to our help.

If I have been vague, it is because we are all vague about everything. Only Tommy and Kunio know, and they are too busy to talk to me. The NC comes out so seldom now that we have no way of knowing anything, and I cannot go to every meeting every day. There is so much veiling, so much politics, so much soft-pedalling in the paper, because it is censored by the RCMP. Only verbally can we hear anything, and then we have to be sure of the reliability.

Shirley and Carol are rapidly becoming conversant with the terms 'camp,' concentration camp, etc. Their nightly prayer is "Please don't let Daddy go to camp."

Tomorrow I'll be 30. There are lines beneath my eyes that were not there in January. My back has a discouraged stoop I noticed in a shop window today, and I drag my feet, the shoe repairman says. I have lost so much weight this month past that I can easily get into my suit now.

Tomorrow is Good Friday. Rev. K. Shimizu is coming to baptize the twins at home tomorrow evening. Doug will be here, and so will Aunt Sei and Janey. They will sleep here. The Reverend has a car permit and a curfew permit so he can go around freely.

(Going to bed now)

April 5:
Well, the twins were baptized. Jon fidgeted right through the ceremony, but Ellen cooed like a cherub. I held Jon and Auntie held Ellen. Shirley and Carol and Janey were goggle-eyed. There is a Council meeting practically every day, but of course I cannot go to them all.

Doug's not working now, as the RCMP won't let him go back to Indian River. He's staying with Seiji [Onizuka] at the Hotel World, but sometimes bunks with the Yanagisawas. Kachi [Yanagisawa] got married the other day.

We have had no word from the Head Office about Eddie. Ed has to report on Tuesday. I'm sick with worry. Frank[46] has to go Tuesday too, so there won't be anyone at the Bank to handle the Japanese customers.

---

[46]Frank Nakamura worked with Ed Kitagawa in the Japanese Department of the bank.

I hear that Taylor is drunk most of the time, and Mead is a mean guy, only MacNeil (CCF)[47] is approachable. Fujikazu Tanaka[48] is causing a lot of trouble at the Council meetings. He's got no brains.

Tomorrow I'm taking the kids to see *The Gold Rush*, a Charlie Chaplin revival. I had the boy next door take some snaps of the twins. As soon as they are developed I'll send them. Well, I'm going to bed again.

Love,
Mur.

April 8, 1942.

Dear Wes:

Got your letter this morning. It is getting harder and harder to go anywhere now on our own, and Ed and I just can't do anything about it. The Bank hasn't given us a definite answer whether or not they are going to do anything for us, like transferring us some other place. Until they have definitely refused to do anything we just can't do anything on our own. Tomorrow Ed has to go for his medical exams, and then he'll know the date of his entraining, and also will get his strip of tickets or whatever it is that they get. He is going to try to get a temporary extension today. Since yesterday afternoon when we heard that the Bank might refuse to help I've been going around in a daze, and cannot settle down to any work, so I thought I would pound it out on this machine, hoping to get some relief from this strain. If the Bank does nothing, then I will have to go to the ghost town with the rest. If Ed has to go to Ontario he will most likely dig ditches or something equally unskilled, because I don't suppose they will need bookkeepers anywhere. I don't know what to do now.

I've lost quite a bit more weight than I thought, apparently, because

---

[47]Grant MacNeil of the CCF party was the Executive Secretary for the B.C. Security Commission.

[48]Fujikazu Tanaka, with Robert Shimoda, spearheaded the Nisei Mass Evacuation Group.

Ed's cousin said I was so thin she hardly recognized me . . . my face has lengthened. However, in the most embarrassing place, I am still much too fleshy. I wish my hips would thin rather than my face. This way I look positively sick.

I had a snap taken of the twins that I am enclosing. The sun got into the children's eyes so they look lopsided. The camera I borrowed is so rickety that the little lever stuck all the time, making the film blur.

I haven't been to meetings of the Council lately, but things have been happening again. The bunch of Nisei scheduled to go last night balked. I don't know what happened yet. You see, there are three general camps, or rather a three-way split among the Japanese here: the Morii gang, the Nisei and Kikajin Council (Kikajin being the naturalized), and the anti-Moriis who are also not co-operating with the Council, the last being the very great majority, and the Council being just a handful of sensible people.[49] It's terrible uphill work for the Council, especially when Tom and Kunio are still under RCMP suspicion. Two Takashima kids were supposed to go last night but haven't heard whether they are in the jug or confined in the Pool or left on that train. You know Wes, unless you are here right in the middle of all this mess you can't realize what it is like. There is a pall of ignorance and fear and uncertainty, which arouses defiant resistance and plain mulish balking. The NC doesn't publish often enough to be of much use. The daily bulletins that are posted on Powell St. are not available to the people in general. Nobody knows the exact details of what is happening, but we know plenty happens every day and everyone that reports it to another gets a different version, and this spreads like wildfire through the town. So the Council is hard put to keep up with forestalling the latest rumours. There is great distrust of the federal authorities, fear of the RCMP, and mostly a kind of helpless panic . . . not the hysterical kind, but the kind that goes round and round going nowhere.

Doug is apathetic too. By the way, Luke [Tanabe], Dan Washimoto, Roy Kumano and a couple of others have been hired by Mitch to work his farm. Perhaps you might get to see Luke.

---

[49]Of the three groups, the "Morii gang" are those who support Etsuji Morii and his Japanese Liaison Committee; the "Nisei and Kikajin Council" are the Japanese Canadian Citizens' Council and the Naturalized Canadian Japanese Association; and the "anti-Moriis" are the Nisei Mass Evacuation Group and people in the community not aligned with a designated group. For a discussion of the "three-way split," see Introduction, pp. 34-42.

Do you mean to say that there are actually Japanese Naval officers in Steveston? Ye gods . . . you wouldn't be mistaken? Maybe they were just retired, or just had to take that course during school, since Japan is so highly militarized that even school kids learn army and navy manoeuvres. Gee whiz, if what that Minister's son said is true I hope to gosh he's told. I hate to think that even we unsuspecting Japanese couldn't tell a fisherman from a sailor. Then all those articles that are appearing in many magazines must be true. They sounded too much like the movies to convince me. I wonder if Tom and them know? Do you think the NC would knowingly cover up? I hardly think so. The trouble with all this spy business is that the usual man on the street, the ordinary guileless man, can't tell which is a spy and which isn't. Gosh, even the secret service men can't. As you say, you can't even trust your neighbour now.

Have patience with us, Wes, if we can't tell you exactly what we are going to do. I can make plans, but they are only plans. So I repeat again, until the Bank definitely refuses to help, we can't go ahead with any plan of our own. As soon as I find out for certain I'll let you know. I'll keep you posted on our affairs anyway.

April 9:

Eddie got a one month extension. It seems to us that all those Vancouverites who are conscientious enough to report when they have to, law-abiding enough to not kick about their treatment . . . these are the ones who have to go first. Those who intend to buck the authorities for no reason that is reasonable are the ones still on the loose. These are single men without a shade of responsibility. So the married ones have to go to fill the quota. Fujikazu raised a rumpus at the Commission offices and got the Council into hot water. He ought to be fried in oil.

Tommy sends this message:

> Dear Wes: Guess we have to take all that is happening in our stride without the help of pulled wires or anything. I know how you feel, and thanks. Times being what they are, much as I would like to write to you, I just can't sit down to it. It is better that even one, such as yourself, stay out of this mess.

This is all he had time for over the phone. He also said that all that could be done in the interests of the people as a whole is being done. More they cannot do, without endangering a lot of innocents. Time, and the good sportsmanship of the Nisei, now will do more to clear things up than a lot of fighting, justified though it may seem. About the Morii business, it is dirty enough, but the tide is turning against him without our forcing the issue, so don't get excited too much about it. After all, in times like these, morale counts a lot, and if the general public found out that certain heroes had terrible feet of clay, who knows but that we, not the deserving ones, will get it in the neck. After all, it isn't the people in general that are doing this to us. We've been fighting like mad here and many times felt that exposure was the only cure for things, but you get right into this tangle, and you find that you just can't do it yet. For there is nothing we can put forward as proof. Even those who have been talking a lot generally shut right up when we ask them to come right out and say it before witnesses. What can you do? Anyway, as I've been told, our letters aren't censored yet, but they might be any time, so it is better to know that a wide mouth gets more than one person into trouble. So let's you and I quit talking about what should be done. You see Wes, things change every day. Even by air-mail I can't keep you up to the minute on the latest.

Did I tell you that Uncle Fred has gone to Tête Jaune? We haven't heard from him yet.

Doug says that the beet fields are terrible. He worked there remember? No nothing. Water so alkaline it is bitter, and you have to dig at least 100 feet for your well. So with the babies I wouldn't think of going there. The ghost towns would be better. The Bank hasn't done a thing for us yet, and there is a possibility that they will not, because the Royal Bank is not doing anything for Mr. Kinoshita.[50] But they haven't said anything definite yet so we have to await their pleasure. Ed says he'll dig ditches if he has to, but I'm afraid he won't last long. He's awfully frail. He needs fresh air and exercise in slow easy doses. He can't dig four square yards of garden without getting so tired he can't work. Whatever would he do with a pickaxe! These white collar jobs sure take it out of a man.

Well, I'm going to post this one as is, and write again.

Love,
Mur.

---

[50]Z. Kinoshita held the same position at the Royal Bank as Ed did at the Bank of Montreal.

Dear Wes:

Just got your letter. You know, Wes, I wonder what I'd have done without you to sort of keep me balanced. Every time I get one of your "preachy" letters I feel as if I'd been hysterical for nothing.

I've been meaning to write Mrs. [Olive] Pannell another letter, but life is so miserable just now that its poison is sure to find its way into anything I say. Right in the middle of a letter the lid is sure to blow off. So will you give her my regards, and tell her how much we appreciate her kindness? We are waiting daily for some definite word from the Bank, for until then we can do nothing. As for that "Record of Dignity" thing—it was only the tail end of a double column of wrathful questionings.[51] Tommy has destroyed it, but I can remember it almost word for word. They told me it was too hot to handle, so they doused it.

Doug was here this morning. He's got an extension till the 28th. Told the RCMP he was going to Alberta.

> "Beet farm?" queried the officer.
> "No. Cowboy. Been there before. Know the people and the work."
> "You the head of the family?"
> "No. Single."

At this point a Morii fellow says:

> "You can't go there on your own."

Doug swore at him:

> "You shut up! Who's talking to you? I'm talking to this Mountie, not to you."

---

[51]"A Record of Dignity" was published in the *New Canadian*, 5 March 1942. This statement appears as the Epigraph to this collection of Muriel's writings.

Then Doug told me he wanted to poke the runt but he was so little, Doug couldn't. Doug intends to go to Alberta and says to the Mountie:

"Who's gonna stop me?"

So, there you are. If they won't let him go to Alberta to work as a cowhand, he's going to "buck." Doug's 28, and I don't feel I have any right to even persuade him otherwise. You see, these boys (or men I should say) are terribly bitter. The Morii gang makes them worse. Trying to explain to them is worse than not trying. They look at you as if you were a traitor.

As for faith—well, it depends on the person. I can't say anything for other people, but for myself it's this. I have faith in this land—not in any political group, not in any MP and their codes (or tricks maybe), not in any system of government—but in the land and the people on the land.

Mickey Maikawa's father came back from Grand Forks where he was stuck. He's bought land for his family and is buying a tomato farm for Mickey and Kiyo. Mr. Maikawa went to see Greenwood, the best (?) of the ghost towns and says the accommodation being fixed for the lowly Jap is worse than Hastings Park. In Greenwood there are only shacks and big frame buildings. No central heat of course. We'll all be in cages, so to speak. Hundreds will be housed in one building. There'll only be double-decker wooden bunks and community stoves. Eddie went to see the Pool bunkhouse for men (the former Women's building) and was nauseated by the smell, the clouds of dust, the pitiful attempts at privacy. The Livestock Building (where the women and kids are) is worse, plus manure smells. Those straw ticks get damp and mouldy. There are no fresh fruits or vegetables. Kiyo Maikawa ate there one day to see what it was like. She had 2 slices of meat, bread and butter and tea. That's all. For supper it was 2 slices of bologna and some bread and tea. That's all. Those who have money go out to buy lettuce and tomatoes and fruit. Nothing for babies, yet. We're asking for improvement in that quarter.

You know Wes, my one obsession is privacy. Ever since I could remember I liked being in a place to myself—in fact I needed it. I'll go nuts if I have to stall with a lot of clacking females and crying kids. If I could have a house to myself and the kids—if Ed and we could be transferred to York—if—if—if—

113

Sab earns about $2 a day at the Pool helping out, minus board, of course.

I forgot to enclose the snaps last time so here they are. You can see that Jon is fairer than Ellen. They are beginning to "coo" at each other.

By the way, how's the drinking water there? Bet you can't beat Vancouver water? That's what I'm going to miss.

I'll have to rent this house partially furnished. Have to leave the chesterfield suite, dining suite, range, refrig, rugs, linoleum etc. etc. We aren't allowed to sell our furniture. Hits the dealers somehow. I don't understand it, but so they say. The Council is representative of only its backers now. Other organizations have their own delegates to the Commission, ever since Fujikazu raised that fuss. Awfully unwieldy business—this evacuating. Very few entrain for work camps. The rest just "buck." There's a "wanted" list of over a hundred names of Nisei. More added every time the boys won't budge. They're chased all over town. Doug may be one of them yet. Will write again.

Love,
Mur.

Hastings Park Description
April 20, 1942.

Dear Wes:

I went to the Pool yesterday to see Eiko who is working there as steno. I saw Sab too who is working in the baggage . . . old Horseshow Building. Sab showed me his first paycheque as something he couldn't quite believe . . . $11.75. He's been there for an awful long time. Eiko sleeps in a partitioned stall, she being on the staff, so to speak. This stall was the former home of a pair of stallions and boy oh boy, did they leave their odour behind. The whole place is impregnated with the smell of ancient manure and maggots. Every other day it is swept with dichloride of lime or something, but you can't disguise horse smell, cow smell, sheeps and pigs and rabbits and goats. And is it dusty! The toilets are just a sheet metal trough, and up till now they did not have partitions or seats. The women kicked so they put up partitions and a terribly makeshift seat. Twelve-year old boys stay with the women too. The auto show building, where there was also the Indian exhibit, houses the new dining room and kitchens. Seats 3000. Looks awfully permanent. Brick stoves, 8 of them, shining new mugs . . . very very barrack-y. As for the bunks, they were the most tragic things I saw there. Steel and wooden frames with a thin lumpy straw tick, a bolster, and three army blankets of army quality . . . no sheets unless you bring your own. These are the 'homes' of the women I saw. They wouldn't let me into the men's building. There are constables at the doors . . . no propagation of the species . . . you know . . . it was in the papers. These bunks were hung with sheets and blankets and clothes of every hue and variety, a regular gipsy tent of colours, age, and cleanliness, all hung with the pathetic attempt at privacy. Here and there I saw a child's doll and teddy bear . . . I saw babies lying there beside a mother who was too weary to get up . . . she had just thrown herself across the bed . . . I felt my throat thicken . . . an old old lady was crying, saying she would rather have died than have come to such a place . . . she clung to Eiko and cried and cried. Eiko has taken the woes of the confinees on her thin shoulders and she took so much punishment she went to her former rooms and couldn't stop crying. Fumi was so worried about her. Eiko is really sick. The place has got her down. There are ten showers for 1500 women. Hot and cold water. The men looked so terribly at loose ends, wandering around the grounds, sticking their noses through the fence watching the golfers, lying on the grass. Going through the place I felt so depressed that I wanted to cry. I'm damned well not going there. They are going to move the Vancouver women first now and shove them into the Pool before sending them to the ghost towns.

I'm getting kind of frantic because we haven't heard yet from the Bank. The manager wrote again on the 17th. If they would only hurry up and say something one way or the other. If they say no, I shall send you a wire and then you know what to do. If only Eddie can get a job that pays enough to make it worthwhile staying out of the work camps, something we can eat on and save a little. He's quick with his hands, but he knows figures best. He's worked 21 years with the Bank of Montreal. If I can, I am going to take Eiko with me as nursemaid. I don't think it would be wise to take Obasan[52] with us

---

[52]Japanese for "Aunt," here a reference to Aunt Sei Toyofuku.

because she is a national's wife, and she is going back to Japan anyway as soon as she can, while Eiko and we have no such intentions.

The other day at the Pool, someone dropped his key before a stall in the Livestock Building, and he fished for it with a long wire and brought to light rotted manure and maggots!!! He called the nurse and then they moved all the bunks from the stalls and pried up the wooden floors. It was the most stomach-turning nauseating thing. They got fumigators and tried to wash it all away and got most of it into the drains, but maggots still breed and turn up here and there. One woman with more guts than the others told the nurse (white) about it and protested. She replied: "Well, there's worms in the garden aren't there?" This particular nurse was a Jap-hater of the most virulent sort. She called them "filthy Japs" to their faces and Eiko gave her 'what-for' and Fumi had a terrible scrap with her, both girls saying: "What do you think we are? Are we cattle? Are we pigs you dirty-so-and-so!" You know how Fumi gets. The night the first bunch of Nisei were supposed to go to Schreiber and they wouldn't, the women and children at the Pool milled around in front of their cage, and one very handsome mountie came with his truncheon and started to hit them, yelling at them, "Get the hell back in there." Eiko's blood boiled over. She strode over to him and shouted at him: "You put that stick down! What do you think you're doing! Do you think these women and children are so many cows that you can beat them back into their place?" Eiko was shaking mad and raked him with fighting words. She has taken it on her to fight for the poor people there, and now she is on the black list and reputed to be a trouble-maker. Just like Tommy and Kunio. I wish I too could go in there and fight and slash around. It's people like us who are the most hurt . . . people like us, who have had faith in Canada, and who have been more politically minded than the others, who have a hearty contempt for the whites.

Fujikazu and his bunch are working with what Kunio calls a 'shyster lawyer' who has told his clients one thing and the Commission another, and in front of Tommy and Kunio, got bawled out by Taylor. There has been some sort of pamphlet they put out that has been uncovered by the police and the stink is rising again.[53]

The cop that nabbed Sab was so drunk he had to be propped up

---

[53]The pamphlet issued by the Nisei Mass Evacuation Group opposed the breakup of families.

by his assistant, and he weaved around and tried to poke Sab. Sab wisely did not retaliate.

By the way, we got a letter from Uncle . . . or rather Auntie got it. He's the gardener, and has to grow vegetables and flowers on the side. Takashima is cook and gets $50 clear. Uncle only nets about $10. All cards and letters are censored, even to the Nisei camps. Not a word about sit-downs, gambaru-ing[54] or anything makes the papers. It's been hushed. Good thing for us. I wondered why I didn't read about it. I haven't been to meetings so long now that I don't know what's going on. Uncle's camp is 8 miles from the station up into the hills. Men at the first camps all crowd down to the station every time a train passes with the Nationals and hang onto the windows asking for news from home. Uncle said he wept.

But the men are luckier than the women. They are fed, they work, they have no children to look after. Of course the fathers are awfully worried about their families. But it's the women who are burdened with all the responsibilty of keeping what's left of the family together. Frances went to Revelstoke, bag and baggage and baby. When I heard that I felt choked with envy, and felt more trapped than ever. Eiko tells me: "Don't you dare bring the kids into the Pool." And Mr. Maikawa says Greenwood is worse. They are propping up the old shacks near the mine shaft. Sab went through there and says it's awful. The United Church parson there says of the Japs: "Kick them all out." Sab knows his son who had the room next to him at Union College. Vic and George Saito and family went to the beet fields. Sadas are going tonight. They are going to hell on earth, and will be so contracted that they cannot leave the place or move. Whites will not go there.

I pray that Kath and Mom are safe. Mom's got to live through this. Now that Japan proper has been bombed they will come here.

Sab told me his father has applied to get to Winnipeg or to Toronto. Sab is hoping to get to Queens.

Eiko, Fumi and I, and all of us, have gotten to be so profane that Tom and the rest of them have given up being surprised. Eiko starts out with "what the hell". . . and Fumi comes out with worse. It sure relieves our pent-up feelings. Men are lucky they can swear with impunity. (Hell . . . I can smell horse all of a sudden . . .)

---

[54]"Gambaru" is a complex Japanese word with many shades of meaning, here suggesting "to hold out" or "to resist."

117

On account of those fool Nisei who have bucked the gov't, everything the JCCL fought for has been lost. Our name is mud. Why they don't arrest Fujikazu I don't know. I kind of feel that the RCMP are just letting us raise such a stink by ourselves . . . that is fools like Fujikazu and his ilk . . . that the rest of us who are really conscientious and loyal will never have a chance to become integrated with this country. It's damnable. All we have fought for and won inch by inch has gone down the drain. More than the Nationals, our name is mud. There's over 140 Nisei loose, and many Nationals. The Commission thinks the Nationals are cleared but oh boy there are a lot of them who have greased enough palms and are let alone.

By the way if you ever write anything for the NC write it to Tom personally.

How are things there? How are the Pannells and everybody? Three Nisei girls are going to Toronto for housework. Maybe you might get to see them, whoever they are. Aki Hyodo is in Hamilton. If Mrs. Pannell doesn't mind the typewriter, I think I shall write to her.

I'll write again soon.

With love,
Mur.

April 28, 1942.

Dear Wes:

Doug leaves for Schreiber on tonight's train (Tuesday p.m.). Was a volunteer. Will write details later.

Love,
Mur.

April 29, 1942.

Dear Wes:

Well, Doug went to Schreiber, and it's a great relief he did, because those who resist are being imprisoned in concentration camps[55]—not interned as they hoped. He came out on Friday to volunteer because most of his friends were going.

(By the way, have you kept these letters of mine since December? If you have, good, because I may need some of the things I've written. They are the only records of what I've written about this business and how it affects us. Eiko is busy taking notes of a different sort.)

It's kind of lonesome not to hear from you for such a long time. Days seems to pass so quickly and yet in retrospect they seem years away.

Many families have gone to Greenwood—first of the ghost towns. Maybe I'll go to Kaslo with the United Church bunch. I don't know. Ed hasn't had any word from the Bank yet. Did you get the "snaps" of the kids? What did you think of them?

The news about your "passed with honors" made the papers here. True it was tucked into a corner but even my Chinese vegetable store owner told me about it. Unfortunately I didn't see it. (Couldn't find it later on either.)

Masa [Takahashi] is at the Pool. She is taking it well. They have a partitioned corner. I felt I could not offer sympathy or pity in the face of her superb 'laugh-it-off'-ness. A Harry Naganobu went to Schreiber, too. Couldn't go to Edmonton. So did Tommy Iwasaki, Frank Nikaido, and a lot of others. Three coaches, two baggage cars, engine and stoker. The train was so old it was peeling. It was so old, when Doug yanked at the window the glass splintered and fell out. It was so old it was rusty. That's what the boys have to live in for the next I don't know how many days. They have to sleep sitting or standing. Doug took no food except sunflower seeds and oodles of cigs. Everyone else had "o-bento."[56] I wish I'd known he might need it, but Doug said he'd be fed so I didn't fuss. I was appalled when I saw that junk pile. Thank goodness Doug was a volunteer. He came on his own, on a taxi to the depot. He and his comrade-

---

[55]Barbed-wire prisoner of war camps in Ontario, at Petawawa and Angler. For a first-hand Issei account of internment at Angler, see Takeo Ujo Nakano's *Within the Barbed Wire Fence* (Toronto: University of Toronto Press, 1980), especially pp. 55-100.

[56]Japanese for "a lunch."

volunteers. The others had to come by a big Pacific Stage bus—locked in with a couple of armed mounties. Aunt Yamada was heartsick, foreseeing like treatment for Steve and Pete and Sam. She just drooped when I saw her watching the arrival of this huge tightly laden bus. I felt so glad that Doug came on a taxi. Such a little thing, but significant. Doug hasn't been what you might call a wholly satisfactory brother, but he and I have never fought, and while we were never as intimate as you and I, still he often came for advice, and I've been careful not to treat him as anything but an adult with adult brains and responsibilities. Of course I've gotten mad at him plenty—but when I saw him go (you know how boisterous he is to cover his soft heart!) amid yelling and shouted good-byes with never a last look at the only family he has, grouped rather forlornly behind the milling young men and girls—I cried. It seemed as if some huge hand had wiped his imprint off the horizon. Now I saw him, half out of the window waving both hands—"Bye Thelma! Bye Kay (Uyeno who got engaged to him on Sunday)! Bye youse guys! Bye Kachi! Bye Otto." I felt then that truly he was some stranger I should have known but didn't. Then he was gone. I never felt so forlorn for I am alone now. Kath in Japan. You in Toronto. Doug in Schreiber. Nobi only a kid, and I'll never see him again either if he does not come of his own accord. Sometimes the responsibilities that are mine are too much. I am trying to keep Aunt Sei with me in case I go to any ghost town, but Janey, being an only child, suffers from having to be one of a crowd, and Shirley and Meiko resent any favours (to their eyes undue favours) given to Janey—who does whine an awful lot because Auntie gives in so easily. They're too much of an age to be under two separate standards. Ed doesn't like the idea of having Janey with us, but I'm willing if I can only keep *one* relative with me to stand by in troubled times and in emergencies. Kids scrap, but they forget. I am getting used to the dread of a ghost town, but be sure I'll try everything else possible first.

I received a box of the darlingest sweaters from Mrs. Clapham[57] for the twins. Please thank her for me. I cannot write just now as I feel too restless. As May 8th comes nearer, my tension tightens.

War, twins, evacuation—honest to gosh! how does one bear up under it all?

---

[57]Marvel Clapham, Deaconness of Carlton United Church in Toronto.

Please write soon. My regards to all and I hope like anything I can get to York.

Love,
Mur.

April 30, 1942.

Dear Wes:

Well the word came from the HO. It was a definite "NO." *But*, don't go rushing around for us yet. We are trying to stay in B.C. somewhere . . . somewhere on a farm with some fruit trees. I have to do some fast work contacting all the people I think can help in some way. Ed doesn't want to leave B.C. If we go too far, we may not be able to come back, because the Bank has given Ed "indefinite leave of absence."[58] When the war is over he can come back to his old desk. He does not want to let go this slim hope for the future unless whatever new job he gets is better in every way, financially steady, promise of pension etc., so that he can continue to save, so that as he grows older his salary will increase, with the bonuses he's been getting. Without those bonuses we could never have managed so far. That is why Ed prefers to get some temporary job close by here on which to eat. We hope to get a little rent for this house. He doesn't want to go to camp while I am so helpless with the twins. As soon as they are old enough, if he has to go he will.

How about you, and your next two years? Please let me know.

I don't feel much like writing any more. For all our sakes and for your own please keep going as long as you can; try to get your degree, and if Doug will send me his pay I will send it to you. He said he would but I am not counting on it till I actually get it.

Love,
Mur.

---

[58]As it turned out, Ed's leave of absence lasted until 1947 when he began working for the Bank of Montreal in Toronto.

121

(May be last letter for some time unless arrangment made to go east—
then will have to do more talking.)

May 1, 1942.

Dear Wes:

I was on the point of sending a wire to you today but newer
developments cancelled it. A detailed letter air-mail might be better. But we've got to work fast. You see we got word only on the
29th, then the Commission puts out a notice . . . "everyone ready
for 24-hour notice . . . no more extensions". . . holy cats! everything
piled onto us at once as usual.[59] And are we hustling around! Trying
to get into Salmon Arm, into Chase, into anywhere livable and which
will let us in. We have to try for a good climate for the sake of the
kids, someplace where we can have a garden to grow enough for
a year.

But I wish you would contact Mrs. Pannell, too, and find out what
sort of job Eddie could get, and where, and for how much. You know
the sort of work he can do, so far as clerking goes, but he is willing
to tackle anything else, farm-work or anything, no matter how hard
the work is. He'll get used to it in a few weeks. He's handy with
his hands, awfully precise and neat, always good-tempered, and
diplomatic. All born here etc., etc. His job at the Bank is open to him
when he comes back. I would like to live where there is lots of space
and a garden, even on the outskirts of the town. Find out the cost
of living, rentals, etc., etc., also the details about the house like electricity (a must), hot water, furnace, bath etc. Doesn't need to be a
fancy house so long as the wind won't blow it away, and it's big
enough for us. Do you know anyone like Mitch [Hepburn] who would
employ Ed similarly? Let us know everything, so that we can make
up our minds quickly. Ed says going east is our last resort, but we've

---

[59]On April 25, the B.C. Security Commission published the following notice in
the *New Canadian*: "Persons of Japanese origin residing in Vancouver should ter-
minate, not later than the 30th April, 1942, all leases or rental arrangements they
may be working under. They must also be prepared to move either to Hastings Park
or to work camps or to places under the Interior Housing Scheme at twenty-four
hours notice. No deferments whatsoever on business grounds may be made to the
above orders" (p. 3).

got to git by the 22nd. Don't breathe the date to a soul though, because officially the deadline is the 8th. Are there grocery stores in need of a clerk? Ed will try anything.

[Hand-written in the right margin:] If they don't want us to settle there perm, we won't. Tell 'em so.

I wrote to Mrs. Pannell to ask if there were any disposable diapers left in Toronto. Wherever I go, I'll need them for the train trip. If you can spare the cash and there are diapers, buy them and send me pronto, and I'll send you money to make up and more. I need an average of two dozen daily, for the train trip anywhere. How long does it take to get to Toronto?

Mr. Lock[60] is coming over Saturday night to see what he can do to help. There never is a friend like him anywhere. He's swell. Gosh sometimes I wonder what I did to deserve a friend like him.

Anyway, you do what you can there and we'll do what we can here. We'll take the winner. That is, we'll go east if there is nothing here.

Love,
Mur.

May 4, 1942.

Dear Wes:

Got your letter. Get my wire?[61] I've been getting my wind up. We've got to get out in the next couple of weeks or get locked up in a ghost town, which heaven forbid.

There's another prospect (for people with money)—that of going to McGillivray Falls, 20 miles from Lillooet. A summer resort complete with outboard motor and mountains and maybe "cats." Fifteen families at $1500.00 a year. That's about $100 per year rent. 1-2-3 room cabins furnished, electricity, a main lodge with huge living

---

[60]Mr. Lock was Muriel's English teacher at the Duke of Connaught High School in New Westminster who first encouraged her to write.

[61]Muriel's telegram sent on May 3 read: "Contact Mr. Pannell for Ed. Outdoor work preferable. Letter follows."

room and bath. On account of the cost (slight though it is, if these were normal times and one had a job), there are no takers. Ed's keen to go there. Fishing in the lake and gardening, maybe work on near-by farms. Only no medico, no school. Maybe I'll have to teach. We'll be cramped for space in 3 rooms—about $12 per month. The lodge is $20 per. They take a $50 entrance fee. Transportation and baggage up to 1000 lbs. is free. Heck! rice alone weighs 300 lbs., but I guess we pay the excess. However, even this prospect is not certain, on account of the cost. We'd have to live out of our own pockets and ours is pretty slim. We haven't heard yet from Salmon Arm. I believe from all accounts that place is the ideal place to go—1000 feet above sea level, dry, fruit farming—invigorating. Just what Ed needs. He's sick and tired of desk work. Wants to work outdoors for the duration.

Then, because we haven't much time, I want to keep a finger east too. Ed wants farm work—outdoors anyway. Since the risk of going east on our own is great, the job has to be something guaranteed so we won't have to go hungry in between. As for a house, so long as it has 3 rooms for beds and a kitchen with running water and electricity for things like an iron and washer and toaster and maybe refrig (we can sell our big one and buy a tiny one when we get there). Also indoor toilet and bath and furnace. Don't mind candlelight for rest of the rooms. Don't care if the paint is peeling or if the house is old, so long as it's got a garden. Big house is okay if cheap. Rental depends on job, too. If we get only $80, then the house has to be cheap. Even if the job pays better, the cheaper the house the better, so we can save. I know we can't be too choosy about the pay but I'm sure you understand that going east is such a gamble it's got to be worthwhile. Though going to McGillivray Falls will eat up everything we got, it's so close to Vancouver it'll just take a few hours to get back to our old job. Of course, this project is uncertain as it's no good unless we get the requisite 15 families.

As for your impression of the authority of the Commission, sorry but you're wrong. If the Mayor and City Council says "No," then it's "No" for the Commission and RCMP alike. They made it clear that they would not permit us to go anywhere the City Council didn't want us. So, you see, York or wherever has to give the Commission a written okay. After that it's easy.[62] We may not need letters at

---

[62]In his letter of May 1, Wes had written: "Six families applied to get into Toronto

124

all. If we do I'll wire again "LETTERS." Those letters must contain the purport that the writers will undertake to see that the Kitagawas will not be a burden on the public. Tough on the kind writer don't you think? It's too much to ask of strangers, I think. Can't take such advantage of their goodness. What they *can* do, is to persuade the City Council in York or any town around Toronto that it would be an act of Christian mercy to take us in. We're Canadian-born, all of us, Ed too. You know how Canadian we are. If we get a job there we won't be a burden. We may be shining lights in our own way— who knows? Education for the kids is the biggest problem, plus medical care.

So don't think the Commission has the last say. Far from it, or our lot would be a hundredfold easier. It's because so many towns bar their doors that we are having such a heck of a time. If the Commission had the last say, we could go tomorrow to Salmon Arm, which is for us the "hopingest" place.

So Wes, the town may be 20 miles from Toronto, but if it lets us in and we are guaranteed a job for the duration we'd go like a shot.

As for those girls you want, I've told Eiko and her sister Yaeko.[63] They've been wanting to go east. I wrote her so I ought to know in a day or so and then I'll write again. They're both Christian— Yaeko is the neater, but Eiko is the more lovable. They can take whichever. Of course it all depends on whether they go. I've told them to go.

Doug went to Schreiber, but I don't know which camp. I won't know until he writes. You see every camp has a number—*all mail to and from censored*. I'm hoping to hear soon, but he's so happy-go-lucky, you can't depend on him. His intentions are perfectly good and he's kind and generous, but Lord! he can forget so easily.

---

by writing the Mayor. The Mayor and a 'committee' decided it was 'inadvisable', but his opinion or decisions don't hold water. The main thing is to get permission from the Security Commission and the RCMP. They have authority over the Mayor as to who can and cannot move to any city." Muriel's understanding, however, is that the permission to move should come from Toronto. The confusion on both sides, common to many Japanese Canadians, reflects the lack of consistent guidelines by the government. Both Wes and Muriel are justified in their perceptions—Wes from outside the "protected area" and Muriel from within.

[63]Wes had written about a request from a sympathetic Caucasian acquaintance in Toronto for a Japanese Canadian girl to work as a housekeeper.

Honest, Wes, if you have to work and if Ed does too—if we can get east you can stay with us and it'll save you board anyway.

As it is now, we don't know which way to turn.

The Bank accountant phoned just now to tell Ed (he's home today because I've got acute pharyngitis, tonsillitis, quinsy and a touch of flu. I'm dosed with some kind of powder that takes the ache right out of me) . . . well, the Bank phoned to say they would use what little influence they had to get Ed a job in a ghost town. The catch is—we won't be a family unit. The Commission isn't having any able bodied male in any ghost town, and even if Ed gets a job there, he couldn't live with us. He couldn't help me with the twins, and we'd have to sleep 6-8 to a room. Depending on the size of the room, they put in 2 to 4 double deckers. I'd have to wash everything by hand which even now with all conveniences at hand I can't do, so I send some to the laundry. I wouldn't be able to keep the babies' milk fresh—and it is more work than ever to make it every four hours. Then most likely I'd have to teach grade-school.

The pay, irrespective of ability, is $2 a day, minus Sundays. Out of which we have to feed and clothe four kids and try to keep them in a semblance of health. Honest, Wes, I wonder if the "Whites" think we are a special kind of low animal able to live on next-to-nothing needing no clothes replacements, disregarding the kids who still outgrow their clothes as fast as you make them, able to survive without the vitamins that they need, money for school books, shoe repair, medicine. (Oh they are going to be sick!!) It isn't as if this place had been bombed and *everybody* was suffering. *Then* we'd be together and our morale would be high. As it is, the wives get $20, the first child $5, the next 4 get $4 each. The rest get nothing. Families of internees, widows, and single women get relief. The families have to buy food at the local stores around the ghost town. Those merchants are bound to raise prices. How far do you think a mother and 8 children can live on $41 including clothing and medicine? And most of those children are old enough to eat a heck of a lot. Not like Emi and Meiko who have the appetites of birds. That's why I have to feed them cod-liver oil and B1 to supplement what they don't get. They don't eat enough to get even their proteins.

We were talking about farm-work. Ed was sighing that he's so out of shape, it'd take him 6 months to get used to hard work. If we could get to Salmon Arm—the work there is seasonal—but being a steady farm hand is another thing the more we discuss it. Ye gods! What *does* one do in times like these?

What *kind* of work is there for Ed to do that would ensure his not getting sick through unaccustomed hard labour—for then we'd be without pay. There are so many complex angles in this business my head aches. Mr. Matsubayashi just phoned that there is no electricity in McGillivray. What does one do without electricity? When have we ever been without it? How do they iron anyway since the old flat irons are as extinct as dodos. How am I to wash for 6? In the hot summer how am I to keep milk and butter and meat fresh?

Another thing that's bothering us is the cost of transportation and freight to Ontario. We can take only our clothes, bedding, pots and pans and dishes. Ed's going to find out. We've sold our dining-room suite and our piano. I'm selling everything else I can't take. Mr. and Mrs. Lock are going to store our valuables for us, our irreplaceables, like books and good dishes (my Japanese ones) and pictures, etc. Also our Hoover.

Ed is so worried he goes around in a daze wondering what to do. We've so little time. The manager was so "yukkuri"[64] about things up till the 30th of April when we got the "No" answer from HO. It's really too late to do much now except hope. I'm afraid Ed's going grey-haired over this. I can see more white now than ever before. What would you suggest? If we go to a ghost town then it's going to be one hell of a life. Waiting in line to wash, waiting in line to cook, to eat, maybe sleeping with strangers. The Yamadas are going to Alberta. Aunt Toyofuku still has a chance to go to Westbank.

At the Pool, confinees have lost as much as 9 pounds in the month they've been there. There's a lot of repressed hysteria, which is so contagious. The red tape is ferocious.

What a hell this mess is. The Bank manager tried to get Ed a place in the more temperate beet fields, but that's out. Once we go to a beet farm we're stuck by contract; the same with a ghost town. If we didn't have to depend on the say-so of every town Council!

Well I've got to go to sleep. We've got to pack yet.

Did you find the diapers? It's either disposable diapers or Kleinerts refill pads (if this last, get two panty covers). Mrs. Pannell or Mrs. Mack ought to know. If we go to McGillivray, we've got to go in a week or so. They won't wait. If you can get the diapers, send them

---

[64]Japanese for "slow."

127

quickly. If they're not available, let me know. I've got to borrow some—somewhere.

Love,
Mur.

May 5, 1942.

Dear Wes:

Ed asked CP how much for all of us.

	Fare		Meals	Tips	Baggage
Ed	$124. + odd cents		$15.	$3-4	
Me	124.	" "	15.		
Shirley	67.	" "	10.		
Compartment	78.	" "	10. (Meiko)		$100 (approx.)
	————		Twins ?		(for least,
	$393.		(need		just clothes
			hot-water) ———		and bedding)
			$50.		

Totals around $550.00

Holy cow! We can eat for almost 2 years on that—in McGillivray. It's a risk. Ed's sat back to think it over several times. So don't rush out there. If we had thousands saved, $500-$600 may be chicken-feed, but ye gods! You see at McG. Falls we intend to buy co-op and save, and then grow our own vegetables, and catch our meat from woods and lake. Except for rent, everything else is free (other than food). The manager is trying to get Ed 3 months full pay—then do something else if we're still loose-ending. The Maikawas want us to go to their brother's tomato farm in Sicamous. Since the 4th, we've had 3 different offers, all costing quite a bit, but with the prospect of a job for the duration. Now we don't know what to decide. Ed got an extension till June 1st today because I'm sick.

We're dizzy trying to decide. Got a letter from Doug. His address is

Milage 101,
Camp SW 5-3,
Jackfish, Ont.

Next day:
Mickey Maikawa wants us to go to his wife's brother's farm in Sicamous. We're considering that, too. Everything is confusion and bewilderment. Ed's getting thin over it all.

Thank Mrs. Pannell for us. I intend to send her something suitable as soon as I get up.

Love,
Mur.

May 6, 1942.
afternoon.

Dear Wes:
Received diapers air-mail 96¢. Phoned Spencer's to price them. Panties @ 75¢ cost $1.50. Refills cost $1.29 per 48 pads. There were 24 pads, so the cost is 65¢. Please give $3.11 more or less to Mrs. Pannell, and thank her a million for all the trouble we're causing her. It makes me feel awfully small to think that (tho' we're in a dither, too) you folks are so helpful in spite of all uncertainties where we are concerned.

Also use rest of the enclosed money to get more Kleinerts' refills, as much as you can with it and send it to me regular mail. Mrs. Pannell sent the first lot air-mail. At the time I wrote I needed 'em pronto, but now we have till June 1st, a matter of 3 weeks. We got the permit mailed to us this morning. Our phone rings several times daily from people offering suggestions as to what we should do. On Monday we were asked to go to McGillivray Falls, Tuesday to Sicamous. Also, yesterday (Tues) the manager bestirred himself at long last to really do something definite. Tuesday, too, we got the official permit (verbal) of a time extension. We were so afraid Ed would have to rush off by the 8th. It was awful. So we have breathing-space to

129

see which way our luck's going to jump. Every day our plans enlarge from despair to hope—from nowhere to go, to several places. Ed wants to stay in B.C. I want to go east. He wants to be as near Vancouver as possible—living and working leisurely somewhere—McGillivray or Salmon Arm.

If we finally decide to stay here, please forgive us. More than anything the horrific cost of transportation bogged us. $550 at least!! With that we could build a shack and eat 10 months. This is what I have in mind, if we go to Sicamous:

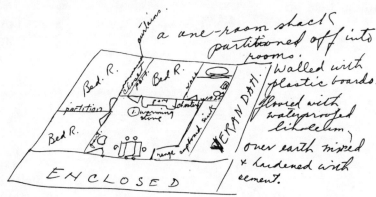

Our plans are still amoebic. Splits or merges or whatever now. If the other plans hadn't cropped up I guess we'd be on the way to Toronto.

By the way, the Takahashis must have had terrific pull to go where the Myedas couldn't.[65] I guess you can expect a letter every day to keep you up-to-date on our fluctuating plans.

Talk of bewilderment! Think nothing but.

Love,
Mur.

[p.s.] How do you remove tonsils painlessly so I wouldn't lose a day's work? Better learn. I need it done bad.

Mur.

The rent at the McG. Falls was reduced for us to $80 per year.

---

[65]The Takahashi family was the first family to get permission to move to Toronto. The Kitagawas were the second.

May 11, 1942.

Dear Wes:

I'm still in bed chafing like the dickens because I can't be up and doing things.

I've been wondering what happened after you sent us that wire. It was a swell offer but a hope dimly lighted because no matter how definite the prospect, how kind the Finlays, without a permit in black and white from Temperance and a temporary one from Toronto we are helpless here.[66] We have only about 2 weeks now. 10 days were wasted by my illness, and Ed is so rushed doing the things I do daily he can't do the things he should be doing.

Ed would be more willing to spend $500 on travelling if he thought we could all live in Temperance. He got $375 cash grant from the Bank (3 months pay). The Finlays sent us a wire confirming yours. Will you thank them? When I am up again I shall write them thanks. Their wire was like a badly needed blessing. I hope you can get us the permits. Get Mr. Umehara to do it. Or shall *we* apply for it? We would like someplace where there is work, whatever the disadvantages.

Anyhow, let us know in a hurry.

Love,
Mur.

May 11, 1942.
39 Harbord St.
Toronto

Dear Mur:

Got your wire Sunday night because I was up north Saturday and Sunday. I borrowed a bike and went to Umehara's farm. I didn't get back till Sunday afternoon and then I went to a "tea" (really a Sunday

---

[66]In his letter of May 4, Wes told Muriel that he would go up north to see George Umehara in Temperanceville (which Muriel refers to as Temperance) about a farming job for Ed, and the wire or telegram was related to the prospect of the Kitagawa family moving to Umehara's farm.

supper because Toronto's Sunday "teas" are really suppers) at Dr. Patterson's—he's head of the YMCA here. Patterson is also helping to find a place for the Takahashis. At present the whole family is staying at the United Church House (has about 50 rooms) with about 48 other guests. They were lucky a family moved out just before they arrived. I happened to know a lady there so I got her and Mrs. Cassidy (a friend of Yukio Takahashi here) to reserve the place for them. The only rentable places are furnished houses from which people are moving to summer houses during the summer months. Mr. and Mrs. Pannell have been answering classified ads for several days with very discouraging results. Empty unfurnished houses don't exist in Toronto, except for some 15-room houses for sale. We finally did get a furnished house which the owner wanted to rent for a year, though it took several days to swing. With Mr. and Mrs. Pannell, Dr. Patterson, and Mr. Finlay, also Mrs. Cassidy and Gertrude Rutherford (head of the United Church Training School) putting the pressure on, she couldn't refuse to rent the place. Just the same, she felt she was being "unpatriotic" in renting a home to a Japanese family when houses were so much in demand. The stupidity of some people! But that's how most of Toronto thinks.

So you see how difficult it is to find houses here. Apartments are out—they don't want families with children.

Your wire says to wire back, but I'm afraid I don't understand what you mean. The tone of the telegram seems to suggest that you would come to Toronto if you could get permission. The "wire back" seems to suggest that you want me to wire back the permission from the Toronto City Council. If we have to get permission from the City Council and from King Township (where the Umeharas have their farm near Temperanceville), it's going to take some time. The Takahashis didn't have to get permission from the City Council. Their permit from the Security Commission was all that was necessary. That restriction about permits is only a voluntary restriction that the Security Commission has placed upon itself. It can make exceptions or override its restrictions whenever it feels like it, it seems. If we have to get permission from the City Council and Mayor, I'm afraid I haven't much hope. The Mayor has already expressed his opinion: Give permission to one, he says, and that leaves the way open for others to come; you know what will happen then. I haven't had a chance to speak to Mr. Finlay yet about your latest wire, but I'm going to speak to him about it. As for the farms up north, there are no available houses near the Umehara farm, and they have no accommodation for a family.

Can't you get permission from the Security Commission if Mr. Finlay wrote that you were coming to his home? Must one get permission from the City Council to invite someone to his *own* home? It's silly, but did the Commission definitely say no? Suppose I got all my friends—Finlays, Pannells, *et al.*, to write letters to the Commission? Would we still have to get permission from the City Council here in order for you to get permission from the Commission? You see, if we put it up to any Council or Mayor to give official permission, they'll all say no and it will create a barrier that may never again be lifted. If you can get permission from the Commission (like the Takahashis), you needn't bother about the City Council. Besides, it may take weeks of negotiations with King Township to get official permission there. Shouldn't a letter from the Umeharas be sufficient, as it was in the case of workers for Hepburn?

But first of all, what I want to know is: are you coming to Toronto or not? I don't want to put the Finlays and Pannells, Patterson, etc. to a lot of unnecessary trouble unless we knew you wanted to come. Do you want us to write letters to the Commission?

There is a terrible shortage of labour on farms, so if Eddie doesn't mind hard work, he can get a job once he gets out here.

McGillivray Falls or Sicamous may be a better place to go, I wouldn't know. But don't distort facts when you're trying to decide, or you'll prejudice yourself one way or the other.

Surely it doesn't cost $550 to come to Toronto! It only cost the Takahashis about $350—six of them adults—coming Tourist. You were quoting First Class prices? Is there no other way of coming cheaply?

By the way, if baggage that won't be needed immediately is sent by freight through Crone Ltd., it costs $3.50 per hundred pounds.

If you come here, the main problem is housing. You could stay at the Finlays for the summer months and then spend that time looking for a house somewhere outside the city. It's a risk I know. The decision will be up to you and Eddie, but I can promise one thing— if the necessity arises, I can get the Pannells, Finlays, Miss Clapham, Pattersons, Miss Werry, Carlton Church, and perhaps the FCSO [Fellowship of the Christian Social Order], and even Agnes MacPhail, to work on it. But without that necessity, I can't approach them for help. I can't get people looking for houses or a job for Eddie unless I know whether you want to come or not.

By the way, Miss Emma Kaufman left this morning by plane for Vancouver to work for the Security Commission. She's secretary of the YWCA here and a good friend of the Pattersons (they've all been to Japan for considerable lengths of time). I was speaking to her last night (she was at the "tea" at the Pattersons' too) and gave her some "dope" on the B.C. situation. She's going to the "Pool" to make a report on it. She may also go to a ghost town to investigate the conditions there too. Her profession is Social Service. I gave her the names of the important Nisei that she may find helpful. I wish I had more information about the dirty work going on there. She may have been able to do something helpful if she knew more about it. All I could do was to warn her about Morii and his crowd.

Let me know which way you decide—and don't get rattled—you have lots of real friends here.

As always,
Wes.

May 14, 1942.
Dear Wes:

I must have tried your patience a terrible lot these last few days. I'm awfully sorry and can only put it down to frantic worry, headache and uncertain fears. I just got out of bed yesterday and still feel kind of floozy around the attic. But I feel better after having decided definitely what our future course will be.

The kids and I are going to Kaslo, the best of the ghost towns. Ed is going to Schreiber. This is our easiest way to get to Ontario because the Nisei going there have been promised that their families will be called one day. We intend to go to Ontario one way or the other, and after days and nights of discussion, scrambling after this frail hope and that, chasing elusive hopes this way and that, worrying, figuring, going bats with indecision because one door after the other closes after we knock on them, we finally decided, that up against a wall, the only way to Ontario is through Ed going to a work camp, and us keeping up a hope that we can join him. For that we must of necessity go to Kaslo.

134

Rev. Shimizu investigated and reports that I can get a small house to myself. There are stores, a drug store, even a soda fountain, and we shall be in the City proper of Kaslo where there is medical service available, and schooling of a sort. Now that we know what it will be like, it is not so much of a risk as we first greatly feared. Better than McGillivray Falls where there are no stores, no doctors, no school, nothing except 15 families . . . out of the world, even though a nice resort. Aunt Toyofuku will be with us to help with the babies. So long as Doug remembers to send me some money I shall be all right. I can take my sewing machine with me, maybe washer too. Please don't worry about us at all now, since once the decision is taken I do not want to be upset all over again by vagrant hopes.

As for the $550 fare, it is all on the level. We asked the CPR and barring cost of food and freight it is the figure they gave us. You see, with twins and diapers and milk and changing, we cannot go by tourist, much as we want to. We intended to cut down on the food cost by taking our own, but freight is $4 per hundred pounds and we had almost 3000 pounds figured. Then there are the inevitable tips, transportation to and from the train etc. Oh yes, Wes it would cost us $550 more or less. It would have been worth it if there was a house in Temperance for us, a job for Ed, school for the kids, and doctors. And we would have been near you and Doug. Never mind now. I don't think I have distorted facts. Perhaps it is the way I see things that is different from yours. And life here is just now as uncertain as all hell. Anyway, the last few letters I wrote were written while in bed, and it is well known that a headache and a swollen throat influence perspective a great deal.

The reasons why we have been so anxious to go anywhere but to a ghost town are (1) the actual conditions at the Pool horrified me to such an extent that I vowed not to go there, (2) reports that the ghost towns were the same frightened me no end, and (3) I didn't know what the hell I was going to do with the twins by myself. Now that there is definite assurance that I can have a small house to myself where Auntie can help with the twins . . . I don't think she and Uncle can go to Westbank . . . and that authoritative reports tell me we shall live in the town proper of Kaslo, the story changes a good bit. You know I can live on next to nothing. Haven't we had experience in New Westminster?

Ed can ask the Commission about this permit business but what's the use Wes, without a house to go to, with rented places so scarce?

135

It's a risk we can't afford. We could not impose on the Finlays, no matter how we appreciate their more than welcome kindness. And if Ed works in Temperance, I take it that this means commuting? Will the job be such that we can afford living in town? Ed and I were talking the other night that you must be chewing your fingernails over us, and the hell-sent indecision of some blankety-blank people would be driving you crazy. Gee, I realize all that, yet I clung to the hope we could go to Ontario. It was the last hope to die in my throat.

Wes, I don't want to go through all the uncertainty of trying again to find a loophole to escape from. I'm resigned to Kaslo . . . and anyway, Rev. Shimizu says it's a nice place. So let's leave it like that until Mitch [Hepburn] says it's OK for Ed's family to join him somewhere in Ontario. We've tried everywhere, and McGillivray Falls seemed to be the only escape from a ghost town and separation. I have cried my cry, I have said good-bye for the time being to home, family life, and Ed, to a reunion with you. All fluttering for escape has calmed down. Just wish me luck. I'll manage and wait till that happy day when we can all be together again. That time I shall yell "Yippee."

Now I must get down to serious packing, selling and buying so I won't write till I'm settled somewhere. Then I shall write to you all. Please give my regards to the Pannells and to the Finlays. I shall write to them too.

Take good care of yourself. Write and let me know things. I asked too much of God.

Lovingly,
Mur.

———————————————

c/o Bank of Montreal,
Main and Hastings Sts.,
Vancouver, B.C.,
May 16, 1942.

Dear Wes:

I really should be concentrating on my packing but I must write this one.

I am sending by freight or express your books, and I am also sending the Rose Cushion Kath made and gave me to give to Mrs. Pannell. The next time I write will be from Kaslo. Yesterday I got my orders to report at the CPR at 5:45 pm to entrain for Kaslo. I wrote to Miss Clapham and to the Finlays.

You see Wes, because we were sort of depending on the Bank to transfer us, we lost valuable time that could have been spent in various negotiations. Now it is really too late for anything if I want to get going before Ed. We think it is better that I go first so that Ed can help to the end, and clean up the house after we go, something I could never do with the twins to look after. I also want to get to Kaslo while there is still time to wire back to Ed in Vancouver for anything I need.

For the time being we will stay in Kaslo while Ed goes to Schreiber. During this time, if it is still possible, we will carry on further negotiations with you people . . . negotiations that will not be rushed and changed practically every day. Once all of us are evacuated the furor will die down somewhat, and we can discuss my moving to Ontario with leisure and thorough investigation. It is the policy of the Commission to spend as little as possible on us, so they will welcome any who will get off their payroll. This rushing is awful business, and something may go wrong at the most unexpected time. I have a letter from Mr. Lock, while Ed has a swell testimonial from the Manager, and I am getting another from the Accountant, and from the Fergusons in Hatzic. I don't know any hakujin minister, and Rev. Shimizu has been shunted (people say shanghaied) off to Kaslo so I won't see him till I get there. When I get to know other hakujin in Kaslo it might be even nicer.[67] So Wes, we shall take it in easy

---

[67]Wes had advised the Kitagawas to get personal reference letters to help them get permission to move to Toronto.

stretches, for I want like anything to get to Ontario where you and Doug are.

Will you tell all this to the Finlays and to the Pannells? As soon as I am settled I shall write them detailed letters.

Doug's new Address is

> DALTON MILLS
> c/o AUSTIN LUMBER COMPANY,
> DALTON, ONTARIO.

It was the time element that defeated us for the present. We won't give up yet, not by a long shot. When Ed goes to Schreiber, and if there is a *good* job for him, get in touch with Mr. Pipher who is the representative for the Commission in Ontario. He is at Schreiber I think. But in this case the job has to be good, so that Ed can call us with a degree of satisfaction and no worry. I mean the wages, of course.

So Wes, I've caused you people a lot of trouble and worry. Thanks a million.

Love,
Mur.

May 17, 1942.

Dear Mur:

I got your wire Friday noon.[68] I meant to write sooner but your wire made me feel so low I didn't want to write.

I wish I were there in Vancouver right now. There are so many angles to this thing, I don't know what to do. You spoke of the risk

---

[68]Muriel's telegram of May 15, sent at 1:49 a.m., read: "No indecision since first wire except waiting for expected permit, but since Temperance houseless and risk is too much, we have decided against going to Ontario for the time being. If Ed goes to Schreiber there is hope we can join him later from Kaslo where Aunt Toyofuku will be with me. Thanks a million for everything you did and don't worry about me now. Also thank Finlays and Pannells."

of coming out here being too great. That's not true. You remember that letter I wrote to Tommy which he published? That's how things are here. Risk—some—but not insurmountable as long as we are level-headed and keep a stable attitude. If you come out here with the kids, you have no worry about them. The whole blooming church [Carlton] is just itching to look after them for you if necessary. The Finlay home is always open to you, and you can have all the privacy you want up on the third floor because they never use it (three rooms I believe).

As for getting permits, if we set the right machinery moving, there's a chance of getting them—I thought we could at least try. The element of time is *so* important. I know you're worried about a job for Eddie. But isn't the important thing a place of security to bring up the kids for the duration? We could never *promise* a job for Eddie, but how can we get him a job until he's here in person? The Takahashis are settled now. The Mayor refused them, but the permit from the Security Commission allowing them to come to Toronto overrode his decision. (The Toronto City Council has not met to discuss this matter yet. The Mayor merely called a committee of some outstanding people in Toronto to discuss the matter—and even then their decision was not official, nor was it an outright refusal of permits—just "inadvisable.")

The Takahashis are living on Cottingham Street, a high-tone district. It was the *only* house available in Toronto, an 8-room furnished house, leased for one year only. They got the house through the combined efforts of the Pannells, Cassidys, Pattersons, and Finlays.

Saburo got a job already working for a dry-cleaning establishment. He answered a want-ad. There's a terrific shortage of labour here in Toronto in non-essential industries. I feel there are so many places that Ed could fit into, if he is willing to take the chance and try hard enough (Sab was turned down quite a few times before he landed the job).

And my friends here have so many connections all over the place they can always find *some* place if necessary.

Coming to Toronto at such a high expenditure of money seems to you a leap in the dark I know, but there's no worry about insecurity once you get here so far as those kids go—I can promise you that outright. We're Socialists at Carlton—it's our creed to help those that need help when we can—and to accept help when we need it and when it is offered in the same spirit. Carlton is known across Canada.

139

Next week the National FCSO [Fellowship of the Christian Social Order] Conference is being held there and delegates are coming from all over Canada. The Finlays and Pannells aren't the only ones worried about you. The whole church is worrying now.

Do you want me to get in touch with Emma Kaufman to see what she can do for you? She's working for the Commission now, and she's a grand woman with a big heart. Isn't there some way I could get a permit for you to come to Toronto? Any possible strings I can pull? Don't you want to come to Toronto if you could get permission? Have you any friends in Vancouver I could correspond with who could look after all the menial jobs of getting references for you, if you can't go around getting them yourself?

But if you feel it's too late now (I still feel there's time to give it a try anyway) and are getting ready to go to Kaslo—would you come if I could get you moved from Kaslo to Toronto? You'd be separated from Eddie anyway—and in Toronto you could live a normal life with the kids. You've never given us the permission to go all out in getting you moved to Toronto so our hands are tied.

Your telegram sounded as if you had given up hope. Ever heard of the saying "dum spiro spero?" It means "while I breathe I hope." Don't give up. If you're sick, hurry up and get better—the kids need you. The amazing part to me is that you've lasted all this time, after all the terrific emotional, physical, and mental stress you've gone through. If you go to Kaslo, I may be along to see you after the summer (or sooner if you want), after I earn a little dough. "They" can't stop me from going to Kaslo can they? I don't come under Security Commission regulations as long as I don't enter the 100 mile area. Only the RCMP have any authority over my movements and that is only a matter of reporting whenever I change my address—same as in national registration . . . .

It's late and I've got to be going to bed now. Send me more of your long letters when you get time. I'd offer words of sympathy to you if I didn't know they were superfluous. You know me, I'm right with you wherever you go. I'll chuck my medical course if necessary. You can count on me. Those kids are the important thing—always remember that.

As always,
Wes.

May 20, 1942.

Dear Wes:

Just received your letter today. I can understand that we've got you puzzled a bit. Our case is so different from that of the Takahashis, who are all adults, and I presume they have enough of what it takes to live. To you it sounds so simple . . . all we have to do is get to Toronto somehow and the rest will follow suit . . . housing, job, etc. To us it is the decision of a lifetime . . . too many pros and cons, too much of cutting a lifeline (the Bank) that we may need badly someday, too much of immediate expense without immediate returns to hold in reserve without being in debt to anyone. It's been the awfullest time in our life so far. No wonder you don't know which way I want to jump. We haven't been able to decide ourselves. But now things are settled. The kids and I will go to Kaslo for the time being, and Ed will go to Schreiber . . . the fare's free you know . . . and from there you have our permission to go all out to find something for him, clerking, i.e., sales clerk in some big store, or his experience in the Bank might come in handy for other things, especially when it comes to handling all kinds of people, or even a farm job. For this last, Ed wants to go first to Schreiber and toughen up a bit, because he couldn't last a day as is. The Manager laughed at the thought of Ed digging: "Huh! You couldn't last a day! Not after being tied to a desk for 20 years."

Oh Wes, I think the Finlays and the Pannells are such wonderful folks! I am so anxious to see them soon and thank them personally for all they have done and all they would do for us. We will be at Kaslo, so you can take your time about getting us there. We'll go as soon as Ed can send for us. And if as you say the third floor of the Finlay house is unused . . . but heck! how I hate to impose our physical selves on anyone! I think it was fated for me to taste the dregs of this humiliation that I might know just what it is that all the women and children must endure through no fault of their own. I don't think I can get off so easy from sharing, for a time at least, all the desperate worry and despondence of their situation. Will you understand that and forgive me for the uncertainties of the last few weeks? Tommy has practically made me Kaslo correspondent for

141

the NC, and I have this typewriter from Steve [Yamada] for the duration. There is a family from Steveston, very good friends of Ed's, that is going to do all the hard work for me, things that only a man can do . . . this Hirokawa is over age and therefore entitled to go with his family to the ghost town. As I said in my last letter, time defeated us. Because, if we are to be separated, it is imperative that the kids and I leave first, before Ed does so that he can do all the left over things after me. Once things have quieted down somewhat in Kaslo I think that chances of my going east are much better than being here where there are hundreds of applications being turned down one after the other, where the officials are terribly harassed with the whole thing and are exasperated with individual demands for attention.

I haven't met Miss Kaufman and I wouldn't think of taking up her time yet as she is terribly rushed. I may see her in Kaslo. She is the same Miss Kaufman that Kath knew at the YW in Tokyo. And answering your question as to whether I want to go to Toronto, what a question to ask! I'm wild to get there. At the moment we are too rushed packing and selling stuff to get around to such things as letters of references and all that but I will get them. I'll try Mrs. Spencer too. If you and the Carlton folks can get me there I'll bless you all, but you've got to understand Ed's position. He will not take a chance . . . not with us. By himself he will try different sources through your help and according to the outcome of that he will send for us. So he is going to let the Commission pay his fare east. Don't forget that a Mr. Pipher is the Representative at Schreiber, and that through him you can get Ed placed in other jobs. My throat is a great deal better but I still talk through a fog, and as you say, it was the accumulation of every tragedy that can happen to one person all in a few months that got me down. My spirit was okay but my body said: Nix, take a rest or you can't go on. Those ten days in bed rested me as nothing could, though I was sick through it all. At Kaslo there is a Colonel Bannan who is the representative there, and through him I intend to continue negotiations to get to Ontario.

Don't worry about me and Kaslo and the Japanese community. I'll be depressed all right. I don't suppose I can prevent that happening, but I will hang on to you people, hoping, hoping for a miracle, and that will sustain me. Anyway, I shall be so danged busy with cooking and washing and whatnot that I may not have time to worry.

So in a way the twins are a blessing, though they are the ones to complicate everything for us.

Goodness I think I shall keep my golf clubs then, and who knows, I may be able to take a turn on the links with the Rev. Finlay someday.

I'm on my way to the Manager's for a last cocktail so I'll write again.

Give my best wishes to all. I've sent those gifts by regular mail. Send all letters now to the Bank of Montreal, Main and Hastings Branch, and they will forward to me until I can let you know my new address. Tell Mrs. Pannell.

Love,
Mur.

[p.s.] I got those diapers. Thanks to Mrs Pannell. Tell her for me. I'll send more money. Get me some more and send to Kaslo when I send you an address. I'll need them to get to Ontario.

May 25, 1942.

Dear Wes:

Well, did you swear when you got the last wire?[69] We're betting you did. We were just as flabbergasted, don't you worry, and I'm still not believing anything until it actually happens. It's the strangest story with the ramifications a mystery I think.

I was all ready to go to Kaslo, and was packed too. Just as a last gesture for my own assurance more than any hope, I wrote to Grant MacNeil, Secretary of the Commission, telling him that I wanted some written assurance that I could continue negotiations from Kaslo. That's all I wanted to know, just the fact that I could hope to get

---

[69]Actually, Muriel had sent two telegrams, both on May 23. The first, sent at 12:04 p.m., reads: "On strength your last letter tried Commission again. Receding hope of going east. Will know definite result next week. Therefore send me air mail two packages Kleinerts refills just in case. Changing places made us nervous wrecks but keep fingers crossed and pray for favourable news by wire."

Three hours later, at 3:15 p.m., another telegram was sent: "Airmail two packages Kleinerts refills at once because distinct hope to going east next week causing rise in blood pressure. Also anticipate your total collapse and profanity. Will write details so wait for favourable news by wire. Will bring own beds."

to Ontario. I had no further aspirations. I was too tired out anyway
to start all over again. Ed mailed the letter for me on Friday morning from the Main Post Office. That was about noon. A little after
3 o'clock the same day Mrs. C. Booth (working there) phoned up
to tell us they'd gotten the letter and would we come down right
away bringing proof that there were accommodations and a job
waiting in Toronto. We were so flabbergasted Ed could hardly talk.
Anyway, he dropped everything and ran. Mrs. Booth, speaking for
Mr. MacNeil, said they were not giving any permits for families to
go to Toronto but that they would make an exception in this case.
She told Ed to return the next day with papers showing his bank
account and references from the Bank, and Ed did. They said the
permit was most likely to be given and told him to get ready to leave.
So Ed went and reserved a drawing room on the train for June 1st,
7:15 P.M. Then he sent the wire to you, hoping you wouldn't cry
"wolf." There! I was all jittery again! I'm getting George Ishiwara
to fix our teeth, and you know your nerves have to be pretty steady
for the ordeal of the drill, but gosh, with only 3 or 5 hours sleep
mine were jumping all over the place and was it awful! We had to
repack all our things all over again and this time I just threw
everything in any old how. I was sick and tired of repacking. So we're
all ready except for the last minute things. Crone is sending our boxed
goods and beds and toys and Japanese food supplies. We had bought
all these things for other projects and they are going with us now
to any place we go and to heck with repacking them . . . dang it!
The written permit hasn't come yet and I'm holding my breath until it does. In fact until I see your face on the station platform I shan't
believe our luck. If this goes through, it will be sheer luck and a
miracle in its way, for while the Takahashis got through, there was
trouble after that and they don't consider applications to Toronto
at all. Even housework girls can't go now. Something's flooey
somewhere. But as for us, I'm wondering what put the balance of
favour on our side, as it certainly isn't us by any means, not with
four little kids! I wonder if the wire from Rev. Finlay turned the trick?
Still, I've got my ten fingers crossed.

By the way there was a terrible miscalculation in our fares that
they gave us at the CPR offices. Remember the prices I quoted? They
were given to us over the phone. Well, when Ed went down to the
ticket office they said it was $83 and some odd cents for adults, half
for Shirley and nothing for Meiko and the twins, and $78.10 for the

drawing-room. The freight is $3.25/100 lbs. through Crone's chartering a car, and we can take 300 pounds baggage free, besides all we can take of hand baggage. There are the expensive meals, of course, and tips. We'll have to spend quite a bit anyway, because our stuff weighs about a ton or more. Since we don't know when the war is going to end, and since we hope to find a place to ourselves, we are taking the necessary china and other things that I wouldn't take to Kaslo, and there's the washer and the sewing machine. The washer has to be rewired for Toronto but there is a system of exchange to get it done cheaply. And I'm bringing your stuff by freight now. The kids are so excited.

Saturday afternoon I phoned Mrs. Booth and asked her if it was safe to transfer my Kaslo papers to Miss Hyodo, and she said: Certainly, we're granting you a permit you know, and all you have to do now is get the Henmis out of here by getting a job for Eiko there, not domestic service. O yes, I meant to write about that too, but Eiko's been terribly sick and could not answer me. Anyway, her brother and her mother think she and Yaeko would be awfully 'oyafuko'[70] to leave the old mother. Eiko's brother is in Sandon up in the mountains past Slocan and wants the whole family there, but Eiko and Yaeko are set on getting out somehow. Eiko will have to stay till the evacuation is complete, then look around, but if she can get a clerical job before then she may skip. Fumi has gone to Kamloops, and she phoned us that from there she'll catch the same train as ours; that is, she'll get up at 4:00 a.m. on Tuesday morning and catch the 5:00 a.m. train. That'll be swell for us. Now Auntie's plans have changed again. She doesn't want to go to Kaslo if I'm not. She wants an extension, which I'm trying to get for her, so that she can continue to try to get Uncle back from Camp to go to some job in the Interior. This is a heck of a life. Somehow I feel terrible about leaving her, but I hadn't intended to stay long in Kaslo and she knew that. She wants to go with the Marpole bunch in the Anglican Church group to Slocan if she has to go anywhere. Life is at sixes and sevens. She may get a job for Uncle at Grand Forks and then everything will be swell for them. At any rate, she's alien and poor and no one can get away from that nowadays, unless you've got pots of money. Heck, do you think I should have stuck by her? Gee, I feel awful. Yet when Mrs. Booth phoned, Ed, who up till then

---

[70]Japanese for "unfilial."

was so darned sceptical I wanted to cry, and who didn't want to go to Ontario because it was so far from the Bank, just ran to the Commission offices without shaving . . . darn it, we got hysterically excited about the whole thing!

Mrs. Miyazaki got a letter from Saburo [Takahashi] saying that I could get a job as cook. Were you talking to him? Ed says that I may have to as a last resort, but after all, the whole point of the matter is that we want to keep together as a family and that is why we have had so much trouble. If we have to break it up, what's the point of going, especially if I have to sleep wherever I have to work and the kids are distributed here and there? Ed wants to earn enough to eat on and keep us all together, even though I may have to pitch in with an occasional hand. The whole point of our going together is that of our staying together, for better or for worse. Now if I have to work as a sheer necessity I shall, but not until then. Not because I don't want to, but because I want to look after the kids my way.

Anyway, Ed's going to the Custodian tomorrow and then to the Commission again. He may get his permit or he may not. Too many of these things are cancelled at the last minute for anyone to feel 100% sure of anything. Will it be hell if I transfer my Kaslo papers to someone else and we don't get the Toronto permit! That's why I want those diapers in a hurry! I'll bring you the money if we come and pay for all expenses of mailing etc. Those diapers are so thin that I'll need more of them than I would of the flannelette ones, and those I need two dozen a day. I shall leave a memento of the twins at every change along the tracks right across to Toronto. Maybe I ought to get a long pole to hang out the washing to let the prairie wind dry it . . . and make it dusty too.

As soon as we get definite word from the Commission I shall wire you date and time. We're leaving this house on the 30th and most likely will take rooms at the Patricia Hotel for Saturday night and Sunday. If you think your mail will reach here by Saturday morning, we'll be at this house but after that we may be gone.

Say, what is it like at the Finlays? We are going to wire them as soon as we get the permit, and if we're still welcome we'll head their way for the time being. Do you think we can have meals by ourselves, or do we eat with the family or what? Is there a bathroom on the 3rd floor and base plugs? How much of our stuff would get in there? We thought we would store our things until we get a place. I'm bringing my mixer and things and may be able to help Mrs. Finlay with

146

the baking and cooking. Is it the Finlays that have this little Donnie? Did they get the gifts we sent? Ed's kind of shy you know, and the children are . . . well you know what they're like. I have to jump every once in a while for something they want. If I could get an electric plate there I could make the babies milk every four hours upstairs. How about chances of getting cribs and high chairs? If we could get it cheaper there . . . but heck, it might be just as cheap to freight the whole darn works.

Oh Wes, I'm not believing this until I see you. The Locks were here Saturday night and they took all our good books to store for us until we send for them. And imagine! Mr. Lock offered us financial assistance! Aren't they swell? Of course we are not borrowing from anyone since we got this grant from the Bank. Ed wants to go straight to the Bank of Montreal to thank the General Manager in person.

I'm bringing shoyu, rice, canned mirinzuke, green tea, and every Japanese dish I have, and trays, and bowls. Can't get any more miso now. So long as we have shoyu we can have chazuke[71] anytime. You can't get much Japanese food now as the stocks are almost gone.

Gosh my stomach has been upset since Friday so I have to rest awhile. Maybe I'll have time to write again. Anyhow, wait for the wire and hurry with the diapers. Two packages . . . that is, 8 dozen.

Love,
Mur.

Ask Finlays and Pannells to pray for us. Will wire them as soon as.

May 26, 1942.

Dear Mur:

Got your wires Saturday at supper time. It was too late to get diapers then—the stores were closed—so I got the two packages today and am sending them with this letter.

I don't know whether Jon and Ellen will appreciate it or not, but

---

[71]Japanese for "tea over rice."

every time they wet a diaper it's going to cost them 6¢ each. If you send a wire, please send an air-mail letter with it to explain things. Your wires have got me so that I don't know whether I'm coming or going (or rather whether you're coming or going).

As a favour, could you keep the $1.00 and 50¢ stamps and bring them with you? Or better still, if you have time, you can slip them into a letter. They're for the post office clerk's daughter—she's a stamp collector—and the post office clerk is an awfully nice feller and has been very helpful to me. Mrs. Pannell and Mr. Finlay have told me about the presents they got from you. They were tickled pink.

Sincerely,
Wes.

May 28, 1942.

Dear Mur:

Got both your wires today,[72] so did Mr. Finlay. You needn't worry about bedding. The Finlays have what you need.

As for your meals, Mr. Finlay was saying that you could arrange some sort of system so that you could eat at separate times if you wished. He said family entity and unity is a valuable thing and should not be destroyed, especially with such little kids.

There is a bathroom on the third floor and Mrs. Finlay suggested that putting a hot plate in the front room upstairs would save you the trouble of hoofing it all the way downstairs each time.

The Finlays don't want you people to feel shy about anything. But you needn't worry—just meet Jim Finlay and he'll sure make you feel at home. Mrs. Finlay is so nice too.

---

[72]The telegram sent May 27 reads: "Received permit today. Entraining June first 7.15 pm CPR. Thanks to you all. Leaving Pender house Saturday for Patricia Hotel. Am bringing most of household utensils and belongings so inquire about storage facilities and transfers to speed settling. Arriving Friday morning. Drawing room accommodation."

Muriel's final telegram, May 28, reads: "Afraid bedding not arriving same train. Advise."

Mr. Finlay may be able to get Ed a job for the summer in Toronto, pushing ice around. Tell him to eat grape-nuts—he may need it.

All the Takahashis are working in Toronto now except Mrs. Takahashi (who's ill) and Kenji (studying for his high school correspondence course).

As for cribs, I know a person who has one which she isn't using. It's been lying idle for years. She says you could have it, if you want. Her brother has a 7-room house in northern Toronto which he may either sell or rent. She's not sure yet, but she wanted to know if you had any ideas about that. I couldn't tell her anything definite, and she doesn't know what her brother intends to do.

The church has another crib which they will loan to you if you need it.

Mr. Finlay will have breakfast ready for you Friday morning. I'll be at the station when the train pulls in.

As for storage, there's empty space in the Carlton Church basement that could be put to use.

There's nothing to feel shy about when you're with the Finlays. They're grand people.

I'll be seeing you all soon.

As always,
Wes.

p.s. Donnie is Mr. Finlay's 9 year old son.

———————

Vancouver,
May 29, 1942.

Dear Wes:

The Bank phoned that the diapers were there. Also got your letter and had a comfortable laugh over it.

Now to explain the last wire briefly: Crone Storage doubts if our stuff will reach Toronto at the same time. Regular freight will be delayed about 2 weeks, while a pooled freight may take 4 weeks or so. Therefore except for our 375 lbs free baggage and hand baggage we won't have a thing. I'm trying to see that our sheets and towels and blankets arrive ditto with us. Do you know of an inexpensive hotel we could go to until the beds arrive? Or will Rev. Finlay have the beds? This trans-Canada moving is terrible. It's awfully complicated. It's a headache, but it'll be worth every bit when we're all together again.

Monday I'm going to say "good-bye" to Nobi and tell him to come to us as soon as he can come by himself. Have you heard from Doug? Auntie has a chance to go to Westbank again, but it's one of those things that swing like a pendulum. If she rushes things (like the Tateishis did) Uncle might land in an internment camp, but heck! try and explain that to her! Though she has till Saturday, she wanted to get a deferment. The Commission said "No," because they had her forms all filed and could only cancel her notice, but if they did, she'd most likely be back to file another application for another ghost town, so she had better go to Kaslo and negotiate from there. Gosh! but the women left behind are just like chickens with their heads off. They rush around aimlessly. I'd be the same too if Ed had gone to Schreiber. Just because Mrs. Tateishi was all "het up" about some place where they could go together, she had Mr. Tateishi come back from Camp only to find they couldn't go within the time limit, and now they've threatened to intern him. 130 Nisei at Petawawa— interned for rioting and crying Banzai, shaving their heads and carrying "hino-marus."[73] Damn fools. Lot of fishy-business I can't find out. Hate—spite—jealousies—malice—revenge—all the things that you read of in novels. Tom and Kunio are right in the middle of it. The RCMP came in person to order Kunio off to camp. Rev. Shimizu and Rev. Akagawa too, to camp, but they've been backed by the Church, so they had to leave immediately for the beet field and ghost town.

So Mr. Umehara is an "Onion King." Tom told us last night. Ed proceeded to weep onion tears. By the way, Ed's permit is for Temperance, while mine is for Toronto. Funny, huh? Anyway I'm anxious to see Hart House and the Museum.

Also a show—*AT NIGHT*.

Miss Woodsworth came to say goodbye and gave us the address of Mrs. Sissons and Mrs. Woodsworth both on Admiral Road. Heard Mrs. Obata's there.

---

[73]Japanese for "rising sun" (literally "round sun"), usually referring to the national flag of Japan.

Yesterday we worked so hard! Steve crated—after taking buggies, wagons apart—Ed tied, labelled, ran to Commission. Ran to Bank. Skidded to Crones, to CPR. I cooked and washed 8 sheets, 2 covers, umpteen diapers and restuffed clothes bags. It's bedlam. This morning I'm relaxing—because my cough is worse and I don't want to get sick getting to Toronto. How I hate to leave Nobi.

The first thing you must do when we get there is to take us out *at night*. (By the way, how do you figure 6¢ per wetting? 8x12 into $2.50 and how much in stamps . . . must see today?)

Oh Wes, I'm just beginning to feel excited. It's been such a long night. Would it be too much to hope you'll be at the station so early in the a.m.? Fumi Shoyama's coming with us, maybe. Got to find Eiko a clerical job somewhere around there. Mrs. Booth asked me too.

See you Friday—

With love,
Mur.

Engagement of Tsuru Toyofuku and Asajiro Fujiwara (Muriel's mother and father), in the summer of 1907 in the Moss Garden of the Toyofuku home; Kurume, Fukuoka, Japan. Back row left: Hiroko, Tsuru's older sister; fourth from left: Asajiro; fifth from left: Tsuru; right: Kameko (Tsuru's younger sister). Front row fourth from left: Fred Toyofuku ("Uncle Fred" in Muriel's letters); fifth from left: Muriel's great grandmother; seventh from left: Junji Toyofuku (Muriel's grandfather); right: Sue (Sada) Toyofuku.

Courtesy Kay Fujiwara Sano

153

Tsuru Fujiwara and Tsukiye Muriel Fujiwara in 1912. Muriel was about one year old.

Standing in front of Muriel, from left to right: Douglas, Kathleen, and Wesley Fujiwara, 1921.

154

Muriel in her early teens, c. 1927.

Muriel, c. 1925 (about 13 years old).

1928 class picture, Duke of Connaught High School, New Westminster, B.C. Muriel is in second row, third from left. Her friend, Ed Ouchi, is in third row, far right.

Muriel at home in summer 1933 (age 21).

Muriel married Eizaburo (Ed) Kitagawa in 1933. In 1926, when this photo was taken, Ed was a member of the famous Asahi baseball team.

156

The first editorial group of the *New Canadian*, 1939. Left to right: Seiji Onizuka, Yoshimitsu Higashi, Irene Uchida, Ed Ouchi, Tom Shoyama.

Japanese Canadian Citizens' League (JCCL) delegation to Ottawa to seek the franchise, 1926. Left to right: Samuel I. Hayakawa, Minoru Kobayashi, Hide Hyodo, Edward Banno.

Ed and Muriel and their four children—Shirley, Carol, and the twins—in 1942. This photo was taken in April, by which time the Kitagawas knew they would be forced to leave their Vancouver home, but did not know where they would end up.

RCMP officer posting the Male Enemy Alien notice, Vancouver, 1942.

Seizure of the Japanese Canadian fishing fleet, Steveston, B.C., December 1941-January 1942.

Impounded at Annieville Dyke on the Fraser River, 1941. In all, about 1200 fishing boats were impounded. They were sold by order-in-council during January-February 1942.

Officer of the Royal Canadian Navy questioning two Japanese Canadian fishermen, 1941.

160

Some 1500 cars, trucks and motorcycles owned by Japanese Canadians were impounded and placed at the Pacific National Exhibition (PNE) grounds in Vancouver. They were sold by the Custodian of Enemy Alien Property in summer 1942.

Courtesy Vancouver Public Library

Many Nisei men were separated from their families and sent to Schreiber, Ontario to work in road and lumber camps.

Courtesy Vancouver Public Library

Courtesy Vancouver Public Library

Hastings Park: workers stuff straw into bags to make mattresses for Japanese Canadians detained in the exhibition buildings.

Hastings Park: men's dormitory.

Hastings Park: washroom.

Hastings Park: men's dining room.

Hastings Park: guard house.

Hastings Park: school classes for children.

Hastings Park: women's dormitory.

The whole place is impregnated with the smell of ancient manure and maggots. The toilets are just a sheet metal trough. The bunks are steel and wooden frames with a thin lumpy straw tick, a bolster, and three army blankets. These are the 'homes' of the women I saw.

Hastings Park: children's dining room.

Hastings Park: women's laundry room.

167

A scene in Sandon, one of the ghost towns in the B.C. interior where Japanese Canadians were sent to live.

Arriving in Slocan, another B.C. ghost town.

Many Japanese Canadians had to endure the harsh Slocan winter in tents while waiting for shacks to be provided by the government.

Tashme, a detention centre built just outside of Hope, B.C., is an acronym for the names of the three members of the B.C. Security Commission: TAylor, SHirras and MEad.

172

The Kitagawa family in Toronto, in the back yard of Ray and Olive Pannell's house, April 1943. Back row, left to right: Muriel, Ed, Wes Fujiwara.

Wes Fujiwara in Toronto, c. 1944, with Muriel's friends (left to right): Yaeko Henmi, Setsuko Yamaoka, and Eiko Henmi.

173

Preparing for the Fund Drive of the NJCCA (National Japanese Canadian Citizens' Association), which was formed in September 1947 to seek compensation for losses resulting from the wartime uprooting.

Muriel working at the typewriter, c. 1943-44.

Muriel in 1972, two years before she died.

II

Other Writings

The Year 1942
(December 1941)

1942 dawns beneath black clouds, and there seems little hope of any lightening of the gloom. Half the world is ranged against the other half in a to-the-death struggle. Each half maintains that right is on its side. And the Japanese Canadians are on the side of Democracy.

Once upon a time there was a great struggle between Americans called the American Civil War. Then, North was ranged against South. Whatever the minor causes, the main issue was a principle. Brother was against brother, father against son, friend against friend. It was a bitter, bitter war lasting four years, leaving in its wake death, destruction, poverty, hatred, and new feuds.

While this new war on the Pacific is not primarily between Japanese and Japanese, yet in this struggle the American and Canadian Japanese are enemy to their brothers, their cousins, even their aged fathers and mothers. Our first loyalties belong to our homes here in Canada, to the land of our birth, our future. It goes against the grain to be disloyal. Yet because of homey, family ties our hearts can be broken.

Active fighting is much easier to bear than this enforced stillness and waiting, being the bait for every agitator, the target of every small Hitler who forgets that he fights for justice and freedom.

That is why it is so very heartening to know who now are our friends. What words can express our gratitude when the milkman says: "Aw, you're OK. You're one of us." Then there is the lump in the throat to prevent speech when the man who brings my eggs offers: "Now don't you worry. You're all right." Then there are the casual neighbours who go out of their way to be extra friendly, who wave a cheery "hello" and smile extra wide to assure us that they are still the same.

These people, whose human sympathy and friendliness bring warmth to the cold surrounding us, bring us a gift that is priceless. We can appreciate it with a sincerity too deep for words. We can only prove with our deeds that they have not wasted their spontaneous offering. A careless, taken-for-granted acceptance can take the shine off any gift. We are not beggars who have to be contented

179

with the patronizing scraps thrown to us. We are people, self-respecting and not sycophantic, who can accept with true thankfulness the many manifestations of the friendships of our fellow-Canadians.

A New Year dawns. It will not be a year for wishful thinking, but we could brighten it somewhat with our undimmed faith in the inherent decency of the little people.

1942! May you be kind to us all!

We'll Fight for Home!
(January 1942)

The tide of panic, starting from irresponsible agitators, threatens to engulf the good sense of the people of British Columbia. The daily press is flooded with "letters to the editor" demanding the indiscriminate internment of all people of Japanese blood, alien or Canadian-born; demanding the immediate confiscation of our right to work as we like, our right to live like decent human beings. One and all, they add the height of sardonic cynicism: if we are as loyal as we say we are, then we ought to understand why we ought to be treated like poison.

If we were less Canadian, less steeped in the tradition of justice and fair play, perhaps we could understand and bow our heads before this strange, undemocratic baiting of thousands of innocent people.

For the very reason that our Grade School teachers, our High School teachers, and our environment have bred in us a love of country, a loyalty to one's native land, faith in the concepts of traditional British fair play, it is difficult to understand this expression of a mean narrow-mindedness, an unreasoning condemnation of a long suffering people. We cannot understand why our loyalty should be questioned.

After all, this is our only home, where by the sweat of our endeavours we have carved a bit of security for ourselves and our children. Would we sabotage our own home? Would we aid anyone who menaces our home, who would destroy the fruits of our labour and our love? People who talk glibly of moving us wholesale "East of the Rockies," who maintain that it is an easy task, overlook with supreme indifference the complex human character.

They do not think what it would mean to be ruthlessly, needlessly uprooted from a familiar homeground, from friends, and sent to a labour camp where most likely the decencies will be of the scantiest in spite of what is promised. They do not think that we are not cattle to be herded wherever it pleases our ill-wishers. They forget, or else it does not occur to them, that we have the same pride and self-respect as other Canadians, who can be hurt beyond repair. In short, they do not consider us as people, but as a nuisance to be rid of at the first opportunity. What excuse they use is immaterial to them. It just happens to be very opportune that Japan is now an active enemy.

We have often been accused of taking the bread out of "white" folks' mouths. Is there anything against the right to enjoy what one has earned? Our little trades and professions . . . what golden loot for our would-be despoilers! No wonder they drool to get at them. These hard-earned, well-deserved small successes . . . for out of the total of our enterprises, how many are there that can be classed as wealth? So few!

"Man's inhumanity to man makes countless thousands mourn."

Right here in British Columbia is a God-sent opportunity for the government and the people to practise democracy as it is preached. Not in panicky persecutions that do no one any good, but with sensible belief in our very real harmlessness, and consideration for us as a much-maligned people.

Ye gods! Can they not see that we love our home and would fight to protect it from the invader!

On Loyalty
(February 1942)

The quality of loyalty is difficult to define in exact terms. There is a oneness with one's country, just as there is the blood tie with one's mother. There is the fighting urge to defend that country should it be threatened in any way. There is a passionate, unquestioning, unqualified affinity with the land that excludes the pettiness of a man-made—and therefore imperfect—government. All this and active service for the country is loyalty.

181

Who can glibly say I am a Japanese National of Japan just because I am of the same race with black hair and yellow skin? Who can rightfully tell me where my heart lies, if I know better myself? Who can assume with omniscience that I am disloyal to Canada because I have not golden hair and blue eyes? What are these surface marks that must determine the quality of my loyalty? Nothing, nothing at all!

Yet because I am Canadian, must hate be a requisite for my patriotism? Must I hate vengefully, spitefully, pettily? Will not hate cloud my good sense, muddy the clean surge of willing sacrifice, the impulse to rally strongly to the flag of this country? Hate never fought as fiercely as love in the fight for one's country. Hate impedes, while love strengthens.

Therefore it is not hate for a country one has never known, but love for this familiar Canadian soil that makes me want to use my bare fists to uphold its honour, its integrity.

Who is there, unless he does not know the quality of loyalty, who will question mine?

A Series of Three Letters on the Property Issue
(July 1943)

Custodian of Japanese Properties,
Vancouver, B.C.
Dear Sir:

This is to register with you our absolute opposition to the proposed liquidation of our house and lot at *2751 Pender Street East, Vancouver, B.C.*

This house, bought out of slender earnings, represents our stake in this country of our birth, but sentiment alone is not for withholding our express and voluntary consent to sell.

Our present earnings are even more slender than before. You are doubtless aware, if you have a family of your own, what it costs in dollars and cents to feed, clothe, and house a family of six, excluding the other expenses incidental to schooling, medical services, etc. With four growing children, that $25 a week we receive from the rental of our house is more welcome than you could ever understand. Without that $25, meagre as it is, we could not meet all our monthly obligations. You know, too, that while cost of living rises, salaries do not. But now you purpose to deprive us of that regular income on which we are desperately dependent. We are not among those who can afford the loss of their dear-bought investment.

Our house, a private residence belonging to a private citizen of this country, is in the capable hands of a trustworthy agent; the tenants are pleasant and punctual. They know they have a bargain, as the house is in good shape, with added improvements to the cost of many hundreds of dollars, boosting the saleable value of the house, too. This piece of real estate is not idle, either, housing as it does the family of a soldier, and also keeping poverty and hardship that much further away from the absent owners.

We cannot understand the official claim that it is necessary to sell over our heads the home from which we were forcibly ejected. We do not quarrel with military measure but this act can scarcely be in accordance with any war measure. Please hasten to assure us that our house is inviolate.

Thank you.

Yours truly,
Mr. and Mrs. E. Kitagawa.

Canada
Department of the Secretary of State
Office of the Custodian
Japanese Evacuation Section

Phone PAcific 6131　　　　　　　　　*506 Royal Bank Building,*
Please refer to　　　　　　　　　　*Hastings and Granville,*
File No. 10004　　　　　　　　　　　　*Vancouver, B.C.*
　　　　　　　　　　　　　　　　　　　2nd July, 1943.

Mr. Eizaburo Kitagawa,
Registration #01842,
Toronto, Ont.
Dear Sir:

I am in receipt of your letter of the 26th instant in which you registered your disapproval of the sale of your property.

The proposed liquidation is of course a general one and not only applies to your particular property. The policy has been decided upon at Ottawa and this Office, acting under advice of an independent Advisory Committee, will endeavour to obtain the best possible results.

You are aware I hope that the proceeds of the liquidation will be available to you from time to time as you have need of same.

At the present moment tenders have not been called on your particular property but I am unable to give you the assurance asked for and it will be disposed of in due course if satisfactory offers are received.

Yours truly,
F.G. Shears,
Acting Director.

———————————

Toronto, Ont.,
July 8th, 1943.

Mr. F.G. Shears:

I received your letter of July 2nd, File No. 10004, yesterday and must say was not too greatly surprised. The reason for writing you at all was because the government had vested in you the final authority to sell or not to sell our homes, and perhaps I took a vain-hope gamble.

Would you give up a legitimate fight to defend what is yours though the odds are enough to overwhelm you? Britain didn't, did she? This war, for the common soldier, is a war for Principle: the rights and liberties and the pursuit of happiness for every man; and I'm on the side of the common soldier, giving his heart's blood that the oppressed may be free. Who would have thought that one day I would be unable to stand up for my country's government, out of sheer shame and disillusion, against the slurs of the scornful? The bitterness, the anguish is complete. You, who deal in lifeless figures, files, and statistics could never measure the depth of hurt and outrage dealt out to those of us who love this land. It is because we *are* Canadians, that we protest the violation of our birthright. If we were not we would not care one jot or tittle whatever you did, for then we could veil our eyes in contempt. You . . . and by "you" I designate all those in authority who have piled indignity upon indignity on us . . . have sought to sully and strain our loyalty but, I'm telling you, you can't do it. You can't undermine our faith in the principles of equal rights and justice for all, with "malice towards none, and charity for all."

Why can't you differentiate between those owners who don't care one way or the other what happens to their homes, and those who, born in this country, hate to lose their homes? If you are worried for our sakes about the depreciation of property values, then why will you not allow the owners a say in the sale price, the choice of prospective buyers? Can you, with a clear conscience, commit this breach of justice, and face the accusing eyes of all bereft and absent owners? Do you think it is logical, after what happened to the boats, the cars, and radios, that we have any faith in any promise of a fair price, which "proceeds of this liquidation will be available . . . from time to time?" What will happen is the gradual dribbling away to nothing of the pitiful price, and then what shall we have left to show for our lifetime of struggling and saving and loving the bit of land we call our own? You may rightly say that wartime sacrifices are inevitable and honourable, but can you say with any truth that this sacrifice forced on us will be sanctified by a spirit of voluntary giving? What are platitudes against this humiliation!

Now you understand a little why I must contest the sale to the last bitter ditch, if we are to hold up our heads. You will concede us that, especially as this is the very principle for which the democracies are fighting.

However, if all fails and you are upheld in your purpose, then kindly send us our "proceeds" in one sum that we may personally reinvest it in something solid . . . Victory Bonds, for instance.

There are still a few personal possessions in our home for which I shall send at once. You would not deny us that, I hope.

T.M. Kitagawa.

I Know the Nisei Well
(Manuscript, c. 1943)

I know the Nisei well. I know them better than do Mr. Green, Mrs. Ralston, or even Mr. MacInnis, though certainly I should not place him in the same category as Mrs. Ralston or Mr. Green. I've known the Nisei when they were happy, when they were sad. I've watched them grow from legginess into adulthood, seen how they developed from childish ignorance and innocence to knowledge, experience, and realization. I have seen them in anger, in exuberant spirits, enthusiasms and despairs, in the quiet stillness of resignation or renunciation. I've seen them obstreperous, known them to be inobtrusive. I've worked beside them in canneries, on farms, in Red Cross groups, met them in the lighter moments of social affairs, argued with them vociferously and heatedly on social, political, economic, or even religious controversies.

I've seen them in poverty and in luxury, in cabins and stuccoed residences; struggling for higher education on meagre earnings, or cushioned through college by a parent's wealth; going the six miles to university on an old "bike" in all seasons and weather, or rolling along in a shiny new Ford, or the other family car.

I've known them as mill-hands, lumberjacks, clerks, dressmakers, stenos, domestic servants. I've watched them waltz and jitterbug, play baseball, tennis, rugby, golf, and ping-pong. I've seen some go wrong and end up in jail, others who rose to become professors at well-known universities, with degrees and honours stringing after their names. I've known them to go to Japan to stay, others who returned to B.C., preferring this land. I know some who are so *British* they are imperialistic, others who are so stuffily Japanese they are intolerable. I've seen them utterly devoted to their parents, I've seen them disagree strongly enough to leave home.

I've known them in love and out, attended their weddings and followed with interest their family life. I've known them in illness, or face to face with death. In short, I know the Nisei in every mood and circumstance, and because of this intimacy with them, I shall discuss some of the accusations brought against us.

·

I was reading a book entitled *The Ports of British Columbia* by Agnes Rothery, when on page 130 I came across this sentence in the section touching casually on the Japanese: "But practically all accepted their evacuation with cheerfulness."

It brought back to my mind all the nightmarish kaleidoscope of the days after Pearl Harbor. I felt again the fears and confusions, the hysteria, the feeling of being caged in helplessness. And if, out of the welter of those dark days, we wrung from our battered resources any cheerfulness, it was the cheerfulness inherent in all peoples who rise above disaster. This is not a peculiarly Japanese trait. No, the same cheerfulness was shown by those Londoners recovering from the first awful effects of the German blitz. Is the comparison ridiculous? Why should it be? In our disaster the bombs were lacking, certainly, but against us there were hatred, mistrust and an unreasonable fear.

December 7, 1941, dawned for us as a peaceful, sunny Sunday, on which we looked forward to quiet and leisure after a working week. It was a nice enough day for morning golf, for friends dropping in to tea, and evening services for those that attended churches.

My first intimation of disaster came from my younger daughter who came rushing in, her face taut with tension, crying: "Mommy! Bombs are falling on the corner store!" My only response was: "That's silly, baby . . . who said so?" She was just four years old and rather mixed up when it came to retelling what she heard, and I thought someone was kidding her along, as usual. Then my older daughter who was seven at the time came in, also with similar news, except she used "somewhere" for the familiar "corner store." She added too, in a slightly worried tone: "Lainey said we had to go into a con-cen-t'ation camp."

She hesitated over the long strange word. Well, I thought the joke was going a little too far, and I soothed both of them out of their fears. This was around noon. I hadn't had the radio on until then, and wasn't intending to turn it on until the Charlie McCarthy program at five o'clock PDT.

But the phone rang insistently. "Hello! Where's your husband? Japan just bombed Hawaii!" I laughed in polite appreciation at this joking, as I thought it was then. I told the other party to stop being flippant. He insisted in all seriousness, until I caught the undercurrent

187

of his shock and listened with a sick feeling as the bottom dropped out of my world. I was one of those people who had hoped against hope that the Pacific would remain peaceful.

From that moment on we lived in daily fear and uncertainty, and I wished passionately that I had not had children to suffer the effects of this new war, for I knew what we would have to endure.

That was Pearl Harbor Day for me, for us.

The night of December 7th, about 48 Japanese were arrested for internment. Of many that were so interned I can only express surprise and incredulity that there was anything against them. That they were later released must prove that they were innocent.

There was one farmer who was returning home to his farm far from populous centres when he was picked up. He was so far from town that apparently he had not heard of the attack on Pearl Harbor. Anyway, the story is that he walked dazed into the immigration detention headquarter and uttered this simple and soulful statement: "I hear that a war has begun." This story has become a gem for retelling, and has the power of invoking gales of laughter.

My Uncle Fred [Toyofuku] said, as he was preparing to depart for the Tête Jaune Road Camp for Nationals: "Someday, when we shall again sit in peace around our home fires, we shall recount and mull over these events, and they shall be tales to hand down to our grandchildren." Uncle Fred came to this country when he was eighteen, and since he has not been naturalized, as an alien he is sure of better treatment from Canada than the native-born or naturalized. He left his growing azalea nursery, and only with misgivings at leaving his wife and children, cheerfully left for the road camp, determined to make the best of it.

The immediate cause for the wholesale evacuation of the Japanese on the B.C. coast was the flooding of MPs in Ottawa with letters and wires from people demanding the removal of all the 21,000 Japanese from Prince Rupert in the north to Steveston on the Fraser Delta, and from every town and village on Vancouver Island, and the Queen Charlottes. The propulsion behind the demand to Ottawa was the united voice of the few people in B.C. who have always resented, and even hated us, demanding further and further restrictions to be laid on us. It was never our next-door neighbour that demanded expulsion, for they knew us through daily contact. We felt a mutual respect and friendliness, and they were sincere in their sympathy for us.

Acting on the demands of the constituents back in B.C., Parliament passed one order-in-council after the other.

In the beginning, the Canadian-born and naturalized citizens were not to be affected. The aliens would be evacuated from the coast, and males only at that. But gradually, as week followed week, the policy of the government changed until every man, woman, and child was to be sent out of the "protected area," and when the actual moving began, the Canadian-born and naturalized were among the first to go.

Before evacuation plans were even defined, we were ordered to surrender all radios, all cameras, all cars to the RCMP if we had not disposed of them privately before the deadline date. Curfew tolled for us, and we were confined within our four walls from dusk to dawn. (This gave rise to many ridiculous situations, and a few very tragic ones; witness the dying father, and a daughter, living in another part of the town, prevented from going to his side, though she had pleaded to be allowed out, and the doctor who was unable to attend to that man, because the curfew also kept him tied in; witness husbands and sons, caught after curfew in other homes than their own, having to bed down on couches and armchairs and blankets on the floor.) It was a terrible blow, not only because now we could not stroll along the shopping centre, or go to movies at night, or to church, or to visit our friends as we used to, but also because within the four walls there flourished an atmosphere of suspicion, unrest, and dark rumours, fears and a sense of horrible impotence, unleavened by radio entertainment to while away the hours to bedtime. There was a wavering yet enveloping mist of hysteria, controlled, but ready to rise, inflamed.

For ourselves, we felt keenly the loss of our radio, which we sold to a friend at a two-thirds loss. Our radio was streamlined and new, and we had scrimped and saved to get it for its rich tone, making symphony broadcasts a joy, and the record player attached was true in its reproduction of recorded music. We never could get the short wave to function properly, and we never heard the news broadcasts at all, after this. As for our little box camera, it cost $3.25 but it took many a snapshot of our children, friends, and relatives, and I do miss it now. We had no car, but our friends had, and after they had either sold, abandoned, or surrendered theirs, it was strange to see them on streetcars.

189

•

From the days when I began to read and enjoy the Curwood tales of the Northwest, and the Royal Canadian Mounted Police, I have idealized and respected that organization of intrepid men with their scarlet coats and superb horses. Their motto, Maintenons le droit . . . Maintain the right . . . is famous the world over. I was proud of them, and in my eyes they could do no wrong, for how could they and maintain the right? However, there were some incidents during the evacuation that made me uneasy, not about the Force as a whole, but at the thought that there were in that Force certain members who were, shall I say, less than generous in their understanding and treatment of a helpless people. Let me illustrate with an incident, which no doubt still lingers like a sore spot in the memory for many an ignorant and harmless alien.

The aliens, those born in Japan and not naturalized, were required to register personally at the RCMP headquarters in Vancouver. To obtain their "parole" papers, they had to report once a month thereafter, wherever they were and at whatever branch of the RCMP was there. At the initial registering, the offices at Heather Street in Vancouver were lined with these aliens, waiting their turn. They were frightened and timid, and they did not know the RCMP as I did, as protectors and upholders of the law. To these fearful aliens the uniformed men were the symbols of war, incarceration, execution. Well, up and down this waiting line tramped one officer, his right hand holding a riding crop like a switch, and smacking the palm of his left hand, regularly as his spurs clinked at every step, until the sound of it beat into the hearts and heads of the waiting people, like the throb of a deadly menace. Can you imagine the pall of dread that lay over those aliens?

Another instance occurred in the Manning Pool right in front of the Livestock Building in Hastings Park. The whole Park had been in an uproar for two days over the sudden proposed arbitrary shipment of young men to Schreiber, Ontario at a day's notice. The young men refused to go because they claimed they needed more time to get ready, to shop for work clothes, and to clear up family affairs for their parents who would be handicapped by a lack of the English language. More than all this, they wished to return to their various homes for a last farewell. These boys had been brought over to the Pool from the Island where they had been employed in logging camps

190

and fishing villages. In other cases they had homes in Steveston, New Westminster, and farther down the Fraser Valley, and had not seen their families for months, or even years. In the uncertainty that prevailed at this time over the fate of themselves and their alien parents, it was natural that these young men were frantic and stubborn about being confined within the barbed wire Pool in the Park, not allowed to see their folks. At this time too, those on the outside were not allowed into the Pool and passes were difficult to obtain. The authorities were threatening imprisonment and internment, but that only made the boys even more adamant in their refusal to be shipped to points unknown. Therefore, there was terrible ferment in the Pool, with mothers especially on the rampage, thinking no doubt of their own sons. There was also reported some mismanagement on the part of the three Japanese Issei appointed to supervise their fellow-Japanese . . . mismanagement and bullying. These three earned the hearty dislike of the inmates, perhaps not entirely their own fault, but because they represented the seeming heartlessness that cracked the whip over the confinees.

At the particular moment which I describe, the women already confined in their building for the night heard some frightening rumour that had swept the place, as rumours usually do, and they had rushed out in a milling mass of cries and protests. They did not know what for, but their hysteria was near the surface. As they came out of the building and down the wide steps, a mountie whirled, waved his crop and threateningly shouted: "Get back in there you. . . ." I leave the rest to your imagination.

At the same moment one of the young Nisei women workers in the Pool came up, and taking in the situation at a glance, stormed up to the mountie with eyes blazing in outraged indignation: "Stop that! How dare you! What do you think we are! Cattle?" She was near tears at the sight of that mob of anxious women who were cowed back, frightened, and uncertain before the threat of that riding crop. This was a nightmare.

When these reports circled through the Japanese still outside of the Pool, and when I heard them, I felt my heart constrict with the shared humiliation forced upon us, and the glory which I had associated with the Redcoats died. It was the death of an ideal.

•

191

Then there were our homes, stores, businesses, and farms. The fishing fleet was the first to be impounded, and the tale of the trek down from Prince Rupert is still told, of the hungry, freezing, fearful trip down the coast herded by gunboats, of fishermen unprepared for the three-week journey, most of them only in shirt, jacket, and dungarees, without provisions, for they hadn't been told they were going down so far. They had been told only to bring their boats to a certain spot where they would be taken over by the authorities. You can imagine the fears that struck wives and children when day after day passed without the return of their husbands and sons, when frantic wires and letters came to relatives in Vancouver, begging for any news.

Small stores were sold in desperation at ruinous prices, and already some were ready to "cash in" on the tears of others. Businesses were leased or sold, farms abandoned or rented to tenants, and last but not least, there was literally a line-up of prospective renters or buyers for our homes.

The Custodian took over all those properties we left behind with the understanding that our interests would be watched over. Many of us had stored valuables, furniture and personal goods in attics and basements, being unable to take more than just the few necessaries for existence in either a camp or a ghost town room. Many never had time to dispose of anything because they had only a few days to get out of that town or village. The fortunate ones sold everything they could, and though what they got was little enough, it was ten times better than having their possessions auctioned off for a ridiculously low price, as indeed those left by evacuees were in the late summer of 1943.

Early in 1943, the government passed another order-in-council, to sell all property held by the Japanese in B.C., including farms, buildings, and homes. This new order was a shock, and naturally we felt outraged and cheated. The proposed sale of our private homes without any regard to the wishes of the absent owners angered us more than anything could. Our homes represented years of work, saving, and dreaming. We were never content with living in shacks, cabins, and rented houses. We wanted a home where we could enjoy living, where our children would have a solid background just like anyone else, be they a Smith, Berretoni, McNab, or a Bernstein. We had painted and repaired and renewed, installed new furnaces, new pipes, planned with care a front flower garden, and a back garden

192

of vegetables or more flowers, shrubs, and smooth grass plots. Our home meant security in our old age, graceful living for the present. All this was wiped out. Even as I write this, we received a notice from the Custodian:

> Please be informed that . . . your property . . . is in course of sale at a price equal to that placed upon it by an independent appraiser.
> While it is not necessary that the title be available in order to complete the sale it is preferred that it be surrendered to the Registrar of Land Titles.

We had no say in the disposal of our house, and the proceeds after the various handling charges have been deducted will not be given to us unless we can prove that we are in need. I have a letter to this effect from the Custodian.

It may be relevant, here, to tell of the sale of an evacuee's Cadillac family car. Mr. U surrendered it as ordered. Months later it was sold through the Custodian for $33. Handling charges came to about $30 and Mr. U received a cheque for $3 and some odd cents as his share in the proceeds from his car. We had a good laugh over that one, and thereupon grew a joke concerning a man who ended up by *owing* the Custodian money, instead of receiving any.

Sometimes, I wonder what democracy means.

•

The evacuation process itself was such a hodge-podge of confusion that it is still difficult to sort out with any clarity what really happened. The first concrete thing that happened was the requisition of the Hastings Park and Fair Grounds as a temporary Manning Pool for the thousands of Japanese evacuated from the outlying districts. The entrance gates were barred and locked and guards placed. The Midway section of the Park was boarded off, so that the area left to house the Japanese contained all the display buildings, the Forum and the Exhibition Garden which was a new building used for various occasions (Duke Ellington brought his famous band and dazzled his fans there). The Main Livestock Building which used to house prize stallions and mares, prize bulls and breeders, champion cows, pigs and sheep and rabbits and poultry, was washed out with chloride of lime and giant hoses. In it were placed at three foot intervals the double-decker steel bunks, each having one extremely dusty straw tick, three army blankets, and a bolster. There was in the corner a hastily erected sanitary convenience, at which sight I shuddered. The poultry section was lined with tables and benches to be used as a dining-room, and back of this was a rough kitchen, cartons and cases of tinned milk, and food. The bunks and dining hall were walled up, and the only outlet was a narrow door on which hung a significant padlock. All entrances on the outside were guarded by constables. This Livestock Building was reserved for women and children only, and menfolk were forbidden within, which fact was explained cynically in a daily paper that "it was to prevent further propagation of this species." The men were housed in another building, and since I had no access to it, naturally, I cannot describe it.

I had occasion to enter the Livestock Building when I went to visit friends that had arrived from Victoria. I lived two blocks from the Park, and had hitherto spent pleasant moments in it, but from that day on, when I visited it in its new form, I shall always see it as I saw it that day: filled with purposeless people old and young, cluttered, faces lifted in everlasting query—What will happen to us next? When I entered the Livestock Building and saw the rows and rows of bunks, hung with every conceivable kind of blanket or coat or even bedspreads to ensure a little privacy from the other bunks, I felt an outrage too deep for tears. I closed my eyes for I could not bear to look on the closed faces of the inmates, daring me to be curious or superior because I still lived in my own home outside the Pool. Here in the Pool they were stripped of privacies, and only a cold pride saved what little they had left of reticences.

Here is the story of one old widow, whose Japan-born son had been sent to a camp near Jasper. Her neighbours, not having the heart to tell her where they were going or why, brought her down with them, and she was registered into the Pool with the rest and assigned a bunk. She came to her bunk still dazed by swift events, but when she finally realized where she was and why, she collapsed into heartbroken sobs: "I would prefer death to this!"

Most of the women made the best of things and proceeded to house clean. The lucky ones were assigned to a whole stall, where in prewar days a beribboned stallion pawed the straw. Here is reported what happened in one such stall. The occupant, a bustling mother from Prince Rupert, accustomed to order and cleanliness, got soap and water and started right in to scrub the board flooring, but she could not get rid of the maggots so she complained to a passing occidental nurse who turned in fury and upbraided with contempt the surprised woman. There was such a strong protest from the inmates that this particular nurse was removed from that section. However, this incident served a good purpose in that there was a more thorough cleaning out of the cracks and crevices where maggots had breeded.

It was reported that a dietitian was assigned to the Pool, but from the accounts of people who were in there, the menu scarcely varied from day to day or even from meal to meal, and it was first come, first served. At first there was no preparation for babies and young children at all, and they got along on what they could eat from the adult fare. It was cold meat or bologna, bread and butter, and tea, which later changed to stew for lunch and dinner. And the inmates were charged for their board.

The destinations of the Japanese were a matter of great speculation and worry in the early days of the evacuation. Of course, the alien males knew they were headed for the road camps in the Rockies, but what of their wives and families, their native-born sons? What of the Nisei? The naturalized Canadians? Now that it had become clear that everyone had to move, just where would they go? Where could they go?

Before the travel restrictions were clamped down on the people, a few families and single men pulled up stakes and left on their own accord for points east, ranging from Kamloops to Montreal. But these were few in number.

At this time Ontario wanted some thousands of single men for her lumber industry and the farms down in the southern part of that province. Ontario wanted Nisei. Then Alberta wanted contract labour for her beet farms. The rest of the country made it embarrassingly clear that Japanese of any kind were highly undesirable.

The B.C. Security Commission had come into being by then, headed by Austin Taylor, and this Commission forthwith began to plan interior housing schemes in those abandoned mining towns, places which instantly became known as "ghost" towns to all of us, despite the aversion held by the Commission for that term. There were four main towns picked for the purpose of temporarily housing the evacuees: Kaslo, Slocan, Greenwood, and Sandon. (Later a new town was built near Hope and christened Tashme.[1]) Certain numbers were allotted to each town depending on accommodations, and immediately began the juggling and manoeuvring for the most desirable of these places. Some said Greenwood was *the* place to go, and they placed their application for removal to that town. Others were for Kaslo, or Slocan, but most of them shied away from Sandon, as it was thought to be too removed from lines of communcations and supplies. Rumours spread about its being tucked away so securely between mountain heights, that it was built right over a mountain stream that would flood in the spring, that the sun never got around to that place.

At the same time that preparations were made to move to these ghost towns, other groups of people, not wishing to be moved to such places, asked and got permission to go in groups to what were called the "self-supporting" projects. These people had a fair-sized bank account, which they hoped would see them through the duration, since they were to be forbidden to engage in any lucrative business. They went on their own expense to Christina Lake, Minto, Bridge River, McGillivray Falls, and a few other places. These people went on the understanding that they would never be a burden on the Commission or local governments. Very soon, however, they found out that expenses and boredom were much, very much, greater than they had estimated, and when the policy changed again to let families move east, some of them came east to Ontario and Quebec.

Another scattered group were the independents who, not wishing to go either to the ghost towns or the self-supporting places, wished to strike out on their own, anywhere. These, at first, found it very difficult to get permission to go, as towns and cities right across Canada made it known that Japanese were not wanted.

Toronto early had publicized that Japanese were undesirable, but this opinion I believe was not officially recorded as a resolution or motion. A few families had already come here before the travel restrictions. I wished to go to Toronto because my brother Wes was attending the university there and I certainly did not relish being separated for the duration from him. We could not afford to go to any self-supporting place, and the thought of living 8 to a single 9 x 12 room in a ghost town, with all my luggage, with twin infants (born one

---

[1]The name "Tashme" is an acronym made from the first two letters from the names of the three Commissioners on the B.C. Security Commission: TAylor, SHirras, and MEad.

month after Pearl Harbor), without the facilities that would ease my daily work, was more than I could stomach. Besides, the maintenance money, should my husband volunteer for the Ontario camps, was less than half of what I would need for my little family of four. Though if worse came to worst, and if I was forced to go to these towns, I was resigned to it. Nevertheless, I did the utmost to go someplace where the children would have a chance of regular education and medical care, and away from that atmosphere of morbid depression that was already beginning to settle on the people. While the expense of travelling to Toronto was great, I felt it was worth the risks, and we arrived nervously exhausted by the tension of the past months. I'm glad we did for we have met some very fine Christians who have made us welcome and who have given freely of their friendship.

•

One picture of the evacuation I can never forget is the day my other brother Doug left for Schreiber, Ontario. He had tried to enlist in the C.A.S.C. three times after Pearl Harbor, but each time was completely ignored, and he gave up trying. Then he applied for a travel permit to Alberta where he had worked once long ago, but there was too much red tape, and he declined being arbitrarily sent to any destination unknown, to be contracted, to be shorn of that freedom so dear to his wanderlust spirit. After this he volunteered for Schreiber because his friends had been ordered there, not because that was his choice. He was determined to *volunteer* and *not be forced*. Forthwith he was confined in the Pool, but standing on his prerogative as a volunteer, he demanded and got freedom of movement. Then the day of departure came. Those young men who had been drafted and ordered out were rounded up into huge transit buses, locked in with two RCMP guard fore and aft, and taken to the railway depot. My brother with three other volunteers declined with thanks the free ride down, and hired a taxi. I saw him alight and enter the station with long free strides so different from those from the bus who straggled in after the guard.

He never so much as glanced at the RCMP, now a symbol of arbitrary restrictions, as he mounted the steps of the rickety old train that seemed to be coming apart at the seams, with no other passengers except these boys. Their families and sweethearts were on the platform, and to bring them closer still, the boys tried to open the windows of the coaches. Some opened after a struggle but others were stubborn and had to be jerked at and strained at. The window my brother tried to raise finally flew up but the glass pane fell out. The RCMP guard strolling up and down the platform, marking a division between the boys and their relatives, had the grace not to notice, or to comment. Then, accompanied by the cries of farewell and last-minute admonitions from mothers and wives and sisters and friends, the train jerked off to a start, and slowly, agonizingly disappeared around a bend.

Letter to Friends
(March 1944)

This letter is especially for all those friends of mine, to whom I haven't written as I should have. I could say I was busy and be truthful but there is still that awful guilty feeling of having neglected those I used to see or phone regularly back in the days of the past. It isn't that I've forgotten them. Oh no! It's just that I would need an extra 16 hours daily to do everything properly.

Harry and Mary's twins have been on my mind a long time, but I haven't sent even a card of good wishes or asked for their christened names, or asked after their health and cute doings. The stork has been busy elsewhere, too, and there are baby brothers and sisters to little children I haven't seen for over two years. How are they all? Have they grown beyond recognition? Are they shooting up like mushrooms after rain? I just read that another Mary has had a daughter, a playmate for big brother Dale . . . but Dale was such a little fellow when I saw him last.

How does one keep up the threads of a past life? They become tangled often . . . how often! I make half-hearted attempts to inquire, get paper and pen to write, then give up because of the pressure of things to do right at my elbow. I think with real longing for the old days when we gossiped over a cup of tea, or picked up the phone casually for some small talk. I haven't seen a phone since January, a year and a half ago.

There are newly-weds in Tashme that I wish were right here where I could see them once in a while. There are former Red Cross fellow-workers now scattered here and there from Bay Farm to the eastern cities. There are cronies now tucked away in New Denver, across the provinces to Ste. Anne de Bellevue, and I wish we could exchange quips and sarcasms together again. There are very good friends in Morris, of whom I read too infrequently in the *New Canadian*. There's an aunt and an uncle in Vernon that I have not seen since May 1942. So many people, once close by, are now strung out on a transcontinental map, all joined to myself, as the hub, by that invisible thread of friendship and intimacy. And each of these people is also a hub from which stretches out those firm but intangible bonds of the spirit.

I ask forgiveness of all these folks.

Chance brought me to Toronto, though I was destined for Kaslo . . . or should I reverse this? Toronto isn't Vancouver, but it is a city and since I have pavement, dust, smoke, and noise in my blood, it is bearable in spite of the scenery (the lack of it, I should say). However, I really haven't seen the town, although I was in the first lot of evacuees to this city. While the later-comers have jaunted to Niagara Falls and hopped the train from one town to another towards Windsor, and even gone back to B.C. for visits, I've stayed here in my rut, hearing in imagination again the clattering wheels of the train, seeing the swift panorama of mountains, prairies and lakes—the journey across thousands of miles that ended at the Union Station.

No doubt you've waited eagerly for the *New Canadian* each week in hopes of seeing a bit of news that touched your life and family. I do. Do you see, as I do, that the various sections of this paper present a composite picture of the younger New Canadians? I see new leaders breaking from their chrysalis to try out their wings on ghost town school life. They are very young yet, and older eyes like mine watch and wait for them to grow.

I listen to the new singer of songs, and hope that someday I shall hold in my hands a volume entitled 'Songs of the Beet Farmer' by M.A.Y. These songs will breathe a richness of sunshine and steadfastness . . . like psalms. I watch and wait for the younger generation in trembling and earnest hope that they may be spared the wholesale upheaval their elders endured; that they may flower in the best Canadian tradition.

Another item from B.C. will keep our closest attention: next year's election platform on the disputed franchise for the spotlighted Nisei.

Seems as if it's going to be used as a lever for or against socialism, a lever alone, so far as the old parties are concerned. The principles won't bother the consciences of the antis, for have they not got away with a whole lot since Pearl Harbor that wouldn't be tolerated under the Constitution of the U.S. that protects our American cousins? And the new political party is going to stake its growing strength and the conscience of the people for a principle that we've heard much of, but seldom seen practised politically. Can you visualize the forces that will battle on the campaign stands? On the left . . . Champions of Democracy! On the right . . . Protagonists of Racism! What a match, my friends! What a match! It's too big for bets. We can only clench our fingers and watch. The outcome touches not only the Nisei but also the whole pattern of Canadian life.

The Hills of Home
(March 1945)

Yesterday I received a copy of the 10th Pictorial Edition of the *Nelson Daily News*, turning its unfamiliar pages with some surprise because I am not a subscriber to it, and the word "Nelson" has unpleasant connotations. There were a great many pictures in it, some very beautiful, evoking memories of other lovely scenes.

One of the pictures was of the New Denver San, a restful picture taken by an old friend, Mark.[2] The reproduction was dark, yet I could see the clear sunlight, the blue skies smudged with white clouds. There, unseen in the picture, off to one side, are more windows out of which some folks I know of, and some I don't, gaze out onto the

---

[2]The "San" is the T.B. Sanitorium at New Denver, one of the detention centres in the B.C. interior. "Mark" is Muriel's friend and photographer Mark Toyama, fellow writer and poet in the *New Canadian*, who died young in Vancouver on May 21, 1946. Toyama's power as a poet is evident in his remarkable poem, "Powell Street," first published in the *New Canadian*, 15 May 1940 (reprinted 8 June 1946), and published again in Toronto in *Nisei Affairs*, January 1947. Muriel's poem "To M.N.T." (*New Canadian*, 21 December 1946: p. 32), written in memory of Toyama, acknowledges his creative potential as a writer and artist:
> Time, that ancient one, heedless of our lost delight,
> Did take to his sombre self thy half-expressed song,
> Finding in thy dreamer's soul a dream too fine to
> live . . . (dated October 1946)

lake in front. Beauty and tranquillity to make easier some of the sadness, the resignation; nature's eternal beauty and earthly strength to inspire hope and courage when the days seem darker than usual; repose, harmony of line and color to soothe the restless hours of convalescence with patience. What fortune it is to be able to see!

On the same page as the San picture was another of Kokanee Creek. When I looked at that one closely, it became not Kokanee Creek but a spot on the North Shore where a creek slipped quietly on its way to join the Inlet; the creek where as a child I dipped eager hands into its clear cloudness, trying to reach the rounded stones seen so plainly at the bottom. Etched unforgettably in my memory of sight and sound is the cool green of the leaves fluttering as each wanton breeze sped through the branches. It was quiet, free from the traffic sounds of city streets, yet full of the secret sounds that even the dullest ear could hear . . . the murmur of the waters as they swirled around and over a protruding rock, the sweet song of a bird somewhere out of sight, little creaks, snapping twigs, the wind through the tree-tops. It was still, without the rush and hurry of the town, but the current flowed swiftly, and the leaves kept up their eternal trembling.

These and other pictures from B.C.'s incomparable natural landscape woke again my passionate longing to see those places back home. I love the grimy cities for their creature comforts, but sometimes their brick, stone, and dry earth become unbearable. One longs to get out into the open, where trees and mountains, not the tenth storey of a building, tower over us, reaching toward the heights as the soul reaches for heaven.

"I will lift up mine eyes unto the hills." (*Psalms*, 121)

David knew the heart-hunger in all of us. He knew when the sated mind and the weary body needed to look up, trying to find the answer to life. Is there an answer? Perhaps, for do we not feel refreshed when our eyes have gazed long and hungrily on the beauty untouched by a mechanical civilization: of trees outlined against the skies, facing a wooded slope across a shimmering lake, of the majestic granite columns of Cathedral Mount rising in stark splendour from the Rockies? Why is it given Man alone to be touched to the core by the contemplation of these?

Each of us has a Haven of Beauty, a secret spring of inspiration. Some find it on the miles of prairie lands, others on the rolling seas; still others find their serenity in the fragrant petals of a small flower. Some shut their eyes to bathe in the melodious notes of music, while still others spend their restlessness in creating. I find mine where trees and colour ascend the slopes, merging in the distance . . . up . . . up . . . toward the snow-crowned mountain-top, sometimes clear in the sunshine, sometimes veiled behind mists or draped in clouds.

I'm glad I got the paper, glad in spite of the sudden ache of homesickness. There are people who have never seen a mountain, or a giant conifer, or a crystal creek cutting through the mountains. There are people who are afraid of mountains, finding them oppressive. They feel hemmed in, threatened. They think the mountain might fall or a tree topple over on them! How deeply thankful I am that I was born in the shadow of the Lions, almost within the shade of the Seven Sisters in Stanley Park; and that, far from falling on me, they are there for me to lean on.

So, here I am, inundated under record snowfalls, waiting for the thaw when the earth will be uncovered again for the summer. Here I am at my typewriter, suspended for a nostalgic moment out of the present, dreaming of the "hills of home."

Solemn Mockery
(March 1945)

> This is my own, my native land! (Sir Walter Scott)

In the March 3rd issue of the *New Canadian* you could not have missed a news report on Vancouver Mayor Cornett's illogical proposal. He would have us sent to Japan (for good, of course!) as "missionaries" of the "Canadian way of life." He suggests that as compensation for expulsion, we be given a sufficient sum to re-establish our livelihood in that country. Aside from the obvious objections to his scheme, I had an ironical thought.

Picture myself in Tokyo trying to convert a skeptical company of Yedokkos![3]

> Me: . . . therefore I urge you all to adopt the ways of the
> land I have left, a land ruled by a system of absolute and
> benevolent democracy!

---

[3]Japanese for "Tokyo-ites."

Q: It is understood that you have been expelled from that country for no other reason than your racial ancestry. Is that absolute benevolence? Is that democratic? If your country is democratic, why are you here? There is a contradiction I do not understand!

Would you understand?

No, I wouldn't either.

Could you, could I, or anyone, recommend the ways of a country that denied its native-born? Could you, could I, exalt the humbug that passes for humanity and love of country among the incredible racists?

Not I!

Then what if I said this:

"Democracy is a shining ideal for which many men died, and will continue to die, yet under its system we suffered such calumny as shamed the conscience of the good; but the good were not strong enough to nullify the evil the few committed. Nevertheless, we clung to a pathetic faith in its ultimate triumph.

"Were the Japanese Canadians the only ones to suffer, it would have been bad enough, but the sad truth was that other minorities, the Negroes, Jews, Chinese, and Indians, they too felt the discrimination of race and economic greed. Democracy may have been the banner and the slogan, but hateful prejudice and propaganda accomplished their evil ends. Hollow words with glib oratory spread the venom of intolerance, avarice, and bigotry. The will-to-good was well-intentioned, but anaemic.

"The Nisei is a Canadian, born in the most beautiful of the nine provinces. He grew to manhood holding on to a deep faith in the integrity, the dignity of the individual. He embraced with passionate optimism the ideals of liberty, equality, fraternity. Then he was exiled from his home, but not content with exiling him, appropriating his possessions, denying his citizenship rights, the forces of racism went further and demanded expulsion from the country as well. To add insult to injury, they blandly proposed that the victim of a very 'un-Canadian way of life' preach to the inhabitants of Japan the tenets of a superior 'Canadian way of life'!"

O solemn mockery—

Yet I would exhort the disillusioned Nisei to have faith even to the end. Hatemongers may shout, may flourish on the feverish

203

fear of the ignorant, but their very pettishness defeats their own ends. Racism is slush, mixed with dirt and refuse, abhorred of men. Slush always melts in the sun and goes down the sewer.

Let us walk with dignity to meet our earnest destiny.

Canada is Our Choice
(June 1945)

In answer to a letter from Mr. Pickersgill, Commissioner of Japanese Placement:.

My Dear Mr. Pickersgill:

Though we have not, at any time, made any application for removal to Japan now or after the war, nevertheless, we received, through the mails, a letter from you accompanied by a notice from the Department of Labour concerning voluntary "repatriation to Japan." The last paragraph of your letter reads:

> This assured assistance from the government, as outlined
> in the notice, will mean to many who desire repatriation,
> relief from unnecessary anxiety and it will allow them to
> plan for their future, and that of their children, along
> economic, social and cultural lines which they fear may
> be denied them were they to remain in Canada.

This very revealing paragraph is another drop in the depth of our disillusion.

We do not ask why you should send such a letter to those who have not applied for "repatriation." Every effort and devious method tries to persuade us that Canada is no place for us, that we would be better off in Japan. Temptation is thrust into lives already uncertain and fearful of the future for which no definite hope, only generalities, has come from Ottawa; temptation to give up the weary struggle for equality; temptation to take the easier way out of a seemingly hopeless situation.

We chose Canada long before you ever thought to ask us to choose. We chose Canada then, and we choose Canada now, with our eyes wide open to the probable consequences of our choice.

Are we not afraid of the future, the "future" you mention in your letter? Yes, sometimes we are afraid. When there are children depending on us, there is fear. But that fear does not lessen our love for our country. Perhaps because of that very fear, and because we are dispossessed and fenced in, we cling to our last reality, our native Canada. Perhaps because events have made our choice conspicuous and because you have never been asked to choose, our claim to Canada has a deeper, more understanding love of country than yours.

In your letter you hold out hope of material benefits for those who choose Japan. Is there any consideration or bargaining for material benefits in one's loyalty to a country? In choosing Canada we take the evil with the good, and taking the good we share the responsibility to eradicate the evil. As long as there is left one minute without full equality of the rights and responsibilities of citizens, there is neither a just nor an equitable government. This is one of the evils against which we struggle, hampered as we are by restrictions and prejudice.

Yet your letter is a not-so-soon invitation to us to give up the fight.

Our forces are pitiful and inadequate, and we may be fools to keep on fighting, but what kind of Canadians would we be if we succumbed now?

Mr. and Mrs. E. Kitagawa, Toronto, Ontario.

Deportation is a Violation of Human Rights
(November 1945)

There is an urgency in the appeals sweeping across this country asking the government to be merciful to those who had been misguided enough to have signed the "repatriation" papers. The urgency is real enough, for on the one hand, the government is eager to get rid of 10,000 "Japs" in one fell stroke, while on the other hand, the adults in that 10,000 are frantically appealing against impending deportation.

Like wheat swaying in every wind, the misinformed, ill-advised people in the ghost towns have expressed the uncertainties of their own life by signing, as the lesser of two evils: staying in B.C. with certainty of food and shelter, as against being ordered east to houseless, jobless, insecure futures. Therefore they signed, and stayed in B.C., looking no further than their present comfort, ignoring the politics of their unhappy situation.

They were leaderless, or maybe they had too many of them who rode hard on the harried men and women and used their tense emotions to confuse the issues. Perhaps there were men who went around ranting (not for any strong convictions, but merely to hear their own voices raised in leadership) about the foolishness of staying where they weren't wanted and the advantages of living where they would be Japanese among Japanese.

But now the war is over, with Japan beaten to its knees, facing starvation and homelessness. A bleak outlook, to say the least. And this aspect has suddenly loomed larger than the abstractions of loyalties. Ah, who blames anyone for not wanting to starve, for shrinking from homelessness? I don't! If those who signed for "repatriation" shrink from certain destitution, they are to be pitied for not having thought of that angle before . . . before they followed the crowd and signed.

When the Rev. W.R. McWilliams takes up his pen on behalf of the vacillating evacuees, I'm sure he does so from the rich depths of his love for people, especially the oppressed ones, oppressed from without and within. When other groups of Canadians take up the cudgel to appeal against deportation, they also are concerned with the bleak future facing those to be deported, the harmless pawns of politics. Papers like the *Winnipeg Free Press*, while acknowledging the hardships of the people, emphasize the precedent-forming injustice perpetrated on the basis of "race" by a supposedly democratic government. They warn against the thin edge of the wedge of the ideology that ruined Germany.

We, too, who fight injustice from the ranks of the oppressed, love liberty too well to be silent under its desecration. If we seem callous with the individual sufferings of the evacuees who signed and their individual reasons for signing, we only seem so because we are mainly concerned with attacking the root of this mess. If Alex Paton, Colin Gibson, Tom Reid and their colleagues are allowed their way, their way of the denial of the rights of man, it is to pave the way for more and more oppressions on other peoples too, not only on the Japanese. If we do not stem them, we shall all pay with blood and tears.

This proposed "deportation" is a monstrous violation of the Rights of Man.

The Thirteen Colonies in 1774 fought for those rights in the War of Independence, incorporated them into the American Constitution, then nobly upheld those principles after Pearl Harbor. France threw off the yoke of tyranny in 1789. Right down to modern times, men have fought against the violation of freedom. Canada, too, struggles for its nation's rights. She has signed international agreements to preserve the freedom of all nations.

But her signature isn't worth the ink used.

The officials in Ottawa have nullified that signature by the treatment of the Japanese Canadians. They have used a method that kept one bland eye on the legal courts so that they can win on technicalities, while using every vile method possible scarcely within the law. Officials claim that "public pressure" is the reason for their acts.

Groups of Canadians throughout Canada are publicly appealing against the deportation. Newspapers are decrying it. Churches plead against it. This is not public pressure? Who makes up the "public pressure" that Ottawa officially recognizes? A group of racists, condemned by World War II, of unknown membership (it must be negligible because unpublicized), but of known bigotry.

The racists can argue that the evacuees signed "voluntarily," but they have overlooked the causes of their signing. Mr. Pickersgill can protest that there was no "coercion," but the fact remains that Ottawa took mean advantage of the war-induced tensions in the ghost towns.

It is horrible enough to send 10,000 men, women and children (innocent children too!) to virtual homelessness and starvation, but to do so with a deliberation that ignores appeals for temperateness, for even mercy, is no different from the action of the Germans in herding Poles and Jews toward annihilation, whether in the ghettos or the gas ovens. A boat chartered by Ottawa to deport these 10,000 souls is no better than the freight trains used by the Nazis. Only the degree of brutality differs.

207

Freedom

(November 1945)

MacArthur[4] stands,
a colossus astride the cursed men
who used the "sacred" name of "heaven-descended"
to gild the scourge that drove a muzzled people.

MacArthur orders: Freedom!
where freedom never lived before,
where freedom died in prisons.

And here?
where Freedom is the motto
inscribed upon the cornerstone of democracy?

The edifice is built so grand,
the busy men-in-office on the topmost floors
sometimes forget their very elevation
rests upon that cornerstone.

The inscription still remains
for brooding fingers to trace again
the imprint of the blood, the sweat, the tears
carved deeply there . . .
each letter carved as deeply on our waiting hearts.

Racialism is a Disease

(January 1946)

Some time ago, an article by Captain Harper Prowse reprinted in the *New Canadian* condemned the B.C.-inspired Japanese Repatriation League. One sentence stands out:

---

[4]General Douglas MacArthur was the American general placed in charge of Japan after the war.

I can't think of a better way to insure World War III than to allow these hate campaigns to have their way.[5]

In *Nisei Affairs*, Pearl S. Buck speaks out against racial discrimination, saying:

Our future depends upon good-will. . . . Future wars are inevitable without such good-will, but we prefer to do without such good-will in order to keep our prejudice.[6]

•

It is felony, punishable by law, if one is caught practising extortion on a fellow man. It is a crime to use mails to distribute pornographic literature, or seditious and treasonable pamphlets. It is against the law to soak the sucker, to pander to immorality, to betray society or country. Yet it isn't against the law to discriminate against race!

But Captain Prowse and Pearl Buck say we must scotch these hate campaigns now, change prejudice to goodwill or look forward to another war—a race war. They are not alone in their forebodings. It is our duty as responsible Canadian citizens to guard against that danger.

Canada and the United States are supposed to be Christian countries. Yes, there are a good many Christians in these countries, but not enough to warrant the whole state any title to the name, if we are to be honest. When we love God without loving our neighbours too, we fail to live up to the two main tenets of Christianity. Lip

---

[5]From "Why Repatriation," by Captain Harper Prowse, *New Canadian*, 10 October 1945: p. 2; reprinted from the *Edmonton Bulletin*. Prowse says he received a letter from the Japanese Repatriation League of Vancouver "which has as its object the Dominion-wide circulation of a petition asking the government of Canada to make certain that all persons of the Japanese race shall be repatriated to Japan. Let us hope that Canadians will not be hood-winked by this version of the 'master-race' theory."

The editor of the *New Canadian* (17 November 1945) described the Japanese Repatriation League as an "openly anti-oriental group, which before 1945 called itself the White Canada League," adding that they "are championed by a number of British Columbia members of parliament whose racial bigotry in most cases antedated Pearl Harbor" (p. 2).

[6]Pearl S. Buck, "The Basis for a Fundamental Attack on Prejudice," *Nisei Affairs*, vol. 1, no. 3 (September 1945): p. 5.

service to God and hatred for our fellow men are strange actions for professed Christians.

No person mindful of his physical health would allow syphilis to take unrestricted control over his body, of which he has only one for only one lifetime. He would beg the best doctor he can get to cure him. In a nation too, there is only one Present, until the future relegates it to the past and history judges whether that Present was either Golden or Dark. As the child is trained in health or humanity, so will he administrate.

The government provides protection for the victims of extortion, does its part to curb immorality, separates the malcontent from the fold, but fails to act against race baiters.

•

Prime Minister King, it is true, made a very diplomatic statement of policy about the Canadians of Japanese ancestry. But his utterances fail to go beyond mere words, when he immediately turns around to speak in support of the disfranchisement of evacuees east of the Rockies, because we never had that particular right in B.C. And apparently, Mr. Norman Robertson, Undersecretary of State for External Affairs, believed he was being reasonable when he remarked to the Co-operative Committee delegates who met him in Ottawa: "Canada had done rather a poor job with the whole matter of the Japanese ever since they have been in Canada, so therefore, it might be better for them in their own interest to go to Japan . . ." (reported in *Nisei Affairs*).[7]

Not only has the government failed to protect us, but it has ordered the unsanctioned sale of private properties which resulted in disgraceful losses to individuals.

Now, the government, to all purposes, is attempting to rid the country of unwanted people by presuming to judge that intangible quality called loyalty through a judicial commission!

---

[7]The quote appears in an article, "Delegation to Ottawa," *Nisei Affairs*, vol. 1, no. 3 (1945): p. 5. The delegation, which included Mrs. Hugh McMillan, Secretary of the Co-operative Committee on Japanese Canadians in Toronto, Kinzie Tanaka of the Japanese Canadian Citizens for Democracy and others, presented a brief asking for relief aid to those relocating, the lifting of restrictions on purchasing property, the option for those who signed for "repatriation" to change their minds, the franchise, and indemnification for loss of properties and income.

Some people who get fed up hearing about the injustices to the Japanese Canadians counter our protests by saying that the Negroes are worse off, so what are we kicking about? In actual fact the Negroes may be worse off, in spite of the absence of apparent restriction on their movements and activities; but what could condemn a people, a country, more than the use of this fact as an argument against our protests?

By accident, I overheard four high school boys arguing with an MLA that the Anglo-Saxons should be the rulers because of superiority in education, etc. Well, the MLA said, educational standards differ here and there, and what might be high in one place might be low elsewhere.

Only through appropriate education can we accomplish what our natural orneriness can't. Anti-discrimination must be taught from kindergarten up to adult education throughout the country. Not only must it be taught wisely, it must be practised as well.

Because the overwhelming majority of us are innocent, we protest against restrictions based on our racial ancestry; we protest against the fine technical distinctions of word and deed to cloak the facts; we protest against the arbitrary judgments on our loyalties; we protest against the indifference to and disallowance of our human qualities, our ability to suffer, our capacity to appreciate good, our weaknesses, our strength, our experiences and our present environment, our mediocrity and our talents . . . all because we happen to be of Japanese descent.

How long must it be before the public realizes that our grievances are not the petty gripes of only one unimportant part of the whole, but are the symptoms of an ugly disease, racial discrimination, which can wreck a nation if left unchecked?

Farewell to a Friend, Olive Pannell
(February 1946)

The Japanese Canadians lost one of their best friends in the east when Olive Jean Pannell passed away in Toronto on January 18th.

She was the wife of Mr. Raymond Pannell, and both husband and wife, from the early days of 1942, did everything in their power to ease the lot of the evacuees, especially those who came to Toronto.

I did not know her until March 1942, when she wrote me a letter full of friendship and hope. She had met my brother at the Carlton Street United Church, and through him heard of the confusion and tragedy of evacuation on the west coast. Mrs. Pannell was Vancouver-born, and lived there for 16 years when her family moved east. Revealed in that first letter was a common ground between us in our love for the snow-capped Lions, and for digging in the garden. She wrote to say we were welcome to take shelter in their home if and when we came to Toronto, that though the house wasn't large, they would manage somehow. That is how we came to depend on the Pannells until we actually arrived in Toronto.

As the train sped towards Union Station in the early hours of June 5, 1942, we were tense with worry. Then, who should come aboard at West Toronto Station but the Pannells. They introduced themselves in a most cheerful and friendly fashion, putting us at ease. Mrs. Pannell had a low, happy chuckle that I will hear every time I think of her. That morning she said: "We thought it might be better if we just rode into the city with you . . . in case there are any nosey reporters around. Yesterday the papers made quite a fuss about the T's, and they reported that another family was coming in this morning . . . that's you folks. You shouldn't be bothered by such things the moment you step off a train, so I thought Ray and I . . . that's my husband . . . would sort of, you know, pilot you past." They helped carry the infant twins, and guided us down into the Station, where my brother was waiting with Mr. Finlay and the young Pannells.

Coming as we did from a West turned hostile, into a city that made it clear we were unwelcome, the thoughtfulness of these first friends warmed every worried cell in our hearts. At once we were included in a circle of friends as casually as if we had known them for years. Then, for almost four years, we enjoyed a delightful and deepening friendship with one of the most intelligent and understanding women we had ever met.

In her passing we lost not only a dear friend, but the Japanese Canadians lost a fearless champion. I mention the Japanese in particular, but to Olive Pannell all races were one people. Discrimination of any kind or degree was a challenge she took up in the face of many obstacles. When a few "prominent citizens" of Toronto met to discuss and deplore the threatened influx of evacuees, Mrs. Pannell tackled Mayor Conboy himself, then the Mayor of Toronto. Before this, both Mr. and Mrs. Pannell had roused the Carlton Street United Church to action by reading to the members of that church some letters I had written her describing the process of evacuation, the confusion in Vancouver, and the state of Hastings Park Pool as I had seen it. Thereupon, with leadership and encouragement from the Minister, Mr. James Finlay, a band of people stood ready to give help whenever we should need it.

The initial support, spurred on by Mrs. Pannell, gradually became the spearhead of the protests against injustice arising all over the country. These separate voices, crying out in the wilderness independently of the Pannells, snowballed into the significant movement today when so many decent Canadians demand justice, and the rest of Canada waits to see the results of the Toronto group's action against deportation.

Canada is now roused to action, proving that the inherent love of justice in the people needed only a spokesman to be heard across the country. I know that once Mr. Finlay heard from Mrs. Pannell certain facts of the evacuation, he needed no further encouragement to cry out in thunderous protest against "man's inhumanity to man."
He is the first Minister to preach those challenging sermons concerning the plight of the Japanese in Canada, to bring out the crusading spirit in those Christians who heard him. For a long time it seemed he preached into a void, but now, after four years of unceasing effort, Mrs. Pannell can know that her work was well done. While the fight is not over yet, still the people have been challenged to prove democracy.

Olive Pannell would be the first to laugh away any credit to herself. She would say: "It's no more than what any decent person would have done."

Weep, Canadians!

(Headline in *Toronto Star*, Feb. 20: RULE SOME JAPS DEPORTABLE)
(March 1946)

The Cabinet stands white-washed.
The judgment reads in banner headlines:
"Japs Deportable!"

Weep, Acadians!
The bitter tears of 1755
You shed in vain.
Evangeline will mourn again for Gabriel;
Gabriel will die again, calling,
"Evangeline!"

Weep, ye murdered Jews!
Ye homeless of this earth!
The total of your suffering is not enough
To pay the price of liberation!

Weep, Canadians!
For now it seems you need the blood
Of one billion coloured men
To bring Christ back to earth again!

Grey Dawn on Another Day

(August 1946)

The second phase of the evacuation is almost over. Now dawns
the grey morn of the third phase, and it will depend on us all whether
this phase shall be long or short. If we forget the past, if we look
not to the future, we shall be long in this grey morning, and our
children will marvel that the sun shines so little on them.

Out of the immigrant past, we were spewn into a war which scattered us to the winds, but in which we had very little legitimate part. The first force of the wind has abated, and things have quieted enough for most of us to take stock of our losses, to count our gains, and to plan ahead. In this planning we must remember the past so that in choosing which road to take at this crossroad of our life, we will not take the one that will lead us back instead of forward.

We must remember that on December 6, 1941, if we wanted to take a train for Halifax we could have, only we didn't. Today, if we wish to go to Vancouver, we can't. Today, we are grudgingly allowed to be citizens (restricted class), and because we are not imprisoned for such words as these, we say we are free. But we are not.

It is painful to remember we are not free. Some would rather forget the unpleasant side of the evacuation, and remember only that many have a better material life now than they ever had before, and they are not going to quarrel with their luck. They do not wish to risk upsetting the precarious balance they hold in establishing a new foothold in life. Who is to blame them? I just want to ask one question: "If your child should ask you why . . . what shall you answer?"

Why can't we do this? Why can't we do that? Why can't we go there? Why must we get permission? Why? Why? Why don't you do something about it? Can't you do anything about it? Have you done anything about it? What did you do? What? Is someone going to do something? Who? When?

Some can answer the question proudly, wearily.

Can you?

Freedom lies not in three square meals a day, not in a pay envelope. Freedom lies in the integrity of one's innermost self. Even if the leash on our privacy is long and loose, still the collar around our necks halts our free step, and our eyes are clouded with the awareness of restriction. We can stand upright only by bearing with strength and courage the burden laid on us, for it threatens our every move.

That burden is tied on us, and we have not the key to unlock the chain that binds it to us. It is not a burden that we bore in our own freedom to hoist over our shoulders for the common good, as others have borne the war burdens of the past years. No, we have been catalogued and typed, tagged and segregated, and the strongest, the best, have carried the heaviest burdens. We have straggled on between the marked out paths on which we could go as far as the leash was long.

215

Don't ever think you are free . . . yet, because you are not.

If I remind you of what hurts, then be proud because it hurts. If it doesn't hurt you any more, God pity you, for you have become used to the cage and the security within, which is not security but captivity. If you wish to maintain your present comfort, your daily well-being, I congratulate you, for so do I. If you wish your children to have what you did not, who does not? However, there is a price for everything.

In leaving B.C., we left family and friends. Many were reunited but it was not the same. Nor will it ever be the same. And in going forward we tried with many a backward glance to keep in sight all that we held dear to our hearts. The time comes when we must lose the last link to these too, and until the moment when one takes the last step into oblivion, one remembers the sound of fading footsteps, the quiet sadness of a silent farewell. So we said good-bye to the past.

Soon it will be another day, and by all the signs, a very grey dawn.

If we keep the fires of faith burning, we may yet see the sun rise in our day. Let the kindling for these fires be in remembering these:

We have had homes and businesses taken from us unjustly;

We have lost personal treasures for which there is no price, not by the ravage of an enemy troop, but by the greed of fellow-citizens;

We have not the right to live where we choose;

We have not the right to move freely from one place to another;

We have not the right to vote in B.C. or in the federal elections;

We are not free.

Perhaps we have better homes now, perhaps we have new treasures, perhaps we don't want to go back to B.C. anyway, and perhaps we don't care much one way or another how an election goes. Perhaps we want nothing better than to forget the raw wounds of yesterday, to cover the scar with delusions of security, but what was once taken away can be taken again. Who knows but that the next time will be made easier for the plunderers because we shrugged and said: "Shikata ga nai" ["It can't be helped"].

If you have fought for freedom in your small way, and you cherish its dream still, then cherish that dream dearly, for you will be called upon one of these days to confirm your faith. Interpret freedom to your children so that they will not be frightened of it someday when they shall be free.

Meanwhile, remember those who fought for you.

216

Growing Up as Nisei
(Manuscript, c. 1945-46)

Just when I first became conscious of *the Japanese Problem*, in this italicized form, I don't know, but when a group of politically minded young Japanese men met to do something about it, I was there at the meetings.

At the beginning, most of the talk went over my head. It was some time before I got the hang of the political and sociological phraseology. Such things as "civic rights," "natural rights," "privileges," "responsibilities" were only words to me, having little to do with my daily life. "Franchise" was something that bothered me a good deal because it was something we didn't have, and I wanted to know why we didn't have what in high school we learned that everyone should have. I remembered learning that taxation without representation had been one of the major causes of the War of Independence, when the Thirteen Colonies broke away from Britain. I learned at school that democracy was the basis of our national life, and that the French Revolution of 1789 gave us Liberty, Equality, and Fraternity, and that the Russian Revolution of 1917 confirmed the condemnation of the autocratic caste of so-called aristocracy of birth, and that there was such a document as the British North America Act defining our rights as citizens of the British Empire. Lastly, I learned that there was such a provincial measure as the Elections Act of British Columbia that denied to all Orientals the right to vote. This last I did not learn in school. I learned of it at the meetings I went to in those days when I was throwing myself heart and soul into this new and fascinating work.

When we organized a group of progressive young people dedicated to fight for our rights in B.C., I was right there eager to do my best, with a dream of a future obliterating all omens of the hard struggle that was coming. In this greater work I lost the petty pain that plagued me. I shed a great deal of the clumsy gaucherie that embarrassed me into tongue-tied silence. I learned to express my thoughts out loud and to speak without too much trembling and stuttering. I began to ask *why*, then to demand *why not*.

Because the average Nisei at that time was aged 11, our work was uphill. Those young Nisei of 18 years and over had been of a necessity associated more with things Japanese than with things Occidental. The very structure of our social life was built on the framework of race segregation, discrimination, and exclusion. We congregated more closely together than we desired for the sake of mutual protection and the human need of companionship. Our livelihood depended on the co-operation of the community. Both our strength and our weakness lay in a communal solidarity that was an offence in the sight of the anti-Japanese elements. Those who broke away from this solidarity had to break away completely to another life, usually a good linear distance away from what we called Powell Street.

•

Our history in Canada began when the first Japanese immigrant came ashore to a strange new country of giant primeval trees and majestic mountains towering above inland harbours. The railroad and the mines needed cheap labour. The Orient had already provided Chinese coolie labour that had drifted northwards to B.C. from the goldfields of California. Gangs of them had come up to the Caribou when gold lured men there. Stories of the fabulous gold washed down the Fraser River reached even the villages of Japan, and a trickle of hardy adventurers were on their way across the ocean.

Here the mine-owners stepped in and actually commissioned one of the first immigrants to go back to Japan and persuade more of his countrymen to come to B.C. to work. Then began an influx of Japanese in the thousands, lured as were the others by tales of easy wealth—much better than starving on tiny rice farms. After the men came in, naturally women followed . . . and picture-brides by the hundreds came into B.C. Some of the men went to Japan personally to bring back brides, probably wishing to choose for themselves and see what they were getting. The qualifications for a prospective bride were hardy health and willingness to endure hard work, strange conditions, and a chance future in a strange country. The men did not lack for such women. They came, the peasant daughters and fishermen's daughters. Later the daughters of merchants, the petty bourgeoisie, came over. Some of the women were the direct products of the soil, brown muscled young women built for work and child-bearing. Others were daintier, having been taught the daintier arts of womanhood, sheltered in comfortable homes; some of these were well-educated, of a distinctly higher class of people, practically unfit, as it were, for frontier life, yet who had their own reasons for agreeing to emigrate.

These were the beginnings of our family life.

The women came to shack and cabin, to boat-house, and city apartments. They came to help their men break soil, till the earth, to mend fishing nets, to do domestic work, to sew . . . all working in one way or another beside their men. And because they came, they brought the softer side of life to their men. Babies were born, the first Nisei, and their birth planted the first seed of a new citizenship, though both parents and babe were unaware of such momentous, such significant events. Babies were the natural fruits of marriage, of family life, and now livelihood was for the young. The instinct of the parents was to make a better life for the child.

The bare surroundings of their first home gradually gave way to niceties that were taken for granted by the hakujin . . . parlour furniture, curtains, carpets, pictures on the wall, bric-a-brac on the mantels, decorative covers on the utilitarian beds. Slowly and inevitably, toast, jam and coffee became the standard breakfast instead of rice with miso soup and pickles. The heavier meals were still Japanese, but in-between refreshments became a medley of Japanese bean cakes, sponge cakes, pastries, and other sweet desserts. As young Japanese women learned from their mistresses, they learned the arts of western cooking, western housekeeping, western clothes and styles. Of necessity they adopted these things until they became the natural heritage of the Nisei growing up in a world more Canadian than Japanese; for in spite of all that parents could do to keep their Japanese identity, the encroaching environment made their children more Canadian than Japanese, not only in superficialities but also and more significantly in the ideology, the culture, the idealisms, and the doctrines of the western world.

Powell Street became the nucleus of the Japanese community, and so it was for the next fifty years. This street, that was a muddy road in the beginning, was paved one day, and the shops lining both sides of the road were brave and new, with living quarters upstairs.

Some of the early stories of those days have been handed by word of mouth to us. I have heard stories of the beginnings of the small shops that became big stores, of small fortunes made, re-invested, to become the solid financial strength that even the evacuation could do little to dent. I heard of scandals forgotten in the mist of time until their very aura was merged with the respectability of the present. I heard of the gradual mixing of the ancients' standards of caste until the peasant was elevated to riches and power, while the scion

219

of the aristocracy became submerged into the grey anonymity of his misfortune. Family relationships and genealogy became more and more complicated, and there was a distinct tendency for certain families to marry amongst themselves, or to take new marriages unto themselves until the relationships resembled an intricate woven net, and one had to know them all to sort them out.

Time brought changes, unnoticed at first, but the moment they were perceptible, the reactionary forces, the die-hard traditionalists became alarmed and tried to stem the tide of progress, while the radically progressive ones raucously pulled the other way. Most of the Issei moved with the tide superficially, but in their most intimate moments reverted back to the old ways.

While their sons and daughters became westernized, talked a different language from their own, the Issei kept the reins over matters of marriage and birth and death, of filial piety, and submergence of the individual into the pattern of the family. Out of this grew the seeds of Nisei revolt, until war came to tear out the roots of our lives, and we were washed down helter skelter on the roaring flood, and those that were lucky found anchorage in new ground, and their own hardiness existed until their roots found nourishing soil to grow in again.

This upheaval was catastrophic.

With it the Nisei came into their own.

•

For long years after we grew old enough to realize the need to change the face of our old-fashioned community life, we were held down by our economic dependence on our elders, on the existence of the Japanese community as a solid bloc. True, here and there a few young shoots broke off to venture east, and reestablish themselves in the industrial cities nearer the Atlantic. But the rest of us stayed in B.C., partly because it was an ideal sort of place to live climatically, scenically, economically, and partly because families clung too hard to the adventurous ones, preventing their escape into individual freedom, into a personal life unharassed by the collective demands of the family. Within that rigid framework of our background, some of the luckier Nisei managed a fairly well adjusted life of their own, in their own homes, surrounded by their own friends of similar tastes and pursuits. But the rites of their marriage were performed according

220

to the old ways, and love was suspected and condemned. If there was love between the pair before marriage, it was hastily legitimized by a pair of go-betweens, dowries, and all the formal panoply of ceremony, of gifts, obligatory banquets, and family-crowded wedding pictures.

I remember particularly two extremes in the act of marriage. The first was a pair of romantics who were married secretly before a haku-jin minister, a marriage that was against all old traditions, against family preferences, against social mores. A narrow group ostracized the luckless pair, while personal friends rallied round to uphold them.

I remember it particularly because she was my friend, and I knew the boy, or young man. I remember it particularly because mother was in a quandary of conflicting desires. Fond of the girl and knowing the boy's parents, she had wrapped a lovely gift for them, but she had been warned by a leading member of respectable society that to recognize that marriage was to incur the displeasure of decent people. I argued and argued with mother to buck the nasty bigots and wish the pair well. She was too used to obeying the dictates of tradition to become overnight a radical, but she compromised by sending the gift with me, and her regrets at being unable to present it personally.

The other incident had in it all the neutral tones of a submerged will, dominant parents, and weak assent. It broke the heart of a sweet girl, and gave another nice girl the task of living in peace and harmony with a will-less son of a domineering mother.

This boy Seiji had all the charm of an amiable personality trimmed and upheld by a modicum of wealth. He had a girl, or I should say that he went around rather steadily with one girl, and it was generally accepted among his compeers that, parents willing, he would like to marry her. Katie, as she was called, was as lovely and as sweet as anyone could be, and if she openly adored Seiji, we resigned ourselves to such patent display. After all, it was their business not ours.

I remember watching them at a dance, heads close together, far away from the noisy crowds around them, Katie never saying much but glowing with happiness. I wondered when they would get up enough courage to defy custom and ask for their parents' consent to marriage. Katie's parents probably weren't loath to agree; what parents would ignore the comfortable fortune that would one day be Seiji's? Katie's parents weren't poor but they certainly had to watch their pennies.

221

On the other hand, we heard rumours that Seiji's parents would never agree to such a mésalliance on the part of their son. That's why we used to speculate on Katie's chances, and wonder if Seiji would have the guts to stand up to his mother. I remember a group of us talking.

"Wouldn't you think that if he loved her he would just tell his parents so, and get married anyway?"
"Mari, you forget he might be disinherited!"
"Well what's wrong with his working?"
"But heck, you have to consider your parents' wishes too you know. After all, they sacrificed a lot for you and they expect you to have consideration for them in such an important matter."
"Is that the way you're going to be, Tak, when you marry? Even if they pick someone you don't like?"
"Sue-chan, you want to know too much!"
"Go ahead and snub me, your garter's hanging."

Tak shook his head and wondered out loud what made women tick in such an empty-headed fashion, but we didn't pay much attention because he and Sue were always ragging each other. We meditated for awhile in silence, each of us wondering if Seiji was weak, too weak to fight for Katie. Too bad for Katie.

Consequently, when it was announced that Seiji was engaged to a different girl, we were both shocked and indignant. We hated to look at Katie's set face, and we were disgusted with Seiji. His misery was apparent too, and he took the weak man's method of treating his affianced rudely by ignoring Katie. Katie's soft brown eyes were blank, the light gone out of them. She never said a word of reproach, nor spoke of the matter again. She had never been a forceful character, taking life and colour from her surroundings rather than imparting her personality on others. Now she became a pale flower in the backwaters of our active life.

The other girl came of a die-hard but respectable family, and she had an irreproachable character. She was not tainted by the active radical life the rest of us rebels lived. She was boxed and refined in the traditional manner, a true prize package for an autocratic mother-in-law. Her individual personality was less important than the fact that she could always be amenable to her husband's people, would never demand equality as other girls had done, and was trained in all the arts of wifeliness and womanhood as the Japanese understood those traits. To us those things were immaterial. What we wanted to know was this: was she better than Katie, what did she have that Katie didn't, and how had Seiji agreed to her as a choice? Or did he have a choice? Did he not put in a word for Katie? We never knew.

Later, we found out that the other girl was really a swell sort of person, given a chance to be herself. She had a lot more character than Katie, certainly a lot more than Seiji did, and probably would be the one to hold him up by the boot-straps as Katie never could. Katie would have depended on Seiji, and he would probably have let her down. Yet, I argued to myself, Katie's very helplessness should have brought out all the protective manhood in Seiji. Didn't he have that in him? Who could answer?

Seiji's wedding was terrific. Everybody who was anybody was invited. I was nobody so I wasn't invited . . . that is, I didn't get a printed invitation, but I went because Seiji phoned to ask me to come anyway.

"But Seiji, I haven't been invited!"
"I'm inviting you now. It's all right Mari, come anyway."
"Well . . . I'll see."
"Mari, you must . . . I . . ."
"Oh all right, but I'm not going to the reception."

Was there panic in his voice? I hesitated about going. Of course, I wouldn't be noticed at the wedding if I sat far at the back, but gosh how I hated to go where I wasn't invited formally. Yet I couldn't deny I was simply itching with curiosity to see him married to that other girl. I also wanted to see one of these super weddings with all the trimmings.

I went. As usual the ceremony didn't begin until a good half hour past the stated time. The church on the corner of Powell Street was full to overflowing with the prominent people of our community. The usual crowd of children hung around the outside doors, as I slunk past them to hide myself in one corner of the chapel. The altar was a bower of spring flowers, potted palms and ferns. A white cloth marked the length of the middle aisle, and the organist was playing some soft music as we waited. Finally, we heard the organ wake into the strains of Lohengrin's Bridal Chorus. We saw that Seiji had come in from the vestry and was standing there very pale and ill at ease, while his best man stood content and ready. A rustle at the back of the church bespoke the bride coming in.

Two little flower girls, painted and curled to resemble china dolls and wearing frilly pink dresses, came down the aisle spraying the white cloth with rose petals, both uncertain of footing and tremendously solemn about their responsibility in leading the bridal procession. Next came the maids-of-honour dressed in pale Nile-green gowns that floated around them gracefully, their arms piled with the long pink snapdragons in season then. Instead of picture hats they wore a short length of veiling that matched the colour of their dresses. Then came two bridesmaids in soft yellow gowns, carrying scarlet sprays of the same flower. Lastly came the bride in white lace, cut on Princess lines, with high neck and puffed sleeves ending where the long white gloves met them over the elbow. She wore a pearl necklace, and her veil was fully six yards long, caught at the sides of the head with simulated orange blossoms. She carried a bouquet of opulent looking orchids with white flowered streamers. The orchids were white with pink veins and yellow centres. Ferns circled them to show off their exotic beauty. A very worried looking page boy held up the long train, all of which looked slightly out-of-place in the shabby, cramped quarters of that old church. The bride's father held his daughter's arm stiffly, unused to this western style of wedding, while wonder of wonders, two pairs of go-betweens, both man and wife, followed the bridal train. It was pretty crowded at the altar.

The ritual was simple, the responses in Japanese. In less than a half an hour, Seiji was married to this other girl.

My emotions were chaotic.

I couldn't help but be impressed with the beautiful dresses, the flowers, the obvious wealth and social prestige of the principals. The bride was calm, almost beautiful in her serenity. Seiji was grey, and he fidgeted right through the whole thing. I wondered if he wished it were Katie beside him, taking his ring, his promises. I wondered if he ever thought of the position of his bride, and her thoughts, her preferences. Would she give him what Katie did, love and laughter, and blind adoration? Obviously not. But would she give him comfort, to make him forget he ever wanted Katie? Would she laugh with him when he needed laughter? Would he be cared for so thoroughly and so competently that any initiative he might have developed would be lost forever in the harmony of his days? Would he ever

224

miss the dependence of Katie, depending on the strength he didn't have? I had seen Katie a week before the wedding. Her face had been dry with a slight fever she'd had from a bad cold, her lips dry and peeling. She had smiled at me as sweetly as she ever did, but it was her facial muscles only. Her eyes were still blank.

Oh yes, it was a very proper and very suitable wedding, with a tedious reception at the best restaurant, where food was abundant and expensive, where sake flowed like water, and dull speeches were dragged out by the hour. I didn't go but I heard all about it. We had the impression that it was a gaudy show, empty of meaning.

It was this kind of wedding, this kind of marriage that was all too prevalent in our lives, and sometimes we Nisei tried to do something about it. We demanded simpler weddings. We demanded the right for the young to choose their own mates. We begged our parents to accept these choices with good will so that there need not be recriminations, heartbreak and shot-gun weddings. We didn't like to revolt for the sake of revolting. We wanted our parents to change their stubborn clinging to the old ways, of leaving it to the matchmaker to pick a mate in a purely arbitrary fashion, with plenty of considerations for family health lines, social standing, and everything but the wishes of the principals concerned.

Occasionally a Nisei would be lucky and the parents would agree to a love-match, but all the ceremonials were the same. Very few Nisei ever got married without going through the whole rigmarole of formal consent, go-between conferences, family consultations, picking an auspicious day, giving and getting formal gifts, and the passing of the dowry from the groom's go-between to the bride's to buy the furnishings for the new home and the wedding clothes. More often than not, the newly-wedded pair started out with a load of debt from a stylish wedding they had to have to keep face, and for the rest of their married life they were obliged to the two pairs of go-betweens. Every critical event must be prefaced with a formal consultation with them. Precedence and obligations formed no small bogey for the young couple. They were not a new team starting out on a life of their own, making and meeting new situations, new friends, new ways of living. They had to comply and conform to the existing pattern around them, pay their dues of piety and social and moral obligations, and only at the risk of their security break away from it all.

There were many enlightened Issei who agreed that the young must lead their own life, uncomplicated by the old ways that were out of tune with the western ways, but by and large they all succumbed to the well-oiled wheels of custom.

The Nisei used to dream of the day when the Issei would be the minority opinion, when we could pattern our lives our way without risking our family relationships, affections and livelihood. While we talked of breaking away from the old days, war was creeping closer and closer to cut us asunder from the old days.

I Stand Here Tonight
(Manuscript, c. 1945-46)

I stand here tonight to plead with you, not for myself alone, but for all of us.

You know, in this life, we have an average of sixty to seventy years of living. We spend about fifty of those years scrambling for a living, worrying over bills, illnesses, clothes, and education. We skimp and save, and borrow and get into debt. If we have plenty, we worry about hanging on to it, or about increasing it.

It's the rare person among us all, and I certainly include the Japanese people in this category, who will take time to worry over the affairs of other people less fortunate. We are much too busy with our own affairs to be bothered with what doesn't seem to concern us except in a vague and general way. We leave such worries to our representatives who are paid to worry and to act for us. Sometimes we do not make an effort to choose people who will *really* help us, and we carelessly choose people who do more harm than good. But we shrug, and let it go at that. We can get used to nearly everything. So, after a lifetime of making the dollar stretch and piddling around in our own pool, we die . . . having accomplished only a very little of the fine dreams that bless mankind . . . if we accomplish anything at all.

Inertia is the most killing ailment of our time. We mean well, but we do nothing about it. We weep for others, but we do nothing about it. We wonder why someone doesn't do something about it, but we don't do it ourselves. And we wonder what the world is coming to.

So here I am, standing here, asking you to do something to save the integrity of this nation we call Canada.

We've heard a lot of speeches these last six years about the Nazi threat to democracy. We're scared stiff of totalitarianism, we sneer at communism, we're shy of socialism, we hate the evils of capitalism, we don't want monopolies or cartels. We want peace, and the right to live as decent human beings, to be as happy or as sorry as we darn well please, and nobody to force us to do what we don't want to do. We hate the thought of regimentation, but we do not think deeply about its import at all. We demand freedom, but we do not think deeply about all that freedom implies.

What is regimentation? It means that one must conform to a set standard . . . a uniform standard. So far as law and order are concerned we are regimented. So far as politics and religion are concerned we are not regimented. That is as it should be, but these are only the broad outlines. When we become specific and define the limits, we find all sorts of inconsistencies.

For example, by law we are not supposed to swindle the other fellow, and if we are caught in the act we are punished. By law we cannot pander to immorality, and there is punishment for that too. By law we cannot betray our country, for such an act is treason. There are other laws. We cannot steal, or kill; we cannot commit mayhem or assault and battery.

There is one other crime that is not included in the list of things forbidden, and that is the inciting of racial hatred. For that crime we have suffered six years of horrible warfare. So far as the German inciters of such crimes and consequences are concerned, they have been hung. If we can hang the Germans who we say caused all this trouble, logically we can hang others, of any other nation, who do the same thing. But do we allow such logic? Do we?

What is freedom? Is it a selfishness or is it a selflessness? Is it restricted only to material benefits, or does it include the spirit? Freedom to make a million dollars, yes, some of us would love that, but is it freedom if in making that million we denied freedom to others? Is freedom the condition where we can do just whatever we like for ourselves, and too bad if what we call freedom for ourselves is slavery for others? Or is freedom that condition where one limits one's own selfishness the moment it impinges on another's freedom?

You, the Anglo-Saxons, the Europeans, you are free in a general way to do as you like, but have you thought at all that *your* freedom

227

takes up a lot of *our* freedom, the freedom of the coloured races? Are you really free when you have to worry about what would happen if all the coloured peoples were free? Why do you take it for granted that if you free us we shall do you harm?

If a nation, like Hitler's Germany, is definitely out for military conquest, the neighbouring states know what to expect (or they *should* know). One can pity a bully, reason with him or sternly punish him. But if a nation says that it is the guardian of liberty, the home of the free and the equal, and at the same time practises such things as economic exploitation, racial discrimination, political skullduggery, well, all you can say in judgment is: What a hypocrite!

We, the people, are not all free from either stigma. There is in all people a bit of the bully and a bit of the hypocrite, but in all people there is also a touch of the divine that makes us nearer to God. Now, which side of our character shall we regiment, and which side shall we free? There is only one answer to that, the answer that all good men seek today. It lies in the people . . . and unless it is in the majority of people it cannot find expression in our representatives.

This is all a very long prologue for what you really want to hear, the story of the Canadians of Japanese race. But I feel that unless you can see our story against a world background, you cannot see it as it really is, a part of the rottenness of the world . . . which results from merciless conquest, economic greed, ambitions for power, and a sad disregard for the rights of Man. After the so-called "white" people conquered the coloured races, made them the hewers of wood and the carriers of water, kept them in ignorance and filth, and degraded their divinity as brothers under the skin under a loving God, they still talk of the preservation of democracy, human rights, free enterprise and minority rights. How God must weep for his fallen men.

Some good came out of the evacuation, not because the evacuation was good, but because the people had in them the guts to make good after misfortune. Let us not be fooled for one minute by the fact that many of my people are better off today than ever before, because evacuation cut the ropes that tied us to a past. If they did not rise above their suffering, if they did not try to get the best out of a bad situation, these people *would not be* better off. The ones who are better off had families of vigorous young people out to rescue their family by their united efforts. They also had that quality which would not be defeated by tough luck. Some of those who are worse

228

off than before, are in that state because the children are too young yet to work, or the breadwinner is too old, or too broken in spirit, or not physically able to start from nothing again. These are pitiful cases in any language.

The loss of a house, the loss of a few thousand dollars, the loss of a fishing boat, or a business or a small shop . . . these items are big only in proportion to how much the victims could materially afford to lose. Many of my people actually need the return of their properties. They need badly the few hundreds or thousands of dollars that represent their loss, and it is only right that for their loss, since it was forced on them unjustly, they should be reimbursed.

But more than the return of lost property, reparation is the outward symbol acknowledging the loss of our rights. Time heals the details, but time cannot heal the fundamental wrong. My children will not remember the first violence of feeling, the intense bitterness I felt, but they will know that a house was lost through injustice. As long as restitution is not made, that knowledge will last throughout the generations to come . . . that a house, a home, was lost through injustice. It is important for you to remember that the loss of this property spelled the last indignity for a people deprived of the right to move freely, to live where they choose, to be what they can be best, deprived of participation in the life and events of their country, native or adopted, and deprived most of all of their integrity. Instead, it was taken for granted that we would be traitors given a chance.

Those race-baiters who flourish in this country, who spread their poisoned propaganda without any restraint, they always maintain that the Japanese—they mean also all Orientals, all coloured men—are a lower order of people, who feel less than Occidentals, who are naturally treacherous. Sometimes, and this annoys me, even the nicest people, people who are kind and generous and sincere, allow a tinge of patronage to shade their words. I realize that it will take some time before the concept of white supremacy is washed out of the consciousness of the world. However, as our individual part toward the end that all men be equal in the sight of God, let us consciously watch our own reactions and guard against toleration.

Yes . . . I said guard against toleration.

Toleration is a conceit based on one's superiority. When we are tolerant we are benevolent, and when we are benevolent we acknowledge ourselves to be slightly better than the object of our benevolence. If "goodness is its own reward," what virtue is in such goodness? Are we good because we are afraid to be bad, because badness brings punishment? That's a negative sort of goodness.

Let there be no benevolence in our consideration for our fellow men. Let us be kind, considerate, because we *owe* that to our fellow men. These are not our gifts to them, but the natural currency between brothers.

Do you know something? B.C. was never in real danger of either invasion or sabotage. If you would just think carefully and try to picture B.C.'s geography, you'd know why. B.C. is full of thousands of coves and bays, canyons and impassable mountains. It is also a young part of the country, hardly developed enough to be of any worth to an enemy needing roads and supplies. Otherwise, do you think that even a country as young and as unarmed as Canada would have left that coast so thinly defended? Some concession was made to the fearful public by putting up a few cannons here and there and chlorinating the best natural water in the Dominion, and the coast guard prowled here and there vigilantly. If B.C. had been on the first line of offence, some surprise attack would have happened long before and the Canadian Army would have retreated behind the impregnable Rockies. However, I'm not a strategist and I can't speak for the military command. There were a few shipyards, and other centres of vital importance . . . but oh my, they could have been protected very well against any Japanese who had sabotage in mind.

The race-baiters always ask you to see 23,000 saboteurs, but any sensible person knows how ridiculous that figure is. More than half that number were children, and the older children would much rather wear a Canadian uniform than sabotage their own country, and most of the adults thought more of their children's well-being and safety than the doubtful success of sabotage, and most of the adults wouldn't even think of sabotage. When it was taken for granted that we would all commit sabotage if left alone, we felt such a disgust as you cannot imagine. It made us spit that anyone could think such a thing of us, and made us wonder if, after all, Canadians did not have faith in their system of liberal education and Christian teaching. If you do not have faith enough in your system to be assured that the Japanese children could not be trained into good Canadians, do you blame us if we feel ashamed for you? Because we had faith in that education, we had faith in the Christian teachings . . . and what happened? That faith let us down.

What kept us afloat after the country let us down? Our faith in ourselves. We knew that our ideals and training were Canadian, even if you didn't. We knew that we had only to live up to our training to keep our integrity and self-respect intact, unsmeared by your lack of faith. It was hard work. Sometimes we almost gave up the struggle. Sometimes we wondered why we shouldn't get out and lick our sore wounds someplace else than here, but where could we go? To most of us Japan is a foreign country full of all the things we learned to dislike, in spite of a lot of things that were good.

Still, through the strain and toil of a few enlightened people who gave their all towards securing us our lost freedom, we've managed to come through this far. On the way, we've lost dreams, and we've learned to distrust. We've also lost pride in Canada. But we know a deeper love for this our native land, and would suffer much to stay here. Through bitterness we learned cynicism, and through frustration we gained new strength to fight for our rights.

When Canada went to war in September 1939, we, too, the Japanese-blooded people of B.C., felt a thrill of fear go through us, but we too were ready to fight, to die if necessary, under our country's flag, whether at home or at the front. I used to have a flag, a pure silk white ensign of the British Navy, and I also had a Union Jack made of light serge . . . beautiful flags . . . I kept especially the white ensign, wrapped up in a heavy white cloth. There was something so gallant about that flag. I loved it, and kept it with me when I started my own home. It got lost during the evacuation. I have no idea what could have happened to it . . . our luggage was packed and repacked so often, stored here and there, unpacked by strange hands, etc. etc. Because I loved that flag, I would not fly it as long as I could not fly it freely. I did not wish it to be flown in defiance or for exhibition. I wanted it to fly bravely and freely when the flying of it meant I was a first class Canadian.

You take Canada for granted. We don't. You hated to lose your sons in battle for this country, but you took it for granted that they should fight and die on foreign battlefields. My people have not died on any battlefield, nor under any bomb. We were pushed to one side, denied the right to fight, to die, to suffer as all other Canadians did. Instead, we were roped and fingerprinted and card-indexed and corralled. My brothers would have fought, my cousins, my friends. My contemporaries might have given husbands too. I would have hated my husband going . . . I would have hated the sacrifice of my

231

brothers . . . but I would have borne it all with what dignity and courage I could muster. Instead of all that, I had to take part in the shameful struggle for our rights within this country.

I say shameful, because I felt bitterly the indignity of squawking about our properties when civilian soldiers were dying elsewhere. Yet I felt that squawk I must, because it was one way in which the Nisei could join the fight to keep democracy safe. We were skirmishing within Allied lines to keep the battle flag clean. We were doing our duty in the only way we could.

Just think of all the coloured men in this world, for centuries exploited and downtrodden . . . just think of how much the so-called civilized people owe to them! Unless we start paying back right now, our civilization will be bankrupt. I want you to be frightened of that prospect, frightened enough to do something about it. You, in your small way, can do something. You can demand that your elected representatives think of the people instead of jockeying for prestige, for power, for personal glory. You can demand that there be legislation in this country that will restore rights to its discriminated minorities, laws that will ensure the well-being of all its peoples, laws that will keep freedom from being outraged in so many walks of life. Let us legislate to encourage the divine in us, and to discourage the bully and the hypocrite in us. Let us prevent the inertia that makes it necessary to fight so hard for justice and equality.

Canada can never be great, no matter how great her natural resources, no matter how strong the Wartime Prices and Trade Board that has kept a better lid on inflation than the American OPA, no matter how varied the genius in her people . . . Canada cannot be great until she *is* great. To that end, to be a great nation, Canada must destroy the virus of rot that affects our national life, and among other vices, race prejudice ranks high. It is the people, not the representatives, who can make this country great. For if the people will not have corruptness in the governing of men, they will be sure to elect such people as would make greatness free, and secure in that freedom.

I ask you to think carefully on all the aspects of the past and the present; not to let a transient emotion guide you, but to be strong in the conviction that strength is to be found only in complete justice, in the complete equality of all men.

Damage While You Wait
(January 1947)

This article is aimed at those who are fundamentally sound but who leave action to other people. It's the rare person who will give time from personal concerns to worry over and do something about the woes of strangers.

Hereafter, let me address myself to you who mean well, who weep for the misfortunes of others, who wonder sadly about the state of the world, yet who do nothing about it.

Have you a definition for "hypocrisy," "regimentation," "freedom," and "equality"? Do you apply the words consistently, or do you use them in the two categories of "me" and "thee"? If you think this over carefully and come to a certain conclusion, you will find an answer for much of today's confusion.

Quite naturally I shall confine myself to the case of the Japanese, henceforth to be called Canadian, but for purposes of delineation, I shall use the racial term. It is understood, in spite of whitewashers and slanderers, that the Japanese are not wholly saintly or totally evil. There is the usual mixture common to all mankind. Without going into individual degrees of saintliness or villainy, intelligence or stupidity, talents or mediocrities, let's sum them all as "just people."

Since we are people, we react to life around us much as anyone else would in the same circumstances. Of course, there is a theory that coloured people have less sensitivity to the finer appreciation of injustice, discrimination, and hypocrisy. However, the disturbances in India, Africa, the protests of westernized Orientals and Negroes, other Far Eastern peoples, seem to belie that assumption of insensitivity.

When the coloured peoples demand freedom and equality they mean just what the words say. They don't mean slogans or handouts or qualified concessions. They don't mean a conscience-stricken benevolence, or generous patronage, or neurotic indulgence. They do mean a self-respecting liberty, a parity of opportunities as human beings.

233

To equality they add this significant note: a chance to catch up with all that was denied to them of the advantages of Progress. This last is the heavy debt owing to all the exploited peoples of this world. Unless repayment starts at once, the chances against peace become larger. Unless the withholders of freedom and equality return them freely, these will be collected with violence and hatred. The headlines in our newspaper, even after discounting them, prove it.

In recent years we have bandied the terms "regimentation," "freedom," and "equality," until they have become unreal. Another word we like to use very much is "hypocrisy."

What is freedom?

Is it a selfishness or a selflessness? Is it still freedom, when liberty for some means bondage to others? Or does freedom need to be regimented the moment it becomes licence, when it imperils the life and liberty of another? If freedom has limits, then what is regimentation? Is it a uniform standard to which we must conform or pay the consequences of violation? Doesn't it depend on the standard?

All countries, all peoples, have certain laws that cannot be broken without penalty. Impartial, uniform laws are regimentation. Usually these laws are for the security of the people. Of course, some manage to get away with murder, as the saying goes, but culprits caught red-handed usually get their just desserts. There are various limits to our freedom and no law-abiding citizen objects to them.

Politics and religion are supposed to be one's private privilege. This ceases to be freedom when they are used to deny freedom of worship or opinion to others. When regimentation is used to deny rights and liberties, used to conquer and vanquish, then we have wars. When freedom is misused we have economic exploitation, political skullduggery, racial discrimination, all ripe material for revolution.

The quality of freedom and the standard of regimentation depend on what you mean by those words.

The power to encourage the *best* for the *most* lies in your hands . . . if you use that power to its fullest capacity. You cannot afford to be indifferent to this power when it was bought for you dearly with the lifeblood of people who had the courage to act on their convictions. You must demand the best from those you choose to be your representative for a sound and just government. When an injustice cries out to be rectified, don't leave it to a few to cajole you into action. Act, and at once; for if you hesitate, your indecision might cause irreparable damage. If you wait until after the

234

injustice is committed before you act, think of the unnecessary suffering inflicted on innocent folk. One little damage that could have been prevented might well be the first link in a chain of horror. It has happened before, and can happen again, unless you are vigilant.

Our losses . . . our homes, our businesses, personal treasures . . . are insignificant when measured against the devastation in Europe and in Asia, except for one thing, which makes our losses smell more rotten than the havoc in vanquished countries: our losses occurred in a country where the flag of freedom flew, a country busy fighting the very thing that happened at home. The stink of hypocrisy is horrible.

The majority of the Japanese in Canada cannot afford the material loss they suffered through prejudice and evacuation. They are justified in their demand for reparation. Losses through personal failure have to be borne; losses shared with their fellow man in a just cause can be borne; but who can bear such losses forced on a helpless minority by order-in-council, losses that have no justification anywhere!

These losses were the last indignity imposed on a people whose loyalty and integrity were impeached without evidence to the contrary, and who were fingerprinted, card-indexed, corralled and driven to scatter far and wide. Deprived of rights, denied participation in the country's danger, they were humiliated until they either succumbed to bitterness and abnegation, or they gained new strength to combat the threat to their existence as proud Canadian citizens.

It is shameful, indeed, that in a country whose principle is democracy, we must struggle so hard for common rights. This struggle is made no easier by all those who mean well, who want what we want, but who do very little about it. These negative qualifications apply to anyone of any race, including the Japanese.

There are many ways in which to act. Progressive action lies not only in organizational work, but in the day-to-day living of us all. It is very easy to condemn a troubling fault in everyone. It is so easy that it requires a strict restraint on our part, if we wish to be fair. Yet I would warn you against toleration, a conscious toleration that still implies a supercilious superiority in yourself and an inferiority in the other.

Here I could disgress and split hairs on the definition of "equality," but let's leave that argument for some other time.

I would also suggest to you that a forthright unity of action toward the restoration of rights and liberties is not belligerence at all, not a chip on the shoulder; it is a much-needed co-operation toward the goal of brotherhood.

To know and guard our rights, to know and value freedom, to appreciate protective regimentation, to beware of and reject hypocrisy; this vigilance is the duty of citizenship. This vigilance is not a temporary state of excitement and fervour, to be forgotten after the first hullabaloo is gone. This vigilance is for life, the abiding passion of a free man; otherwise there is no point in our struggle.

Therefore, if you believe in these precepts, don't sit back and wait for someone else to do the work of translating them into action. Join in, contribute your effort without stopping to underestimate the worth of your trying, for, little as it may seem to you personally, when added to a nation-wide campaign it becomes great.

Today the Japanese—Tomorrow?
(April 1947)

> I do not agree with a word you say, but I will defend to the death your right to say it.—*Voltaire*

The champions of a literal interpretation of democracy have lost another round in the struggle against race discrimination and the denial of civil liberties. After a contentious three-day debate on the question of extended controls over Canadians of Japanese ancestry, Labour Minister Humphrey Mitchell's Order-in-Council to continue restrictive regulations prevailed by a vote of 105-31.[8] While the

---

[8]A CCF motion on April 24, 1947 calling for the annulment of Bill 104, a bill which would keep in force for yet another year two Orders-in-Council, P.C. 251 (from January 13, 1942), prohibiting fishing licences for Japanese Canadians and P.C. 946 (from February 5, 1943), authorizing the Minister of Labour to control their movement, employment, and place of residence. The continuation of these Orders-in-Council resulted from pressure by Liberal MPs from B.C., such as Ian Mackenzie, who wanted to prevent the return of Japanese Canadians to the province. As Ann Sunahara points out, "The CCF saw no justification for continuing to prohibit Japanese Canadians from returning to the Pacific Coast as the Japanese Americans had been allowed to do two years before" (*The Politics of Racism*, p. 148). The CCF motion was defeated, with only two Conservatives and four Liberals voting in support; 107 MPs were absent from the House of Commons.

Province of Saskatchewan outlawed race discrimination, Ottawa made it official federally, creating a "precedent that will plague us for years to come" (David Croll, Liberal, Toronto-Spadina).

While those who voted against the measure argued from their staunch belief that the government must be consistent with its professed democracy, it is to be noted that the supporters of the bill based their arguments on the presumption that the Japanese who moved east of the Rockies would flock back to B.C. in droves, were the controls lifted now.

Most of the members voted to support the government. Only a few of them, other than the solid CCF group which voted against the bill, broke party lines to stand with the dissenters. From this we can surmise two things: one, that too many of the MPs see nothing wrong with race discrimination within their country, though they are at great pains to denounce it abroad; two, far too many of them rely for their facts on the avowed racists from B.C., and not from first-hand enquiry among the people most concerned, the Japanese Canadians. The MPs seem to prefer believing the worst, and that worst is but a thin cover for personal prejudices.

The vote was a clumsy mockery of statesmanship.

Mr. Mitchell, in defending his bill, said he would take second place to no one "in a humane way," and that he came of a people who were noted for their good treatment of minorities. He also stated that his government had been very generous in giving $200 to each adult and $50 to each child of the Japanese who 'returned' to Japan; that the Japanese government had made no complaints about the Canadian treatment of the Japanese. Perhaps not, but in Japan this same treatment was propagandized to discourage any faith in the democracies. And Mr. Mitchell failed to give any figures on how much was given to those evacuated eastward, to help the needy to start from scratch again.

Concerning the fear expressed that we would trek back to B.C. like homing pigeons if the restrictions were cancelled, a more observant eye than the prejudiced glare of Mr. Ian Mackenzie would see many barriers which would prevent many, if any, from returning to the west coast. Our former homes are gone, perhaps beyond any legal restitution. Our stores, our businesses, our boats, our farms, and our small savings are gone the same way. It took years to accumulate such possessions, not including at all the lost furnishings and treasures and accessories. Our association with our former life

237

is stained with the bitter war years which we might want to forget.

Then, too, most of us just cannot afford the expense of moving back to start all over again for a second time; to search for a house to live in and a job to live on in that economic world of B.C. which was once closed to us through custom and habit of prejudice. Even our new-found right to vote (east of the Rockies) which we have used since we left B.C. is still denied in that western province.

Whatever our nostalgic longings for a once familiar home in B.C., here in the east we are building a new life again, even though stripped of most of our possessions, even though restricted and regulated by orders-in-council and RCMP permits. We did not choose this life voluntarily; it was thrust on us—but we have made the best of it, even improved on it.

Mr. Mitchell also said that according to his information, the evacuees are happier now than they were in B.C. If so, they would not return to any unhappier past, and this seems to eliminate any need for a ban on returning. We know that many Japanese who left the pest-holes they lived in formerly are glad to be out of them. They certainly would not go back to them. As Secretary of State Colin Gibson stated, referring to Japanese-owned properties, most of those former homes are unfit for human habitation and this unsavoury truth was well-known to the unfortunate tenants, but such places were all that could be afforded that was available.

Many others will not return to the coast because they are better off now, no thanks to the evacuation, but because they resettled here before the east had a chance to work up a case of prejudice such as existed on the coast. Some might think of returning but the odds against it are too high, and an important restraint is lack of money to finance such a move.

The only evacuees who might return, given a chance, are those who will have a legitimate reason: if they have a better chance of business in B.C. because of the moderate climate, or if their employment depends on the position of B.C. on the Pacific. These might return, if they thought they would be successful. Then there are those who wish only to revisit the scenes they left so abruptly, having in their wallets a return ticket to their homes in the east.

The Japanese now scattered in the interior of B.C. are often the bone of contention with the racists, who use them as a lever against any proposal to lift restrictions on the Japanese Canadians. But these folk too have been accepted into their new neighbourhoods, more or less, and they do not contemplate a return to the segregated colonies they knew in Vancouver, New Westminster, Victoria, Prince Rupert, Steveston, and elsewhere. These people have literally made the ghost towns come to life again, and are now well-established as part of the community they serve.

There will be no large-scale rush back to British Columbia.

Another point of interest brought out in the three-day debate was that the 50-odd parcels of property still unsold, belonging apparently to the Japanese, will not be disposed of without the original owners' consent. If these owners refuse to sell, and if the refusals are respected, and if those 50-odd pieces are to be considered as belonging to the Japanese owners, even *in absentia*, then what about those owners whose homes etc. were sold over strong protests? What about the total disregard of their refusal to any consent? If the Japanese owners of those unsold properties, no matter how depreciated and unsaleable they may be, can give or not give their consent to a sale, why could not the others whose homes were of such real estate value that they could be sold so quickly, so profitably for all, except the owners? Here is an inconsistency to be questioned.

Does the value of the property decide the right of the owner? We assume that the 50 parcels are unsold because no one wants them. In this day of shortages, surely 50 places to live would not go untouched on the market, unless they were unfit for sale.

•

Veterans Affairs Minister Ian Mackenzie says: "There is not the slightest trace of racial tinge in my attitude toward this matter." He said that the only basis for this legislation was the security of the Pacific coast (*Toronto Star*, April 23).

How would the return of a few Japanese to the coast affect the security there? The war is over. Japan is defeated. Her ships are sunk. Her Air Force is gone. Her atomic research equipment was smashed. The Allies won't let her re-arm. Her fanatic military clique is crushed (we hope), but even this group had no plans for using resident Japanese on this continent or in Hawaii as agent saboteurs. And not even the most ardent anti-Japanese racist in Canada has found any saboteurs, or even plans for any sabotage.

We have heard a great deal about the unfair Oriental competition in the past. We shall probably hear of it again, if we surmount our present handicaps and become too successful in any line. We have been accused of ousting the white fishermen, the white farmers, the white storekeepers, etc., and no amount of facts and figures could convince the malcontent of the injustice of those charges. From the colour of our past experiences, we assume from Mr. Mackenzie's statement that the B.C. coast must be protected from the hard-working, persevering Japanese, who have shown a talent to make the desert bloom, a barren land produce, a ghost town revive, and to endure the beet fields.

How else are we to interpret Mackenzie's oratorical outburst in spite of the fine words about the right of B.C. to determine its own internal security? Any threat to this right would "strike at the heart and soul of confederation." Just how the return of a few courageous Japanese Canadians to those hotbeds of prejudice will endanger the internal security of B.C. is not shown at all. Proponents of the restrictive bill speak soberly or excitedly of a mass return without going any further than that general statement. Therefore, we conclude that, until a more rational reason is found to use instead of an outright and shameless racial discrimination, this vague "fear of mass return" will be used to stir up "fears for the internal security" of B.C.

Benoit Michaud (MP, Restigouche-Madawaska), voted against the bill saying: "As a member of a minority race in Canada I must oppose such legislation." M. Michaud, a scholarly barrister, is a French Canadian from Quebec speaking for the rights of Japanese Canadians. This is an illustration to benefit the Nisei who is concerned solely for himself. No one can decry discrimination against himself if he is not ready to battle for the rights of other minorities.

If we look around us we will see victims of many forms of discrimination, not all racial or religious. If we are to be consistent in our demand for equality, we must show a fine impartiality and denounce discrimination wherever we see it, whether the victims are rabid communists or stubborn reactionaries; whether they be white, black, or yellow; whether they be Catholic, Protestant, Jew, or of any other religion, or no religion at all; whether they be unskilled, exploited workers or something else.

In every phase of life there is a choice between expression and suppression. That choice will have to be made with a clear understanding of how it will affect others as well as ourselves.

The restrictions today are directed against the Japanese in Canada; tomorrow they may be against someone else. Their effect is to loosen the existing curbs on baiting and persecuting any group, any race, for any reason or no reason that excites the minds of the fearful and the bigoted. These controls are, without doubt, dangerous precedents to future issues unless the Canadian people rise now to demand an airtight legislation to protect minorities from persecution by the majority.

Story of the Japanese in Canada
(Manuscript, c. 1947)

The very first Japanese immigrant came to Canada like any European adventurer. He had the itch to travel, to see the New World for himself, and to see if that world would give him a better deal than the old country. But these first immigrants were followed by a mass of a different type . . . a whole pool of cheap labour, contracted by the collieries, and other big business interests. The men who first brought in Japanese labour had thought only of cheap labour. These labourers were not considered human beings at all. They represented only a pair of hands to wield a pick and shovel, and there seemed to be an inexhaustible supply to offset the shortage of other labourers in that province who would not work for such low pay when there was gold in the hills for the picking.

It wasn't long before this group of immigrants, naturally enough, yearned for their lost family life. They wanted their wives and children with them, and the younger men wanted to get married. They had originally intended to make a fortune and then go back to Japan, but that fortune just did not materialize as fast as they expected. Coupled with their low pay, their living expenses were a good deal higher, proportionately, than what they thought they would be. Dollars translated into yen seemed a lot more, but then in Canada, a dollar only bought a dollar's worth, not two yen's worth, so they had to spend more. Then too, in the beginning, B.C. seemed like a paradise to these people who knew only a meagre living in Japan. They felt that their families would have a better chance at life in this rich undeveloped country, where trees were so huge they dwarfed the imagination, where the streams were full of fish, and where the soil would grow anything. Such abundant land, still uncleared, unpopulated!

That's how these immigrants began to think beyond the limits of barrack-like living, and dreamed of homes, and flower gardens, and a front room for company, and the comfort of one's own household. Their wives came in a wave, healthy, adventurous women in the prime of young adulthood, who risked the unknown in coming to a barbarous land. There were no old folks, and children were still to come. That's when the bogey of the high birth-rate started.

When you figure out a birth-rate, you take into account the number of folk past child-bearing and the number of children. These represent the balance fore and aft of a chart. However, the immigrant group . . . and this is true of any immigrant group, Oriental or not . . . had no old, and no children. Their graph-line looked fabulous, because there was no beginning and no end, just the middle, the very peak of child-bearing years. There were the odd cases of a family with more than twelve children, but they were the exception rather than the rule. Five and six were the average figures, and many couples had no children at all.

Well, after the wives came, naturally, they began to want homes. And when they had homes, they wanted the trimmings which couldn't be bought on the low wages, so the men broke away from gang labour and started businesses for themselves. They knew land, and they knew fishing. Hard work was nothing new . . . in such a rich land work was a nice change from the drudgery on worn-out rice-fields they knew in Japan. Because of the language problems, they went to work at jobs that required only a minimum of talking. To learn the language and western ways of living, they worked as domestics. They watched and learned and grew from ignorant immigrants to self-sufficient citizens of a new country. That's when the real trouble started.

Almost overnight, a strange batch of black-haired children were ready for school, children with little if any knowledge of spoken English. White society was contaminated and white superiority was threatened. Down came the iron curtain of discrimination . . . and that curtain has been down ever since. All the superficial reasons for discrimination are of no importance at all. I don't have to list them. You've heard the same ones dressed up to sound real but they are only bogeys.

The primary and driving impulse behind the prejudice and discrimination that dogged our footsteps these fifty years and more was this:

The white man found B.C. first, discounting the Indians, and even if he couldn't work and develop all of it himself, he regarded every advantage, every profit, every blessing as his sole prerogative and right. When another people of another colour tried to stand up proudly, the white man slapped him down for daring to presume they were as good. How dare the cheap coolie labour aspire to stucco homes, cars, fine furniture, and higher education! That is the basic and the vulgar snobbery behind all the technical and fine-sounding phrases used to describe what is called the "Japanese problem" . . . which isn't a problem of the Japanese, but the problem of the white man's queer idea of exclusive superiority. Now, I have been told many times that you don't like being called 'white man', the same as we don't like being called 'Japs', but in the days when the colour line was so definite, the term was logical and proper.

That's when the B.C. government denied the franchise to Japanese.[9] That denial had far-reaching consequences, for not only was it a mere matter of our not being able to vote, it became a sinister bar across our lives. It made us into sort of bastard Canadians. We couldn't do this, we couldn't do that. Every way we turned we felt the shadow of that law. As long as we were very young and didn't know the difference, it was all right with our parents, to whom the matter of a vote was unimportant. They couldn't vote in Japan; they didn't miss it here. They were content in their little jobs and businesses, and expected no more of fortune than to see their children grow strong and healthy, marry some day, and settle down in this wonderful land.

The children had other ideas. As they grew up, went through high school, learned the ways and thoughts of European culture, learned about the Magna Carta, the French Revolution, the Secession of the Thirteen Colonies, the rights of citizens, pride of birth, and love of country, the burden of their restricted lives became more and more unbearable until they questioned the right of the province to deny them their birthright. This awakening happened about 1930, when the Nisei organized into a group which was to spearhead all later actions in the struggle for our rights.

---

[9]The denial went back to 1895 when the B.C. government "extended the clause in the provincial elections act which had deprived the Chinese of the right to vote to include the Japanese" (Adachi, p. 41). Since the exclusion was on the basis of race, citizenship was of no importance—a situation that rankled the native-born Nisei generation.

We were a pitifully small group, bucking our stubborn heads against an incredible mass of ignorance and obstinate prejudice. We had friends among the Occidentals who gave us wonderful support. But these friends were later called traitors to Canada for defending our rights. It could be said of any righteous cause: "O what crimes are committed in thy name!" It was said at the foot of the guillotine in Paris: "Liberty, what crimes are committed in thy name!" Or . . . "God, what crimes are committed in thy name!" That small group of Nisei was to become the voice and standard-bearer of all the Japanese in Canada when war came to the Pacific.

At the time of Godesberg and Munich, and after the start of the war in Manchuria, we started a little weekly paper called the *New Canadian*, which became a voice crying out for equality in the wilderness. This paper also tried to give the Japanese themselves a clearer picture of what Canadian citizenship meant. Its high standard of policy rated praise from all over the country, not only in Canada but also in the United States. When Pearl Harbor wiped out our past, our homes, our community life, and our businesses, we clung to that paper, as we would to a spar, a raft, the beacon of a lighthouse, though for a time that paper was censored by the RCMP, as was all our private mail. The Japanese language papers which had kept our parents informed were wiped out, closed down, forbidden on December 8, 1941. Overnight the *New Canadian* took on the work of all three former papers. It was the only link between us and the events that swept away the troubled pattern of our lives into confusion. Without it we would have been even more lost.

•

After all those years during the 1930s, the British Columbians hadn't bothered to find out what we were like as people, as Canadians. They just believed every rabble-rouser that came along with wild rumours and false figures, who scared the daylights out of the Whites by calling us all traitors and saboteurs, without rhyme or reason. They called us names, impeached us for treachery without evidence, without one glance into our side of the story. Here we had spent nine years trying to reach them, but found that the little group we called the JCCL [Japanese Canadian Citizens' League] hadn't reached very far in that time. The public just wasn't interested in us as people, as Canadians. When war came, they foisted their fears

244

onto us and made us their scapegoats. There is something wrong with a people, any people, who will use a minority group of people as scapegoats. The habit of suspicion, of snobbery, of intolerance, of greed, found a good excuse in Pearl Harbor to tar all of us . . . innocent Canadians (75% were Canadians by birth or naturalization) . . . with one brush as "those damned treacherous Japs."

So, because of ignorance, unwarranted fear and the vicious hatred of a few racists, 21,000 persons were uprooted and scattered to the four winds . . . to lose their hold on security, familiar places, homes, belongings, jobs, families. Naturally, Canada, on the side *against* the brutal Nazis, couldn't quite descend to massacre, but I am telling you, the will to descend was not lacking . . . the will was not lacking, for fear makes brutes of people. There were enough instances of rape, brutality, and callousness to show us that too many British Columbians would not mind exterminating us. One young Nisei was shot in cold blood by young robbers, one of whom was in uniform, and at the trial someone for the defence said: "Why find the four young Canadians guilty when all they did was rid the world of one more Jap?" It was murder in the first degree, but these four got off with light sentences.[10] Our young women dared not go out without escort. These were exceptions, I grant you that, but there they were.

But short of physical violence, we were inflicted with every kind of torture under the guise of lawful procedure. The torture on our nerves . . . you've heard of the war of nerves? . . . was something you would not believe until you've felt it yourself. That is why we simply cannot abide people who say to us: "After all, you ought to be thankful to be in Canada where you aren't treated like the Jews in Europe." We cannot abide people who say to us: "Well, aren't you glad that the war solved the problem of mixing you up with the rest of the country?" All I can say back is: what good we got out of this evacuation was not the intent of it. People have to get the best out of a bad situation or they might as well give up and die. Dispersal was not our major problem. Our major problem was to get the Occidentals to treat us equally.

This forced evacuation, accompanied by so much unnecessary loss of property and increased bitterness, was a backward step for our people. Now, on top of all of their former worries, they have the new task of overcoming this terrible bitterness, and if the bitterness

---

[10]See note on Yoshiyuki Ono above, "Letters to Wes," January 21, 1942.

is passed on to the children, the task of far-seeing leaders is so much harder in their efforts to counteract its consequences.

•

When we were ordered out of our homes on the west coast, only a few came east. The majority stayed in camps in the interior of the province, in abandoned mining towns. These were like a concentration camp without that formal title. Ottawa called it the Interior Housing Project. We just called them the ghost towns. My . . . my . . . what a backward step that was. All the outgrowing Canadianism in the children was forced back into themselves, into a revival of Japaneseness as a defence against the bitter disappointment in democracy. They were confined and card-indexed, fingerprinted, and roped into these crowded, psychologically unhealthy camps.

I might digress to mention that early in 1941 we were all card-indexed, fingerprinted, and registered under a special National Registration, and no matter how much the race baiters counted us over again, they could find only 22,000 of us, instead of the 100,000 they *said* were in B.C. You can be sure the RCMP did not miss one black head. Even the Eurasians, of which there were a few, were counted.

After the government gave orders to the Custodian of our property to sell our homes and business, to auction our furniture and other small possessions, another terror swept through us. Early in 1945, a letter came from Ottawa to every one of us, 16 and over, asking us to make known our decision: *whether or not we would go to Japan*. The advantages of going to Japan were printed on a separate sheet, but not a word of encouragement was given for going east of the Rockies. Those who were already east ignored the letter, but to those in the ghost towns, that letter was a frightening thing, for it became an axe over their heads.

Go east at once or sign to go to Japan. Failure to choose would be interpreted as non-cooperation, and would be regarded as a sort of disloyalty to Canada before a tribunal to be set up to judge the degree of our loyalty. Do you think that for one moment anyone able to get out of the ghost towns would stay there? Except for the people who wanted to go to Japan anyway and were determined to sit out the war, the majority hated the ghost towns . . . but going east, without some job to go to, without a house to go to, with hostile strangers waiting there, with small helpless children or invalids to hinder their free movement. What could they do, especially when the government help to those going east was $40 against the $200 given to those who signed to go to Japan? How can I explain to you the terrible effect this had on the hearts and minds of the ghost towners? They had to choose between the devil and the deep blue sea. Neither prospect was enticing, but they had to choose or be charged with something horrible . . . and all the time the RCMP marched up and down the streets of the ghost towns giving a dreadful air of unnamed threats over their fearful heads.

Those of us in the east had to go down to the RCMP offices to register our choice. I chose to ignore the letter. Why should I register such a choice, when the mere fact of my coming east was half the solution to the letter? Well, I got a second letter, with the notice to report underlined. I ignored that too, especially because I had no way of going so far from where I lived, with no one to look after the twins, and it was impossible to take them both. A third letter came, with the notice in red, and a date stamped on it . . . a time limit. I ignored that too, and waited to see what would happen. Why should I, a Canadian, be required to do such a ridiculous thing, I of all people, who from way back was pounding my typewriter in the campaign for real citizenship, who advised my fellow Nisei to stand on their rights as Canadians. Well, I found out that other Nisei like myself felt the same way and ignored all three letters.

One day, a very handsome, pleasant young man came to my front door, and said simply: "*RCMP*." "Ah . . . " I thought, now here's my chance to tell them what I think. I had no fear for myself, as I knew I was in the right. Well, do you know that half the battle of winning people over is to have a very pleasant diplomat speak for you? He was the nicest RCMP officer I ever met, and I thought that if only the rest of them were as friendly and as pleasant, there wouldn't have been half the heartache and trouble in the ghost towns, and during the process of evacuation. But in spite of the fact that he was such a pleasant young man, I gave him an earful. He had come to put down in black and white against my name on his card-index, my choice. I chose Canada. And in a letter to the one responsible for these repatriation plans, I said that because we chose Canada knowing that the choice entailed further hardships, further discrimination, we were better Canadians than he who was only born Canadian, and who had no choice to make.[11]

---

[11]See "Canada is Our Choice," above, pp. 204-205.

The deportation orders created quite a storm among a now aroused Canadian public. It had taken us all of four years to rouse this public opinion. The spearhead of pressure came from that group of Canadians in the Co-operative Committee on Japanese Canadians, which had branch committees all over Canada. What happened to those orders you know. To date about 5,000 have been sent to Japan, allegedly voluntarily, but that is not the real explanation at all. The rest of us will stay here, about 18,000 of us, to fare as well or as badly as the country will allow us.

When we first came east we couldn't do anything without a permit. The RCMP dogged our every footstep, and the Department of Labour ordered our every move. We couldn't buy a house, or lease one for more than a year. We couldn't start any businesses. We had to go through a special process to get a job. We had to get a permit to travel. Fortunately, most of these taboos have been lifted, but still there are enough restrictions left to make us only second-class citizens. We can't travel without permits over any provincial border, or go to B.C. unless some relative is dying, and we can't get fishing licences. We still can't vote in B.C., and there are recent reports that the Chinese and the East Indians might be allowed to vote, but not the Japanese. How stubbornly they cling to foolish prejudices! Inconsistent and dangerous in precedent. Their original denial of our rights long ago brought on this train of injustices on a very helpless minority. They intend to go along on their path of hate and destruction, while with lip service they dedicate themselves to democracy . . . a principle they know nothing about.

We cannot erase what has happened in the last six years. We CAN prevent a repetition of those events. It will take many years yet to educate the Canadian people to accept the practice of equality, but there is an immediate job to be done, and that is reparations.

We made a survey of property losses of those who now live in Toronto and vicinity, for 200 cases only. These are only the actual dollars and cents lost at the time of evacuation, not the loss sustained over the six years, when we had to buy furniture, clothes, and other things caused by having to start a new life over again. Some of us had it worse than others, farmers and fishermen especially.

In the States there is a Bill before Congress that will, if passed, pay for all losses sustained by American Nisei and their families; a recent development is a plan for across-the-board payment of $1000 each for adults and $500 each for children of a certain age group.

This Bill was presented by prominent members of State and Federal legislatures. In Canada, on the other hand, Mr. King himself stated that he thought the prices we got for our lost homes was fair and only those who could *prove* that they were entitled to more *might* get a hearing. Well, that is a loophole to be sure, small as it is. The judgment on whether the government had any right to sell our homes in the first place is still pending. Judge Thorson seems to have forgotten about it.[12] Meanwhile all our homes have been sold for half their real estate value at best, and in some cases, especially among the farmers, less than a tenth of their value. And this does not account for the irreplaceable lost articles.

When we demand reparations, it isn't a question of Japanese whining for material losses when Europeans who have lost home and so much more are still terribly starving and destitute. But how can you help those Europeans with a clear conscience if you have our despoilation darkening and staining the sincerity and the integrity of your effort? Our losses are part of the world pattern of losses and despoilation, and as long as one part remains anywhere, you cannot say that justice prevails.

Reparation for our property losses will lift the burden of grudges from our shoulders and heal a little of the damage done to us, and only time and a determined effort of all decent Canadians will wipe out the stain of our psychological hurts.

Who Was the Custodian?
(August 1947)

(Actual terms of reference for the New Commissioner [Justice Henry Bird] define the Japanese claims to be considered as those in which it is found "that by reason of

---

[12]Early in 1943, the Japanese Property Owners' Association formed to challenge in court the Custodian's authority to liquidate properties he held in trust. The outcome of this case was held up by Justice Joseph Thorson for years, until August 1947, when he reached a negative decision. Adachi explains that "Thorson's rejection turned, not upon broad constitutional issues, but upon a legal quibble: that is, that the Custodian was not a servant of the Crown but a statutory officer who happened to be the Secretary of State. In others words, the property owners had sued the wrong person" (p. 323).

249

the failure of the Custodian to exercise reasonable care in the disposition of the real and personal property vested in the Custodian, the amount received by the Custodian for such property was less than the market value thereof at the time of such disposition."—July 23, Toronto *Globe and Mail*.)

God in heaven! What is the Custodian of Enemy Alien Property to me? What was left of mine that could be left in "protective custody?" There is no record here on earth of my loss, except engraved upon the hardening shell of a hurt and sensitive heart!

There is a difference in the loss I bear from that I would have borne with calmer acquiescence. Had I been robbed, despoiled, made homeless and adrift by the bloody arms of war, 'twere better borne than to be likewise done by my own countrymen. Were I the victim of the conquering madmen from Berlin, my hate of oppression would give me strength to fight for liberty; but to be bound and gagged in legal verbiage by the *honourable* men, the *respectable* men who govern us in democratic freedom is to struggle in despair of bitter taste.

And who is the Custodian who should have protected what I had, before I lost them to greed and stupid prejudice?

Who is the Custodian of my freeborn rights, if not the government of my native land? Who is the protector of my own chattels from looting, if not the laws of this land? Who is the sponsor of my dreams, of all the hopes and plans, the confidant entrusted with what lies ahead of me, if not my own, native land?

> Breathes there the man with soul so dead,
> Who never to himself hath said:
> "This is my own, my native land!"

God! God! were my soul "so dead" I could not thus agonize for the land betrayed!

•

Did I not *have* solace in my nativity? Did I not one childhood day, one unforgettable day, discover that which is mine, my Canadian birth? A once proud possession . . . mine! Shall I be shamed for it? Does not shame despoil the pride? Did I not *have* faith that my citizenship would be honoured?

250

"Pass, Canadian!"

Instead, was I not tagged, restricted in my walk, a hand of warning upon my shoulder?

"Keep out, Jap!"

And did I not *have* the sanctity of my home, the comfort of my earned chattels? Ah, real estate, furniture, accessories . . . these by the negotiable bonds of legality. Imbue these inanimate possessions with all the dreams and hopes, the sweat and tired nerves, the toil of meagre years, the laughter and tears of human hearts.

List the treasures among the lost! List the lovely iris opening to the sun; the roses blooming through the touch of loving hands; the sturdy fence put up by a brother's care; two snow-capped peaks [the Lions] framed by window curtains facing north; weedless lawns and young evergreens.

What is the market value of such loss? What *are* the shining walnut furnitures, the immaculate enamel of the modern electric age, the crystal and silver and the plush, but the outward signs of man's endeavours? Did they not go down the greedy maws of scornful bargain hunters filling up on loot? Custodian of Enemy Alien Property! Hah! What has this Custodian to do with what I lost? My house? And if I were to get a certain sum, a cheque upon the taxpayers of this land, could it restore to pristine pride my citizenship, could it restore unbroken my faith in honourable men, could it restore the lost years? [Sarcasm]

What account within the Custodian's files has any knowledge of those possessions, costly and not, old and new, replaceable and irreplaceable, of real and sentimental value, all labelled once upon a time as belonging to someone—does it matter whether that "someone" be of prominent note or obscure? Where shall we list the many things sold with haste, blind despairing haste, to greedy men intent on gaining much for little? These things never saw the Custodian's files at all! So, shall the Custodian be judged by these that he did not fail the owners? How else can he be judged within the barren terms of reference of the order to investigate our loss? And shall the honourable commissioner be paid his good round sum per day to find the Custodian's hands are clean of failure, and that our loss is really not a legal loss at all but the petty complaints of a people who

251

did not know what was good for them and who were always putting the government to a great deal of unnecessary trouble?

God! it is no blasphemy to laugh aloud at the hypocrisy of it all! I, being mortal, do laugh at hollow men, but Thou, being God, do weep for Thy people.

There is a difference in the loss I bear from that I would have borne with poignant grace. The loss I bear is not the same that other Canadians bear, for mine and that of all my people, bear the mark of racial prejudice.

God, must all the coloured of this earth endure the iniquities of greed and prejudice? Shall we then only stand higher in Thy final presence? We would forego divine superiority could we but find an earthly equality.

Who was the Custodian of all we had, and how shall he judge the market value of our loss?

Who was the Custodian?

Go East!

(Manuscript, c. 1947)

In 1930, at the Powell Street Young People's special summer meeting with a United Church official from the east, we heard one of the first public exhortations to go east of the Rockies.[13] The white-haired and amiable gentleman spoke of the opportunities to be found . . . ah . . . say in Toronto . . . and he went on to say that the east wasn't as far away from the west as we might think it to be. Thus we went on, touching lightly on the subject of discriminations on the Pacific coast.

Being young and impressionable, I was struck with a parallel situation in American history, when Horace Greeley said casually to some adventurous young man: "Go west, young man, go west!"

Tickled at my great discovery I piped up: "Go east, young man, go east!"

---

[13]The Young People's Society (YPS) of the United Church was a group made up predominantly of Nisei who formed in the late 1920s to overcome the racist barriers separating Canadians of Japanese ancestry from other Canadians.

The genial speaker chuckled at my impertinence and agreed in a laughing voice: "That's right, young lady. Go east it is."

How little we knew then what drastic measures would be used twelve years from that innocent time to ensure that we really did go east of the Rockies!

•

1930 was an eventful year for the Nisei, as the younger generation born in Canada were called. That year saw the first large public dance sponsored by a 'respectable' group called the Nippon Tennis Club, and this broke the barrier of the custom that forbade the mixing of the sexes outside the family circle. Oh, I'm not saying that we didn't do a lot of dancing in private homes where the parents were more broadminded than the others. We did, and some of the youngsters even patronized the commercialized dance halls in the city, and we found nothing wrong with the dance pavilions on the many picnic grounds.

But once our elders had reluctantly chaperoned our first community dance, they couldn't very well condemn the next or the next. Simultaneously, with this new social freedom won from our parents, the more serious-minded younger men and women were studying the economic and political handicaps that barred us from many a career in British Columbia.

Orientals were denied the franchise in B.C., and this in turn kept us off the voter's lists, which in turn kept us out of such professions as law and pharmacy, right down to jobs in civil service and public works. Prejudice on both sides, of Occidental against Oriental and vice-versa, prevented any solution of the so-called 'Oriental problem'. In those days it was 'Oriental', and did not become narrowed down to 'Japanese' in labelling the impasse of discrimination.

While most of the Nisei were still too young to appreciate the depth and variety of their troubles, present and future, the older ones organized into a Japanese Canadian Citizens' Association with the purpose of fighting for the franchise, and to work for a better understanding between the races of people that made up the west coast province.[14] It was a very large order for a very young and very earnest group of people, and only after ten years of heartbreaking effort and many

---

[14]The first Japanese Canadian Citizens' Association (JCCA) was formed in 1932.

failures did we realize the immensity of the problem, which was not so much an Oriental problem, but a problem in human weaknesses.

At the end of those ten years the world had changed, and war had come again. We hadn't got the franchise, and more, we were threatened with mass expulsion from our homes. Only those who experienced the first confused months of the Pacific war can appreciate their deepest tragedy and their hysterically comic moments.

One of the first incidents that made us dread our unenviable position was the cruel separation of a daughter from a dying parent because the curfew would not allow her to go to his bedside in spite of pleas to the local authorities. This dusk-to-dawn curfew came upon us on February 27, 1942, with other restrictions and orders that marked out those of Japanese race from the rest of the Canadian citizenry.

One of the first laughs we got, and we had to have plenty of laughs to lighten the burden on our lives, was the story of the elderly farmer who was arrested by a zealous police on Sunday night, December 7, 1941. According to the story that went around, this farmer, after a visit to another farmer neighbour deep in the Fraser Valley, was trudging home, unaware of the momentous events of the day. He had read no paper, heard no radio bulletin. Imagine his surprise at being suddenly arrested while ambling home!

Then, the story goes on, when he was taken to the immigration detention building on the waterfront in Vancouver, he met with sundry other Japanese morosely imprisoned there, city men in fine business suits. The farmer, still slightly surprised at his own arrest, remarked politely, in lieu of more formal greetings:

"Senso ga hajimatta so desute ne!"

(It is said that a war has begun!)

Today, that story has lost its freshness, its connotations, but at the time we first heard it we laughed till the tears came to our eyes, laughed because it was better so than to cry. Other incidents, which really had a serious undertone, made us weak with laughter. We had to laugh at the spectacle of sober citizens milling around on Powell Street (the main street, so far as Vancouver's Little Tokyo was concerned) grasping at wild rumours, uttering wild threats against a fellow Japanese who was reputed to have been profiting on our troubles, phoning home to their anxious wives the latest news handpicked on the streets.

One gardener, after reporting to his family what was being heard and said in the cafes on Powell Street, added his own commentary:

254

"Some day, we shall gather again by our hearths and laugh over this tempest, and tell many a story to our grandchildren!"

But in spite of the laughs we managed to find in the anything-but-funny situation on the west coast, we went through the days in a dread of uncertainty, with new fears rising daily with the fast-coming orders from Ottawa. The Nisei, who had tried to do their share for an ideal called Democracy, now shied away from the word, if they did not actually laugh at it for its hollow pretensions. Yet, our little weekly paper, the *New Canadian*, the only survivor of the shut-down orders on the local Japanese press, kept on repeating editorially: "Have faith in Canada!"

Keeping our faith was an uphill job, when our cars, radios, and cameras were impounded, our homes taken over by the Custodian and sold over our protests, when our freedom to move, to assemble, to work, to find homes, was curtailed, restricted and administrated by both the RCMP and a new office called the 'Japanese Division, Department of Labour.'

From 1939 on, the young Nisei men tried to enlist in the Canadian armed services. One of the first statements from Ottawa concerning this willingness to serve said:

> . . . if Canadian citizens of Oriental racial origin were to
> be called upon to perform compulsory military service at
> the present time, unfortunate incidents might occur. (O.D.
> Skelton)[15]

The possibility of a war with Japan had not escaped our observations, and I remember some discussion on just such a contingency. After dinner conversation sometimes turned like this:

> "Would you enlist against the Japanese, should there be
> a war with Japan?"
> "Why not? It's no different from the fact that an English
> Anglo-Saxon wouldn't hesitate to fight a German Anglo-
> Saxon. It's been done before."

---

[15]In January 1941, members of the Japanese Canadian Citizens' League (JCCL), in response to a government decision to exclude Japanese Canadians from the Armed Forces, wrote Prime Minister Mackenzie King with a motion asking for the right to serve. Dr. O.D. Skelton, Under-Secretary of State for External Affairs, wrote back with the government's answer, quoted in the *New Canadian*, 31 January 1941, where Muriel would have seen it.

Then there would be speculations on the position of the Japanese Canadians should such a war begin in reality:

> "Would we be interned like the Jews were in Germany?"
> "No doubt there are some people who would like to see that done, but I hardly think that the Canadian government would allow such a thing. After all, this is a democracy, you know."
> "Yeah?"
> "Well, isn't it?"

A rueful laugh would close the topic.

•

The Japanese Canadians (and Japanese Americans) will not forget Pearl Harbor day, because for us it spelled a great failure: the failure of democratic countries to live up to their vaunted slogans, and more serious, the failure to implement the principles of freedom and justice by which they were governed. That fateful day came like a thunderclap to us, despite allegations to the contrary (that we knew all about it beforehand), and a friend of mine, coming in from golf, said quietly: "Well, I'd like to join the air force. They can't do this to us and get away with it."

By "they," he meant the Japanese airmen over Hawaii. But this young man did not get to enter the air force at all. The Nisei were rejected from all branches of the Services. Only the odd one here and there throughout the country was accepted into the army, navy, or air force, and these were mostly from the Japanese Canadians who had settled in the east. Towards the end of the war a few Nisei were recruited for the Intelligence Corps, and of these, some saw service in Asia. Captain Llewellyn Fletcher said of these volunteers:

> The Officer commanding the far eastern section of the Intelligence corps says the Nisei personnel in the corps were the best boosters Canada had in the Far East, and in addition were good advertisements for the Dominion because of their conduct and their ability, not only in their special work, but as soldiers. They made a good impression everywhere.

They did a good piece of work. It is too bad that their willingness to serve the war effort could not have been utilized as early in the war as was the willingness of the American Nisei. British Forces had to borrow heavily from the American Nisei at the stage of the war when the British Intelligence needed them most.

Denied a share in our country's danger, we watched from the sidelines, ticketed and registered as we were to enable an official finger to be placed on us at an instant's notice. We watched the 442nd Battalion of American Nisei fight their bloody way through the prejudice in the United States. We wondered what it was like to crawl from foxhole to foxhole, from dugout to dugout, on the Anzio beaches, cold, tired, wet; wondered what made a 100-pound Nisei G.I. brave enough to attack a German machine-gun nest with only a shovel; how it felt to be among the company that went to the rescue of the Lost Battalion near Bruyères in France, to be the spearhead for so many attacks, to lose so many brother G.I.s, to be so wounded as to be called the Purple Heart Battalion.

We never knew.

We never knew either, what it is to lose a son, a father, a brother, a sweetheart, or a friend on the battlefield; the anguish that must for a time embitter the bereaved for the poignant loss of a beloved one. That this bitterness was usually taken out on the people of Japanese ancestry, we understood, much as we deplored it. But that this bitterness should be exploited into a 'hate' campaign against us was something else. It was a poison as sure to corrode the doer as well as the victim.

The Nisei, supported by intelligent Canadians throughout the country, fought that poison as well as we knew how. Through the help of such friends as the Co-operative Committee on Japanese Canadians (in Toronto), the Consultative Council (in Vancouver), through the churches, through trade unions, university student bodies, liberal newspapers, and even some Members of Parliament, provincial and federal, the Case of the Japanese Canadians was brought to national attention.

We had accepted the evacuation with what good grace we could muster. We had moved east of the Rockies onto the beet fields, farms, small towns, large cities, in low-paid jobs, in domestic service, in farm service camps, in road camps, in hostels, private homes, dingy flats, crowded rooms, wherever we could squeeze into without displacing anyone. We filled the manpower shortage. Those unable, for many reasons, went to the interior of B.C. to live in shacks, in abandoned houses and hotels, in tents (until wooden houses were built later) in the ghost towns that once were mining centres, and in box-cars at road camps for single young men and male Nationals.

In one such town, Slocan, a row of tents housed the evacuees until the snow came. It was bitter cold, with the tent collapsing often as not from the weight of the snow on it. The mess hall, converted from a skating rink, was large and drafty, the bare earth that was the floor, wet and cold. "It was awful," said a former inhabitant of a ghost town, "one night when we heard cries and screams from the tent next to us. We went out and saw that the snow had collapsed over the sleepers' heads and frightened them out of their wits."

Unable to cope with the upheaval in their lives, the ghost town evacuees expressed their frustrations against the petty inconveniences that never used to bother them before. The confusion and the hysteria that overtook them after the war began affected their thinking and reactions to current events that touched on their limited lives. The consequences of this confusion were sadly apparent in the "deportation" issue of 1945. In March of that year, Ottawa published plans for a "voluntary repatriation" of Japanese Canadians to Japan. Those signing to go would have ample financial assistance from the government. No provisions were made for assisting people who preferred to go east, but couldn't for various reasons.

Every one of us sixteen and over received a letter from Ottawa, concluding with the paragraph:

> This assured assistance from the government as outlined . . . will mean to many who desire repatriation, relief from unnecessary anxiety and it will enable them to plan for their future, and that of their children, along economic, social, and cultural lines which they fear may be denied them were they to remain in Canada.

As for those who wished to remain in Canada:

> Failure to accept employment east of the Rockies may be regarded at a later date as lack of co-operation with the Canadian Government in carrying out its policy.

While the first quotation mocked at our desperate faith in our native land, the second one brewed new fears among a people already suffering from the stresses and strains of evacuation, family break-ups, losses in income and property. This particular sentence sounded like a threat, and it, coupled with the presence of RCMP walking up and down the ghost towns' streets before and during the registration of intention, seemed like the sword of Damocles hung over the heads of a harried people. Many signed the "repatriation" papers, only to regret it afterwards. But to those who signed unwillingly, the officials gave assurance that they could cancel their signatures any time by writing to the proper authorities. Meanwhile, having signed, they could still enjoy the hospitality of the ghost towns, and the uncertain security of that sequestered life.

However, when Ottawa moved to deport those who signed, a great outcry rose from all quarters of the country, an outcry strong enough to question the actions of the government through the legal courts. The following are some news headlines:

VARSITY STUDENTS OPPOSE JAPANESE CANADIAN DEPORTATION.
VETO DEPORTATION, ROEBUCK URGES CABINET.
WOMEN OPPOSE DEPORTING CANADIAN-BORN JAPANESE.
RACE DISPUTES PLAY GAME OF NAZIS, SCIENTIST CLAIMS.

These were but the titles of reports from many sections of the nation decrying the proposed deportation of some 10,000 Japanese Canadians whose only crime was their ancestry, for Ottawa had stated through its officials that our record was clear.

The Supreme Court of Canada upheld the orders-in-council for deportation, but qualified the judgment by excluding from deportable status the wives and children of deportable men. This qualification didn't help much, for what could the wives or children do but follow their husbands and fathers? An appeal carried to the Privy Council in London only confirmed the government's power to do what it liked with its citizens under the War Measures Act. Though legally Ottawa had the power to deport the males who had signed the "papers," this proceeding was halted by the public outcry, and the orders were cancelled. Only those Japanese still wishing to go to Japan were enabled to do so with some assistance.

As I look back on these happenings and compare the Canadian scene with the American, I see why more and more Canadians are demanding a Bill of Rights for Canada. In the U.S., from January 2,

259

1945, citizens of Japanese race were freed from all federal or army supervision, allowed to go back to their coastal homes, and assisted to relocate wherever else they chose to go, with Dillon S. Myer and Harold Ickes going to bat for the evacuees' rights. The American Constitution supported the rights and privileges of the citizens of Japanese blood, their government spent about 500 million dollars on the whole evacuation (removal, administration, food, shelter, welfare, education, medicine, resettling, etc.) and Congress passed a wide Claims Bill for losses *rising out of the evacuation.*

I thought, too, of Mike Masaoka, that impassioned young lobbyist for the Japanese American Citizens' League, with his Anti-Discrimination Committee offices in Washington, D.C. He had come to Toronto to advise the Canadian Nisei on forming a similar national organization in Canada.[16] He had said:

> Many of us Nisei in the States, who took on the thankless task of leading our people into the camps and out again back into civilian life, did so only because we knew that someone had to do it. Some of us were beaten up by our own people, but that didn't stop us from fighting for our rights as American citizens!

Mike, incidentally, was called "Moses" for his efforts. He was one of the first to enlist; his younger brother was killed in Italy, and another brother is crippled for life from wounds received overseas.

In Toronto and elsewhere, wherever the evacuees had settled, heated discussions were held about our specific trials and tribulations. Our lost homes and businesses in the west were a sore point with all of us who had lost them.

The S. . .'s, who used to be neighbours in Vancouver, and by an odd coincidence are our neighbours again in Toronto, told me of their particular losses. Mr. S. had worked hard for years to own his own lumber camp. He was just about to make his last payment on the loans that enabled him to run a logging camp, and soon he could call it his own business. War came, and he was arrested and interned. There were no charges against him, and for over a year he was separated from his wife and family, his business frozen and taken

---

[16]The national organization formed in September 1947 as the National Japanese Canadian Citizens' Association (NJCCA).

over by the Custodian of Enemy Alien Property. Though he was released from internment, he had lost his lifetime's work. His daughter tried to salvage some office equipment, but could get nothing except a decrepit old typewriter. The mother mourned to me: "All that scrimping and saving for nothing!" They have rebuilt a new life here, but can you blame the man when he wants the government to honour his loss claims in full?

Mr. S. isn't the only one who lost home and property, the work and accumulation of years of hard work. Most of us lost both home and possessions, not only through the Custodian's office, but through the hasty selling to bargain hunters that haunted us as we began the long trek eastward. There was a time limit to our stay in B.C. We had RCMP orders giving us the date by which we must leave our homes, or be arrested, if we failed to do so.

Who could forget that dismantled home, with the remains of possessions packed in "Imperial Ice Cream Cones" cartons, tied with manila rope, and ticketed for "Toronto." Who could forget the last tryst with the empty shell of a home standing dark and bereft against the outline of mountains in the distance across the inlet? Or the trailing roses that would burst into pink and scarlet glory in June, roses planted with loving care from slips of a parent vine? Or all the familiar things about a modest home? What can we itemize on a legal loss claim form, except the bare dollars and cents that represent only the real estate, the furniture that was lost?

After arduous campaigning by the Co-operative Committee on Japanese Canadians, a Loss Claims Commission was set up, under Justice Bird, which will investigate losses sustained on property vested in the Custodian. The terms of reference are much more limited than those for the Claims Commission proposed for the American evacuee losses. There, investigation will be made into *all* losses suffered on account of the removal.

The thing about these losses is that they weren't the legitimate losses due to war. We could have stood damages and losses that were honourable, losses shared with our fellow Canadians. But marked out and practically looted as we were . . . well, it's been a smelly business. Some day, the whole story of the evacuation will be told in a manner impossible in a short article.

•

261

Back in prewar days, the Nisei were vaguely aware of the terrible colour prejudices that wracked the world, but we were too concerned with our own troubles to cast more than a cursory glance on the artificially imposed inferiority of those races that are not Caucasian. Today, through eyes still fresh with the images of our own suffering, we see with astonishment that what happened to us was bad enough, but it wasn't anything like what had happened to the Jews in Europe, the Negroes in the United States, in Africa and in Australia, the Indians both East and West, the Chinese, the Indonesians, and other coloured people throughout the world.

Still, the lesser degree of our suffering hadn't justified it in any way at all. Rather, it was a symptom of a disease that endangered every citizen of Canada and the United States. There was too much stupid prejudice everywhere . . . prejudice against race, against religion, against politics. Prejudice was not so much a superiority, with the privilege of looking down on someone or something else, but an inability to look up and around with a smile.

That's why the Nisei who had worked with the many co-operative committees to help their people now stress the need to work with other minorities across the country, to try and help solve jointly the ills that beset us. What happens to the Indians in Kashmir, the Negroes in Georgia, the Jews and Arabs in Palestine, concerns us as much as the troubles in our own Canada concerning her minorities, whether these be racial, economic, religious or what-have-you.

One of the amazing paradoxes of the status of the Japanese Canadian is illumined by several incidents that happened to Nisei in the east.

A young man, fresh from B.C., looked for a room in Toronto. He tried a few houses that had a vacancy sign in the window. At one such place, to forestall embarrassing questions he took the initiative and told the landlady: "I'm a Japanese Canadian, evacuated from the coast, and I'm looking for a room." The lady looked doubtfully at him (this being in 1942), but she said, grudgingly, as she let him in: "I suppose it's all right, so long as you ain't Chinese."

The same thing happened in the public amusement places. A Nisei wishing to enter a dance hall with friends was told curtly: "We don't allow Chinese in here." The Nisei objected that he wasn't Chinese but was Japanese Canadian. Much to his surprise, he was allowed to buy a ticket and enter.

This pattern was repeated many times in only slightly differing circumstances. While Negroes, born in Canada, and under no legal restrictions such as hampered us, could not get into hospitals as nurses-in-training, the young Japanese women were allowed to become "probies," and eventually to get their R.N.'s. There was a Nisei miss as a senior nurse at the Toronto Western; there was one on duty at the Sick Children's Hospital. And a young Nisei woman, our first woman doctor, became a senior intern at the Women's College Hospital.

Of course we met many rebuffs and heard some strange rumours during those first months in the east. A close friend of mine had found a temporary home in a Caucasian home. The neighbours of this good landlady asked with much concern over the advisability of letting rooms to "the awful Japs": "I hear they have six toes, and aren't you afraid you'll get stabbed in the back one night?" Trying to find a house, too, had its handicaps. The owners of the prospective homes wanted to know: "Are you a Chinese or a Japanese?" If we had been Chinese, we might have been refused too, if some of the above instances of prejudices were general. Often as not, the owner would say he himself had no prejudices, but his neighbours might. Many an option on a house was lost through our being Japanese, but then we met many a citizen who was more than friendly. Many a hesitant owner or employer put the burden of his decision on the possible attitude of his neighbours, or of his Caucasian employees, even when no such prejudice existed in actual fact.

Just to show how strange and incredible neighbourhood gossip can be, let me tell about a suspicious neighbour to a new Japanese tenant of a suburban home. In this particular house, the furnace was all shot, the draught not pulling right in the chimney, the plumbing had to be fixed, and the unpacked parcels of goods strewed the basement floor. From what flimsy evidence spy stories are built up! In this newly acquired home, the young tenants were banging away on the water pipes, on the furnace pipes, changing washers, elbows and what-not, shovelling coal out of the way, yelling over the noise to each other:

"Get me that screwdriver, willya?"
"Where is it?"
"Why the blankety-blank-blank don't you take the box out
of the way of the stairs!"

263

Etc. . . . etc. . . . just an ordinary settling down into new quarters, but it was transformed throughout the neighbourhood, as witness this account: "Them Japs next door make a helluva lot of noise in the basement, and there's a lot of them down there talking. Could be they're making bombs and having secret conferences." A bulky parcel of sandwiches and a thermos was likewise transformed into a "time-bomb." Happily, the new tenants were unaware of all the surmises that flew around the block until three years later, when through new friendships formed on the block with practically all the other inhabitants of all the other houses, both former resident and new tenant could laugh over the first suspicions. Nevertheless, the evacuees made the best of the situation and, as usual, improved on it.

Back in B.C., the narrow community life of Orientals was due to segregation socially and discrimination economically. So many avenues of livelihoods were closed to them that they were in a distinct danger of becoming a mass of unskilled labour. The hopeless ones would argue: "What's the use of education or training. You can't get a decent job here. No matter what degree you get at a university you'd still have to work in a sawmill, or a garden, or any old dirty job that the Occidentals don't want." But the enterprising ones would retort: "What's keeping you in B.C.? Why don't you go to Ontario or someplace else? I'm leaving this dump as soon as I can. What's the good of scenery and nice weather, if you have to starve in it? Sure, B.C. is the land of opportunities for everyone . . . except us."

It was easy to talk, but not so easy to do. Many a Nisei longing to leave the west for the freer air east of the Rockies could not do so, for family reasons. The traditional ties of family obligations (and some of them are very good indeed, for they kept many an indigent Japanese *off* the relief rolls) kept them in B.C. The lucky ones did manage to leave, and their record is very impressive.

One of the first to leave the coast (only in this case the whole family moved with him) was young Sam Hayakawa, who went to Winnipeg first, then to Montreal, and thence south to the U.S. He has a Ph.D. in literature, and at present lectures at the Armour Institute in Chicago. He is well known for his articles in various magazines and has written a Book-of-the-Month choice, a book on semantics, *Language in Action*.

An even more outstanding Nisei to leave the west coast was young Shuichi Kusaka, winner of the Governor-General's Gold Medal in

1937, and recipient of a scholarship to M.I.T. (Massachusetts Institute of Technology). He spent the next decade getting his M.A., his Ph.D. in physics, with one scholarship after another, studying under Dr. Oppenheimer in California, doing research work at the Advanced Institute at Princeton, where Albert Einstein works, and then teaching physics at Smith College in Northampton, Massachusetts. He enlisted as a buck private in the American Army, was posted at the Proving Ground in Maryland, and won his American citizenship. Finally, he was appointed to the staff at Princeton University, where he continued with his research in nuclear physics, being considered an international authority on cosmic rays. But young Dr. Kusaka, brilliant scientist, was accidentally drowned late this summer [1947], thus cutting short the promise of a Nobel Prize winner.

Not every Nisei who left B.C. attained the fame of these two young men, but the others who left the coast had more opportunities to develop their talents than they would have had in B.C. And just as true, not every gifted Nisei could leave B.C. and therefore seemed doomed to frustration because they were Oriental in race—not only Oriental, but during the war years, having the additional handicap of being of the Japanese race.

Though the majority of the young men came east via the road camps and farm services, and the young women had come out to domestic service, it wasn't long before they took the initiative and hunted for jobs in more congenial lines. With or without (and generally without) the help of the placement officer (an official appointed by the government to supervise the comings and goings of the evacuees in certain districts), these Nisei found jobs wherever their special talents were needed.

Back in the fall of 1942, a young physicist, down on the farms in Essex County, decided he had enough of farms and would try his luck in the city where his gifts could be put to more constructive use. He tried to leave the farms, and was all but forced to stay there, but by dint of arguing and getting the help of loyal friends in the city, he managed to get away from the long rows of tomatoes destined for the cannery. Once in the city, he spurned such jobs as bottle-washing and the like, which were the only sort of jobs on file with the placement officer. He began, instead of depending on that official to find an opening for him, to look around for himself, and finally found a place where precision instruments for the navy were being assembled. From there he went on to better jobs until today,

265

he is lecturing at the Ajax extension of the University of Toronto while at the same time studying for his higher degrees.

Other young Nisei followed suit in looking for their own jobs instead of asking the Placement Officer to find a job for them. These young people, male and female, soon found out that energy and initiative brought their rewards of congenial, well-paid jobs, in firms, offices, and shops, where prejudice was conspicuous for its absence.

An interesting angle to this job-hunting was the wave of independence that swept the Nisei women out of their prewar reticences (some would call it sheer backwardness) into a variety of jobs. Back in B.C. there used to be lively arguments about women's place in the world and in the home, with the balance favouring the Hitlerian slogan of "children, church, and kitchen." And because the women themselves saw no opportunities then for anything else, they frowned on the enterprising female who wanted a career and independence.

That attitude has gone the way of past fashions . . . into limbo. Slowly but surely, the Nisei women are emerging from the custom-bound past and catching up with their Caucasian sisters. A sociologist once said that the women of today were twenty years behind the times, and that the Japanese women were twenty years behind that again. The change hasn't come about without many tears and recriminations.

The old-fashioned mothers wailed that the marriageable values of their daughters were lowered by their being too well educated, too independent in having professions and trades and skills that sometimes surpass the earning power of the men. These daughters, who once would have sighed and stayed at home because there was no other place to go to in B.C., now give their mothers fat shares in the weekly paycheque to make up for the loss of marriageable values, if such values were very valid in this country.

Today, there are Nisei women who are fashion illustrators, fashion designers, expert tailors and dressmakers. They have gone in for ceramics, for political science, for art, optometry, biology, chemistry, soda-jerking; they've increased the numbers studying nursing, become efficient secretaries, clerks, machine operators; they take up social service, campus editing, salesmanship with ease; they plan to become doctors, dentists, teachers. So far, I haven't come across a candidate for engineering, or law, or for the ministry from among the women, but probably they will appear in good time.

Some of the Nisei males are worried about the progress of the traditionally inferior females, and make scathing remarks concerning the loss of delightful femininity, the illusions so dear to men of the frailty of women. I suppose the men do miss the old-time all-enduring, silently suffering, humbly deferential and usually neurotic woman who was too often quite capable of a last stand by committing suicide, thereby ending her intolerable position, especially if she happened to be superior in intelligence to the male and was forced to remain undeveloped and frustrated.

However, the intelligent Nisei men welcome the advance made by their contemporary women friends, and contrary to parental fears, the marriage value of these young women has gone up. There is much less one-sided servility and more companionship in Nisei marriages.

The Nisei men are also doing fairly well, despite having started from practically nothing on their arrival in the east. One young chap is making quite a name for himself as the president of a firm making all manner of consumer goods, beginning with a record player. He started with nothing but his own ambitions and ingenuity, plus a lot of get-up-and-git. Others have gone in for art, photography, machine-shops, accounting, mechanics, contracting, selling, manufacturing, servicing, clerking, engineering, science, economics, politics, law, dentistry, medicine, social science, journalism, cooking, teaching . . . etc. etc. One young man, last reported in Winnipeg, has even gone in for that peculiar trade of panhandling, hitherto unknown to us.

One well-meaning person summed up our situation with the remark: "Well . . . the evacuation was a good thing after all, wasn't it?"

But was it? Is anything that is fundamentally wrong ever good? No, the evacuation was *not* a good thing; it was the undefeated spirit of the evacuees that was good. They turned a misfortune that was embittering into the incentive for progress.

Would we all rush back to B.C. once the last restrictions are lifted? Would we go back to a province still denying its Japanese Canadians their citizenship rights and privileges? After we have enjoyed those rights in the east, whatever our private opinions and comparisons on the climate? The opinions freely expressed run from an outright "No sir! I wouldn't go to B.C. again for anything!" to "It might be nice to see the place again, but I don't think I'd stay very long." And there are the few who wish to go back, *but only after all restrictions have been lifted*, and the franchise granted, and opportunities equal, and discriminations banned.

Seventeen years ago, in 1930, the Canadian Nisei were a fairly idealistic group, just beginning to explore their consciousness of being Canadians. In 1947 we are more sceptical, sometimes cynical, especially of fine-sounding slogans and catch phrases. We prefer actions to words, spend less time arguing, and more time doing.

We look at the coming generation of younger Nisei, who were too young to know much of our background prior to 1941, and who won't be going to B.C. to live with the past again. There is the third generation outgrowing their cribs and prams. They're born easterners. What we do now will affect the lives of these children. What we do now must be done with wisdom and foresight. Education and training they must have, naturally, so that they will have a better chance of getting economic security. Culture they'll get from their environment, according to their inner selves. And faith.

But shall they also need special training to bear the intolerable burdens of race prejudice in their future, as we had to endure yesteryear?

The Problem of the Japanese in Canada
(June 1948)

I am very glad to be here this morning to speak a little on "The Problem of Japanese Canadian citizens in Canada." I was born in Vancouver, and am therefore a Native Daughter of B.C. I speak to you, then, not only as a Japanese Canadian, but as a Canadian woman.

In my remarks I shall not dwell on statistics, or exact documents, which, if you desire them, can be obtained upon request. I shall also refrain from giving you details of our specific hurts and losses, for these are but the instances of a pervasive evil, and are necessary only when we examine them for a particular purpose, such as for our claims for material losses sustained through evacuation. I shall confine myself to the overall picture of race discrimination. As a member of a minority race, I cannot plead for my people without pleading the cause of all who have experienced this discrimination.

That 21,000 Japanese Canadians were displaced persons within their own country is now an unfortunate page in Canadian history. The evacuation of these citizens from the coast of British Columbia, the sudden upset in their lives, marked a distinct cleavage between the dark past of discrimination and a possible future of race equality not only for my people, but for you all. This forced removal of a racial minority from their homes and birthplaces was the proof positive that a vociferous group of race-baiters can upset the just balance of a normally sane people. It has happened in other countries than this. It must never happen again.

It is the sort of history from which we must learn a severe lesson in racial equality which stems not so much from legal condemnation of discrimination, though that helps, but from the genuine goodness which is in every man—but which must be encouraged to positive action. At this time it is not for me to say whether Canada should outlaw race discrimination or not, for that is another topic from the one I am asked to present to you here. I merely ask you to view the rest of my remarks in the light of this preamble:

1. That Canadian citizens were displaced within the borders of their native land;

2. That innocent people were stigmatized as dangerous saboteurs;

3. That unreasoning fear makes cowards of us all;

4. That the guilt for any injustice lies on the head of every one of us, and not only on that of the most violent racist.

Therefore if we, as Canadian women, are to search for and cure the source of this evil, we must know facts, not rumours; we must use our common sense and intelligence, and not rely on our prejudices to help solve this problem . . . this problem of racial discrimination in Canada, and throughout the world.

Canada, as well as the United States, is made up of a multitude of races from many lands. We have the native Indians, descendants of the original North Americans who were here to greet Cartier and Columbus. There are the many European races including the Celt, the Scot, the Briton; there are the Negroes and other Africans, Orientals and other Asiatics, South Americans, Polynesians and others. All these people of many shapes, sizes and colours, are now Canadians in nationality, for as the late Mr. Roosevelt said: "Americanism [or Canadianism] is a matter of the mind and heart and not of race or ancestry."

That is how the Japanese Canadians felt in 1939, when war brought nationalism to the foreground of our thoughts. Since then, for seven years we have taken the distrust and suspicion turned against us: from the time our volunteers were rejected from the Canadian Army because of their racial ancestry, through the confusion and hysteria of the evacuation, until today, three years after the war's end, when we are still officially forbidden the complete enjoyment of the prerogatives of our citizenship. For fifty years previous to these seven, we were regarded as aliens, undesirable as ranking citizens, but very convenient as a source of cheap labour. A hangover from this past remains today in B.C., where only those of the Japanese race are denied the franchise.[17]

The majority of my people are glad to be out of B.C., and not even the tourist climate can lure them back to the scenes of their humiliation. Still, the fact that we are glad to be out of B.C. does not excuse the evacuation in any way. Let us say, instead, that now the thing is done, now there is no way back to those former times. And now that most of our bitterness (for a while it was bad!) has thinned out, we can look on our displacement more objectively, and make the most of our present circumstance. However, whether we wish to live in B.C. or not, we should be able to travel there as freely as anyone else not of our race. There are places back home which are dear to us through some happy memory. There are graves and friends and scenes we would like to visit again, for the west coast was our home for fifty years.

The present government in Ottawa, for no valid reason, has extended for another year the Orders-in-Council forbidding any of our people to go to B.C. without a police permit . . . I emphasize: *a police permit.* Another Order forbids the issuance of commercial fishing licences, even to a veteran of this war, if he is of the Japanese race.[18] He cannot even ship aboard a fishing vessel. This ban is another hangover from the bogey stories of "spies" in the fishing fleet. There may have been spies . . . I don't deny the possibility . . . but surely

---

[17]When Canadians of Chinese and East Indian ancestry were given the vote in B.C. in April 1947, Japanese Canadians were excluded. They had to wait until March 1949 to receive the provincial vote. Vancouver City Council permitted the vote to all Asian citizens in January 1949.

[18]In March 1948, the government received approval to continue some 27 wartime orders relating to Japanese Canadians, and these included Order-in-Council P.C. 251 of January 13, 1942 and Order-in-Council P.C. 946 of February 5, 1942. The first prohibited fishing licences to be given to Japanese Canadians and the latter gave the Minister of Labour power to control the movements of Japanese Canadians.

they were the responsibility of the proper authorities. Their crimes need not have been saddled on the rest of the fishermen of the same race, thence to the rest of the 23,000 Japanese Canadians.

These are the two immediate problems that face the Japanese Canadian today: the travel restrictions and the denial of fishing licences. Our material losses, such as can be inventoried on a dollars-and-cents list, are now before a Claims Commission, whose terms of reference are still so narrow as to exclude many legitimate losses caused by the evacuation.

You might say of the extensions of these restrictions: what of it? Even if they were removed today, how many would actually buy CPR or CNR tickets to take the train back to B.C. at once? Very few. You might ask: what hurt is the fishing licence ban? After all, it affects only a handful of people, and surely these people are earning their livelihood in some other line today. Why the fuss?

Let us make a comparison.

Suppose a similar tragedy happened to Englishmen: for some reason or other, London thought it best, for the sake of the victims and for the country (of course!), that all the brunettes of a certain shire should be ordered out of England to any of the Dominions, and told not to come back on pain of arrest, but when conditions became favourable a certain percentage of them "might" be allowed to return. To continue the parable: these dark-haired Englishmen are the bane of the blondes who insist on the perfect Anglo-Saxon colouring for the natives, and are afraid that if something isn't done the blonde Anglo-Saxon type will become extinct. Besides, the blondes insist that the brunettes are marrying off the choicest blondes, and that this sort of competition is highly unfair to blondes who simply cannot look as darkly romantic as the brunettes. Therefore, the brunettes are undercutting the sex appeal of light-haired types. Well, the dark-haired Englishmen are outraged; they protest the absurdities of the discrimination. What's the use? London calls in the Metropolitan Police and Scotland Yard to implement their government's orders. The brunettes feel like fighting . . . but the government assures them that such an attitude, while understandable, would cause civil war, and surely the brunettes were loyal enough to abide by orders for the time being, until the blondes had cooled off a bit. So the brunettes shrug. They co-operate as best they can. Besides, they had always wanted to travel anyway, even on a police order.

The years pass, and the emigrants make a new start in many places in the other Dominions and decide to stay there. Still, it would be nice if they could see the old country again, even if they have to see the blondes too. But the blondes [in London] won't have it. They don't want to see a brunette again in that shire, not for a long time, if ever, because they must keep it for blondes only. The Dominions are large places. The emigrants are settled fairly well. Maybe the evacuation was a good thing after all. At least it keeps the blondes quiet in that shire . . . and what a fuss they can raise on this issue! London is sensitive about the votes commanded by the blondes. Let the ban on brunettes stay for another term! Something might turn up by then.

The comparison is silly, isn't it? But it is a reasonable facsimile of what happened in Canada, aside from the significant violation of democratic principles.

Once in twelfth-century England, the barons thought King John was abusing his kingly powers. The Magna Carta resulted. Later centuries saw the rise of such men as Eliot, Pym and Hampden in England, Thomas Paine in America, Voltaire and Rousseau in France, and Gandhi and Nehru in India. The people come into their own with the right to question the abuses of power committed by their rulers. Today the pendulum of liberty seems to be swinging back as people let go their hard-won prerogatives, having taken them too much for granted.

We, the people, are too apt to stay in our comfortable, our safe shells, no matter what is happening to the other person, as long as our own sight and sensitivity are not brutally assaulted. We feel badly, of course, when we hear of wrongs committed, injustices inflicted, but since we do nothing more than talk about it, we allow the evil to exist.

Therefore, I repeat again and again: racial discrimination of any kind in Canada, whether it be against the Japanese, the Negro, the Jew, the Chinese, Indian or anyone else, affects not only the victims but the aggressors as well. While the victims become highly sensitized, while their perceptions become keener, their reflexes faster, their characteristics more and more pronounced, the aggressors become hardened to brutalities, which in turn brutalize their finer sensitivities. They become so accustomed to lethargy that they do not wake to their serious responsibilities as citizens until it is too late, and by then they have lost the liberty gained by the blood of their ancestors.

At no time in our history was this fact as apparent as it is today.

At no time in our history is the united strength of women so necessary to preserve the peace of this world, so that we may not again be witnesses to the bloody tragedy of war. In our hands lies a terrible power either to do good or allow evil. A short time ago women were not allowed to take an active part in the life of their nation. They were cloistered within their kitchens, parlours and bedrooms, veiled in ignorance. Now we must be the power for good (not the source or the channel for intrigue) *behind* our men, *with* our men. To get a good government tomorrow, we must train to-day the children who will be the future rulers.

The Local Council of Women have as their motto: "Do unto others as ye would that they should do unto you."

If you would have a better world, you cannot start early enough to train the children from their cradle toward a constructive good, not only your own children, but all children, toward that rich cultivation of mind and heart and body, so that we may be spared the ugliness of children aping the contemptuous malice of their elders. It is no joke to hear a 6-year-old call the junk-collector "that sheenie man." We must not call close-dealing "Jewing." If my son, at four years of age, wept bitterly at being called "a dirty Chink," then he must not call a Negro baby "little nigger! little nigger!!" Children must learn new words for "eenie-meenie-miny-mo," and adults must look for another expression than "nigger in the woodpile." Children must not grow up to regard the Indians as a degraded race, but must see them as the victims of exploitation. Every Oriental is not the sinister character depicted in movies, radio scripts, stories and the comics. In all phases of our daily life there are these poisonous racial barbs. They must be uprooted.

If we are to save our future generations from making the mistakes of today, we must first train the children, then mould the community attitudes, then influence legislation to prevent the recurrence of the tragedies stemming from racial hatreds. To so act, women must first know and understand the problems that exist within and without our homes. We must find out for ourselves, and not depend on hearsay. We must take an intelligent stand, without emotionalism, in accepting people of varied races as equals, whether we like them as persons or not. We need not feel obliged to marry each other as the corollary of acceptance. Marriage, our private life, our person-to-person likes and dislikes should not affect the larger issue of racial equality.

The minorities do not seek patronage or tolerance. Both are gratuitous charities. As Thomas Paine wrote a hundred and fifty years ago: "Toleration is not the opposite of intoleration, but is the counterfeit of it. Both are despotisms. The one assumes to itself the right of withholding . . . the other of *granting* . . . ."

The minorities desire not patronage (though kindly meant), not tolerance (which rises from the conceit of superiority), but acceptance as people, in spite of any and all faults.

Looking Back
(Manuscript, c. 1945)

It is now three years since Pearl Harbor, and that tragic event seems as far away from my present life as is Japan, the country that fired the fuse that led me and all the rest of the North American Japanese away, hundreds of miles inland from the salt-sea coasts. Looking back over the years that led up to all this, my mind registers kaleidoscopic pictures, all aslant and mingling one with the other, jumbling movement and sound with the flash of accompanying thoughts. When I try to concentrate on one picture at a time, the very trial brings out a host of other pictures woven into a piece by the same cord of time and place. To sort out these pictures, to put them in their chronological order and sequence, to explain how each one is related to the other, twined and intertwined through events and personal ties, is a dizzy, back-breaking job, made all the more difficult by the incompleteness of memory, the blanked out portions that I never saw but only heard about, the other blurred visions that must be guessed at and filled in with only the outline of the facts. The story of these pictures is one that has filled my heart and mind for many years, and now finds expression with what amateur skill I have.

I would pick, as my first picture, that of my mother bending over her sewing machine, the needle whirring over the cotton work gloves she made to sell that we might eat. Sometimes she paused in the monotonous work to tell us a tale of bygone days, of days when she was a young girl, just come to Canada from a growing railway town in Japan. She would pause, her thin hands still taut on the fabric beneath the needle, to raise her pointed face to us who were all

274

around her at the big table where we turned the gloves as fast as she made them. She would look inward to her past, and a ghost of a smile would light her soft brown eyes at unseen images reflected within. We always waited, our fingers still busy, turning out the cloth fingers right side out, pressing them into flatness, pairing a glove with its mate, and piling them with eleven other pairs to make a dozen that would be secured with a string. We waited, our hearts turned to her eagerly, our ears purposely deaf to the shouts of other children outside, playing and running around freely while we worked with Mother. Then gently, not breaking the steady rhythm we made, she would begin, her dry and cracked lips forming words of gentility and refinement for the many tales that beguiled away the weary hours. Our young hearts beat with a fierce pride in her and a passionate affection that roused our defiant protectiveness toward her. She was our mother, our sole support for food, clothes, shelter, and morale; hooligans that we may have been in those awful days, we recognized the innate breeding in her fine bones, felt in our own marrow some part of her indomitable spirit, and dreamed of the day when we would clothe her in velvet, rest her on cushions while hired minions served her delicious foods. Once she got in one of those precious and peaceful interludes between one dozen and another of those gloves, she would tell this story:

"When Mother first came to this country, and everything was strange, your grandfather would tease me about many things. He was a fine man, your grandfather, and a pity he was not related to you by blood, for he was only the stepfather of your father.[19] Now, in Japan, where I used to live, there are no toilets like the ones here that flush when you press down a handle, or pull on a chain, so of course I did not know what they were for. Well, on the first day I came to this city, I almost washed my face in it."

We chuckled in delight and appreciation, for this was a twice-told tale, and though we knew as well as Mother did, it always made us laugh, and in laughing we left our cramped, undernourished bodies, and dwelt again in the past with Mother. My littlest brother would ask, as he manfully strove to emulate his older brother in speed and neatness, with his preternaturally solemn face:

---

[19]Muriel's stepgrandfather is Kisuke Mikuni who made a considerable sum of money by getting the contract to supply gravel and boulders for the CPR dock in Vancouver. He married Muriel's grandmother Sano Fujiwara in 1904. Their photo accompanies an outline of Mikuni's achievements in Toyo Takata's *Nikkei Legacy*, pp. 78-79.

"Why . . .?"

"Silly!" my sister would cry out in superior disdain, ". . . because she said that was where she was to wash her face, of course!"

"Y'mean, that's what Grandpa told her," interposed the older boy, not for a moment stopping his task of separating and turning and sorting the five-or-six dozen unturned gloves piled before him.

Mother listened without interrupting, the faint smile still on her face, and I would look at her, projecting myself with her in that incident, forgetting the glove still clumsy in my hand.

Grandpa was such a nice man, with a kind twinkle in his eyes. He must have taken one look at the lovely aristocratic young bride and recognized a kindred spirit, yet his natural impishness could not forbear playing a joke on her. She was dusty from travel over dirt roads in a horse-drawn buggy. He could see her struggling with her shyness as she hesitated to ask for something. Finally, blushing as she did so, she asked him:

"The place where one washes . . . where is it, please?"

Grandpa must have measured her with his eyes peering over his glasses, his face friendly and quizzical, as he answered slowly: "Upstairs down the long hall, turn to the left, there is a small room, which has a large porcelain bowl wherein the water runs at the pull of the long chain."

She looked up at him receptively, acknowledging his silently offered friendship just as silently, as she bowed her thanks and departed towards the stairs with a light tread. Grandpa stroked his long moustache, beginning to grin, when a sudden compunction sobered him, as he thought of the guileless smile she had given him. He could hear her footsteps going towards the left, and a little reluctantly he hurried upstairs too. He caught her just as she bent down her face and hands over the bowl.

"It was a joke . . . I didn't mean . . . I realize you wouldn't know the difference and that's why . . . but my apologies."

The young bride turned around in surprise, looking at him slightly perspiring there in the hallway. She could not understand.

"But . . .," she stammered, " . . . there is water in this white bowl."

"Yes . . . yes . . . I know, but that is not the one. I mean, that is the . . . well . . . you don't wash there. Here! come this way. The bathroom is the next room. Come here and I will show you. See? This is the hot water tap and this is the cold water, and that is the

276

bathtub, and here are some towels, and this is the soap, and you lock the door this way."

"But, Honoured Father, what then is that next door?"

"That, my new daughter, is the . . ." but a sudden gust of chuckles choked him, and he shouted to a completely bewildered girl: ". . . Hell! that's the toilet!"

After we shook with laughter at the joke on Mother, we went to work with renewed vigour.

How often that scene recurs, again and again in my memory, each time with the same beginning, but sometimes with a different story. After a little while, one of us would ask:

"O-kah-san . . . Mother . . . how old were you when you first came here?"

"Seventeen, as you count years in this country." Mother did not look up from her work, but added gently: "Why?"

"Just wanted to know . . ."

Seventeen? We could not yet get the sense whether 'seventeen' was young or old or just right, because such an age seemed too far from our present reckoning of twelve years down to four years. However, that didn't bother us. Mother was seventeen when she came to B.C., and that was a million years ago so far as we were concerned.

Seventeen? I turned that over in my mind and without conscious effort, started counting up from twelve. Five more years! My goodness, only five more years! Why, I thought, I'd be seventeen in five more years! For goodness sake! I'd be grown up then! For a moment I was appalled to have my future suddenly staring me in the face! Would I be married, too, when I was seventeen? My mind instinctively recoiled at the possibility, and in sheer self-preservation I shoved that spectre away from me.

But I could not get away from the subject and I had to ask: "Mother, why did you marry at seventeen?"

Mother stopped for a moment to remember why. The memories came to cast a shadow on her face, and I waited tensely for her reply. It came slowly, as if the words were picked with care in consideration for my tender years.

"In Japan, a girl is grown-up at seventeen, counting Japanese-style, which is really sixteen here. It is a disgrace to her family if she is not married by twenty at least."

"But, Mother, did your mother *make* you get married?"

277

"Well, I had very little to say about it, whether I would or not. Everything was arranged for me."

"Gosh!"

I thought in dismay about Prince Charming and the Sleeping Beauty, Robin Hood and Maid Marian, and Tom Mix and the beautiful girl he rescued. Oh gosh! Parents made you get married! Right there and then awoke in me a reflex against being forced to marry at seventeen.

My younger sister who was already clothes-conscious wanted to know: "Did you wear a wedding dress, Mother, and a white veil?"

"No, not the kind your auntie has on in her wedding picture. Mine was a black 'montsuki,'[20] the kind you see in those Japanese women's magazines, you know?"

"Uhuh! It's got all kinds of flowers and birds on it, all pretty colours . . . and did you wear that big white kind-of-a-hat too?"

"Oh yes, That's the 'tsunokakushi'."[21]

"What's that?" asked the youngest boy, intrigued at once by the odd name.

"It's a custom . . . the white cap is supposed to hide a woman's horns."

"Horns . . . oh Mother!" Unbelief in his voice.

"It's just a saying," laughed Mother, and did not explain further.

Only a saying. Well, that was a relief. It slipped from our minds at once. My sister continued in her queries: "Where is your wedding dress, now?"

"In Japan."

"Why?" asked the youngest, that being his favourite question.

"Yes why, Mother?" echoed Kiyo, adding, "why didn't you bring any Japanese-clothes with you when you came? You haven't got a thing."

"We-ell, I didn't think I would need them here. I was told clothes were different . . . and they are. You don't see anyone wearing 'kimono' and 'geta,'[22] do you?"

"No-o-o, but I wish you did bring them."

"Someday perhaps, Kiyo-chan, you can go to Japan and wear them too."

---

[20]The most formal Japanese kimono which was decorated with a family crest.
[21]Decorative cloth worn around the bride's hair.
[22]Japanese wooden slippers.

278

"Will I really go to Japan?"

"When you're grown up."

Kiyo mulled that one over in silence.

All of a sudden, Tomu who had not said a word for a long while exploded with: "Aw . . . who wants to go to Japan!"

Silently I agreed. That country seemed too formidable for me. Then my mind went off on another angle and I wanted to know: "Did you know Father before you married him?"

"No, Mother didn't know him at all, but I saw him once before the wedding."

"Golly, Mother, that's awful!"

"O but . . ." Mother said gaily, "it's vulgar to be friendly before you marry . . . like they do here in the movies. They don't do things that way in Japan. It's all very properly done, and a girl must be maidenly and refined."

The whole thing became too much for me. It was the unknown in too big a dose and I was overwhelmed. Above the blurred confusion in my mind I heard my name called: "Sue . . ." Mother was looking at me speculatively.

"Hai . . . yes?"

"This summer holiday, do you think you could work on a farm?"

I gazed at her, troubled at once at her tone. There seemed to be apology in it and a restraint that clutched at me. Work? On a farm? Peasant work? I? A chasm yawned around me now, and an unexpected burden seemed to be lowering itself on my back. In a flash I saw the long, heat-baked, endless rows of Chinese farms on the other side of the road. I saw the Chinese farmer in faded blue trousers, patched and worn, hoeing all day long. I saw him jogging between rows with that long pole braced on his shoulder and the two baskets hanging and bobbing up and down with every step he took. I saw his brown, shiny, sweat-streaked face, his leathery brown hands. I saw the pile of manure beside the shed, smelled it, and the heap of rotting leaves and discarded vegetables, and the dry dust rising in the sun's shimmering haze. I saw the Japanese women in khaki coveralls, floppy straw hats tied under the chin with thin towelling, their dirt-stained fingers showing through the holes purposely cut in the discarded lengths of winter stockings they used to cover their arms from the sun and mosquitoes. I saw them on their knees, weeding, or squatted between rows picking strawberries, or peas, or reaching up between the shaded dew-damp rows of raspberries, pole beans. I heard the early morning truck call around for the strawberry pickers, all chattering and calling loudly, shouting jokes and good-humoured insults to one another, clutching their lunch pails as they clambered into the open trucks. They would go miles out into the countryside and come back at night, their knees aching, their backs weary, their fingertips stained red . . . sweaty . . . dirty . . . but with the fruits of their labour for ten hours tucked into their socks. Some of the younger kids got only $2 while the oldsters got $3.50. Oh, I knew about, and accepted our poverty, just as I accepted the fact of Mother's working on those endless dozens of gloves, yet, till now, I had not consciously thought of ourselves as a compact family unit, isolated from the other people by our poverty, and the fact that this poverty was not our usual status, but was a temporary affair which would cease to be as soon as we were able to return to our rightful place in the world. Now I had to relate poverty to farm work. Now I had to orient myself among those khaki-clad people who were our present neighbours. I don't remember being aloof from them. I do remember *they* put us apart from the very first: first because we talked differently, then because we acted differently, lastly because we looked ahead differently. They seemed to *know*, as we *felt*, without once talking about it, that someday we would leave their neighbourhood for different fields.

My brothers and sister were staring at me as if I were alien now, and I felt a wild fear at the thought of separation. Mother was still waiting quietly for me to say something. How long had she waited? It was in another time. Poverty meant we needed money. Farm work, from what I gathered from the other girls I knew, might bring me $2 for every ten hours I laboured. $2 . . . $2 . . . that sum revolved around and around me . . . $2 . . . $2.

I sighed, and mumbled: "I don't know."

Mother turned back to her sewing for a moment without a word. She seemed to be hardening herself for some duty she hated. Then she sighed deeply . . . such a deep, tortured sigh that it cut through me as I waited for her to explain.

"This house is now poor. Your father is not here, won't be here for a long time. Mother must work to feed you. You must have books for school . . . and shoes. Always there is not enough money to go around. You cannot depend on your grandmother or her store. We must work together . . . work hard . . . if we are to get anywhere in this world. In Japan, in my family, your position would have been

280

assured . . . assured enough so that you could get your education and become part of the family pattern. Here we have no one to help us, and we must help ourselves. Until you are adult enough to go your own way I must help you, but as you know very well, my little is not enough for all. It would help such a great deal if you could earn enough just for your books for high school. This autumn you will enter high school. You will need much new books. You haven't got a winter coat this year. You need another pair of shoes. If you work two months . . . say 50 days, not counting Sundays, you might be able to get about $80 to $100. $80 is a lot of money. Of course *you* would get less than that this year because it is the first time for you, and the farmer might charge for your lunch."

I waited still, wondering what farm she had in mind.

"Mr. S. is willing to try you."

"Mr. S." I cried, "why, he is on Annacis Island!"

"Yes, you will have to get to the dykes by quarter to seven in the morning and he will come across in his gas boat for you."

I was horrified! Mr. S. . . . that miser, that skinflint, that awful cackling man who worried Mother for the rent to these three rooms in this ramshackle frame house that he called apartments! "Oh Mother . . ." I cried out in fear, "must I go there?"

"I know it is an unpleasant ordeal, Sue, but unfortunately he is our landlord, and you are so thin that other farmers might not like to hire you. They don't think you can stand the work."

However, the mind of a twelve-year-old is elastic, is resilient to changes, and now my thoughts and calculations turned to the $80. I did not even consider $100. It was not within the bounds of possibility. $80 could buy so many things! I made up my mind at once. "All right, I'll go, Mother. When is it to start?"

•

That first summer when I hoed weeds around dwarf beans and my hands blistered and my head ached with the hot sun's rays, when I lost hours of work because my nose bled, when I had no appetite for the coarse, poorly cooked lunch they served in the farmhouse whose kitchen had no floor but the mud caked hard and uneven, where the well-water stank, and we drank river water . . . that first summer introduced me to hard, back-breaking labour that was just a part of life to the people around us. To them it was summer, summer

281

meant profits, pin money for the winter. Incidentally, I earned about $30, deductions being made for meals, and work hours lost through this and that. I took $10 of that money and ignorant of relative and comparative prices, bought patent leather Hurlbert oxfords that cost me $5.75. Mother wept. I went without rubbers that winter, and the sleek lines of that pair of shoes became ragged all too soon from the rigours of walking four miles every day to and from school. That summer too, Tomu, who was nine, began to deliver papers, to chop and pile wood for the winter. When he was ten he was also to dig a patch of ground in the empty lot next door, to plant seeds for corn, for cucumbers, for carrots, for onions. He too began the pattern of work that slowly hardened him to any and all kinds of physical labour. In the years when we looked back to our days of poverty, loneliness, and being called 'stuck-ups' by our contemporaries, it seemed that only Tomu and I shared with mother the terrible need to earn money at the cost of playing time, of weary bodies strained to their limit, the fear of debts and the sudden need for doctors, the hidden but agonized dream of a shining goal. Some part of the carefree childishness shrivelled in us, and we never knew the protectiveness of a sheltered home life.

One of the chief joys of those hard years was to hear again and again the stories of Mother's childhood home, her parents, her brothers and sisters, the things they used to do, and the early days of her arrival in B.C. We loved hearing the stories about our grand-father who was a gentleman even though he gambled in the thousands of dollars, who owned lumber camps, rice mills, a big general store and contracted labour for the building of the railway, the wharves that even now remain, though few know about him now. We loved to hear the legends of old Japan, the tales of heroes and daring deeds. One of the odd angles about the interludes of story-telling was that we exchanged stories. Mother told us of Japan. We, that is, I told her about Robin Hood, about the legends of Asgard, King Arthur and the Round Table, Cinderella, Tom Thumb, Hansel and Gretel. One story in particular I remember telling mother was Daudet's Tartarin of Tarascon.[23]

I must have been about fourteen when I told that one. I had read about it in the *Book of Knowledge* and had loved it, so I went to the public library to borrow the book. How was I to know then that

---

[23]Alphonse Daudet (1840-1897) was a French novelist.

Daudet was a French writer who poked dry fun at people and things? What difference did it make anyway? I loved that story. I brought the book home, read it cover to cover, and one day when the sun shone softly outside and the yelling of the boys and girls was unbearable to us who longed to play but could not because we had to turn the gloves, we began telling stories as we worked. This was the usual thing, but this particular day, with the story of Tartarin fresh in my mind, I began to retell it, acting it out with a glove in one hand and a rounded stick in the other. This stick was used to push the fingers right side out.

"Listen everybody, I read a funny story. It was good!" I savoured for a delicious moment the chuckles that ran through the adventures of Tartarin. Mother looked up with a light in her eyes. She was always afraid for me, because she thought I read too much, that I would die young like her older sister. Tomu looked up too, expectantly, as did Kiyo and Jun. How dearly they loved a story!

Then I started: "Tartarin was the name of this French man and he was supposed to be brave and he went to hunt for a lion in Africa."

I talked in the mixture of English and Japanese which was our medium with Mother, though our English was idiomatic and unaccented in contrast to the speech of the kids in the neighbourhood. You see, up till then we had always lived among the 'hakujin' as we called the European races, and our English was natural to our tongues. Our Japanese, in the first years of our sojourn on that [Lulu] Island street, was clear Tokyo-ben, the refined language of the textbooks and polite society . . . which you could compare, I suppose, to Oxford English, the King's English. Later, out of sheer necessity, to keep from being called down as 'haikara'[24] and too good for the neighbourhood, we had to drop the refinements, the polite phrases, and learn the colloquialisms, the blunt and vulgar speech of what is known as the lower-class speech forms. Then later, when we tried to recapture the lost ways of speaking, we found we had lost them, and they came hard to our rough tongues.

I continued to tell the story.

It has always been one of my shining memories, for Mother laughed and laughed till her tears came. The others hung on every word I uttered, and they laughed and shouted with appreciation at the antics of the brave Tartarin, who came back from Africa to his home

---

[24]Haikara is Japanese for "too refined," literally "high collar."

village with the carcass of a lion. What villager cared to examine that animal to find that he was toothless, mangy, and so old he was easy prey to Tartarin? I aimed my stick as a man sights his rifle, and I puffed with pride when the villagers hailed me as a great hunter. Oh, I was Tartarin as I sat up on the big table, waving my stick and the unturned glove. My family was so absorbed in the story neither they nor I, for that matter, noticed I held but that one unfinished glove in my hands, while the sewing machine roared and the gloves piled in six separate piles. They never noticed, and I like to think that they never knew that they worked as I became a raconteur, my one unturned glove waving in my hand from start to finish of that story. I like to think that the story I told recompensed the fact that I did but that one glove, a half of a pair; that Mother laughing in hearty enjoyment made up for my neglect towards duty. Yes, that is one of my shining pictures of those years.

•

Once, back in the days when our daily food depended on the dozens of gloves Mother sewed, we had a piano. The neighbours said we were a crazy lot . . . having a piano when we were beggars! This piano, we found out later, was an old concert upright grand, built somewhere back in the 1890s, as the date on the inside testified. We got it for $300 second-hand, in the days when everything was very expensive. My uncle put up the money as a gift to me, and I loved that piano as I loved no other thing, and when I had to part with it later . . . oh much later . . . for $40, it hurt. This piano was a wonderful and huge affair, carved in the grand style and dwarfing everything else in the room. I have my suspicions that it was palmed off onto us because it was more or less a white elephant for the store, being so huge when the public demand was more toward apartment sizes in everything, pianos included. That piano was decadent aristocracy, once proudly a part of gilt and plush, but now reduced to the bare wall of a shabby, dusty, chilly room in a tumbledown building. But oh, how its tones rang through our childhood with richness and glory.

That piano was our dessert, it was our new dresses, it was the picnics and parties we never had. It was company, it was comfort, it was confidante, it was comrade. It was the outstanding thing that set us apart from our environment. It was of another world, a world of music, of art, of drama, a world where minds talked and hearts were enchanted and the earth was beautiful, as the day is beautiful when it is looked at by the soul, and not by the sightless eyes of noses too close to the ground.

That piano stayed with us through five years of a threadbare existence, through later years of plenty, right through to that fateful day of evacuation, when I realized bitterly that this huge piano could never come with me to any crowded ghost town, and that lack of means prevented me from storing it, that its gigantic size would never fit into any friendly house. There was only one thing to do, and that was to sell it, but buyers were scarce. Finally, a furniture company took it . . . for only $40. How I remember its scratched surface, the long gouge mark that my youngest brother left with a toy chisel, nicks here and there from toy saws, from nails, from boot kicks, a bubbly finish on one side where it stood too close to a heat register (yet there was simply nowhere else to stand it). It had weathered many times the rough handling of amateur movers. Its felt was moth-eaten, and in 18 years it had never been tuned because it had never gone out of tune, or if it did it was so slight no one ever noticed it in any of its resonant keys . . . keys slightly yellowed with age, and worn by the pounding of many fingers.

In the beginning it gave forth timid sounds, discordant, uncertain. In time the melody was smoother, if not more expert. At times it rang gloriously with Beethoven when a friend's trained hands met complete co-operation from the keys, and then that piano was fulfilled for a time. Yet the very next day loving but clumsy fingers coaxed the keys to sing, and I doubt not the piano was as happy with those stiff fingers as it ever was with the nimble ones. Why? The nimble ones condescended to decrepitude but the clumsy ones adored. I remember the times when Mother bent her aching back over the keyboard and picked out with her forefinger the tunes of hymns she loved best: "What A Friend We Have In Jesus" . . . "Peace, Perfect Peace" . . . "I Need Thee Every Hour" . . . "Saviour Like A Shepherd Lead Us." She used to sing to us in her sweet, thin voice those songs we learned at Sunday School: "Jesus Loves Me" . . . "When He Cometh" . . . "Listen to the Voice of Jesus." I remember the times she stood over me as I played those hymns with faltering chords. The dark circles under her eyes and the weary droop of her shoulders seemed to lighten, supported by some Unseen Strength.

Yes, that piano may have seemed to others a shameful extravagance, but to us it had been a sweetening of the breath of life.

This is My Own, My Native Land!
(Manuscript, c. 1946-47)

One of the lessons of citizenship, clarified and confirmed in the last five years is this:

> It is not enough just to have a birth certificate, certifying one's birth in Canada. It is not enough to be a native Canadian and expect that mere birth alone is everything: privileges, responsibilities, pride, allegiance. One must grow into citizenship; one must shoulder the responsibilities before there is any real joy in the privileges; one must be vigilant for the honour of one's country, its integrity, else how can one say with pride: *I am Canadian*.

I can tell you almost the exact moment when I realized for the first time a thrilling identification with one's native land:

> Picture a classroom, the 8th Grade, and I, only twelve. I am enduring the literature period by passing notes across the aisle. We've just finished a Canto of "The Lay of the Last Minstrel" by Sir Walter Scott, and the teacher says, "Memorize the opening stanza of the next Canto."
>
> Bored but patient, I look at the page to make sure which piece to memorize. It's routine work: I declaim aloud at home, swinging the book around in large gestures to emphasize the grand rhythm, and I get it word and punctuation perfect. The next day I'm bypassed, and other pupils are asked to recite it to prove they did their homework, but those other pupils haven't got it letter perfect, and I prompt them . . . silently of course.
>
> The oftener I repeated the lines, the clearer they became, until the sense of the words knocked loudly on my young consciousness.

Up till then, Scott's poem had been only a mental picture of an ancient and white-haired minstrel, with an ancient harp, singing a ballad to a company of lords and ladies of an ancient day. Now I heard clearly these words:

Breathes there the man with soul so dead,
Who never to himself hath said:
"This is my own, my native land!"

Whose heart hath ne'er within him burned
As home his footsteps he hath turned
From wandering on a foreign strand?

It was a breathless moment, and being only twelve I didn't know what to do with it. But from that moment those lines haunted me.

So many times after that . . . many times in later years . . . I had occasion to repeat those lines: proudly, belligerently, sadly, desperately, and bitterly. I had identified myself with Canada; bitter or sweet, my tag was '*Canadian*'.

At first I was rather shy about it, though very proud, because in spite of hardships, of hunger too, there was this feeling of *belonging*:

"This is my *own*, my native land!"

Then as I grew older and joined the Nisei group taking a leading part in the struggle for political liberty, for economic equality, I waved those lines around like a banner in the wind:

"This is my own, my *native* land!"

Ten years later, when our struggle hadn't brought any tangible results I wept those lines with the slow grief of knowing that the ten years would soon be twenty.

"*This* is my own, my native land!"

When war struck this country, when neither pride nor belligerence nor grief had availed us anything, when we were uprooted, despoiled, and scattered to the four winds, I clung desperately to those immortal lines:

287

"This *is* my own, *my* native land!"

Later still, after having been ordered out of my home town, having got permission to live in Toronto, after our former home had been sold over our vigorous protests, after having been re-registered, fingerprinted, card-indexed, roped, and restricted, I cry out to you:

"*Is* this is my own, my native land?"

Well, it is. My Canadian birth certificate wasn't enough, and my record . . . in a very small way . . . as a fighter for TRUE Canadian democracy wasn't enough to prevent all that happened to me, because racially I am *not* Caucasian. I have to have something better than that. I have to have a deeper faith in Canada, a greater hope for Canada. My daily life and my future must be an integral part of Canada. I have to be a better Canadian than most of the Celtic or Anglo-Saxon variety . . . which hasn't been too difficult lately . . . but which ought to be difficult if and when you, and I, succeed in our work.

288

Bibliography

I. By Muriel Kitagawa: Letters and Writings Selected

"Canada is Our Choice." *New Canadian (NC)*, 23 June 1945: p. 2; signed "Mr. and Mrs. E. Kitagawa."

"Damage While You Wait." *Nisei Affairs*, vol. 2, no. 1 (January 1947): pp. 3-4.

"Deportation is a Violation of Human Rights." *NC*, 3 November 1946: p. 2; signed "T.M.K."

"Farewell to a Friend, Olive Pannell." *Nisei Affairs*, vol. 1, no. 7 (February 1946): pp. 4,6; unsigned.

"Freedom." *NC*, 10 November 1945: p. 2; signed "Dana," a pen name Muriel reserved primarily for poems.

"Grey Dawn on Another Day." *NC*, 10 August 1946: pp. 2,8; published in a regular column, "Hello There"; signed "T.M.K."

"Go East!" Public Archives of Canada (PAC), Muriel Kitagawa Papers, MG31 E26, circa 1947. Two other versions of this unpublished essay are extant, one in PAC and another in the private manuscript collection of Dr. Wesley Fujiwara.

["Growing up Nisei."] Untitled manuscript in the private collection of Dr. Wesley Fujiwara, circa 1945-46. The manuscript is an excerpt from an unfinished autobiography written during the 1940s. Another section, called "The Crucible," suggests that Muriel intended to give this title to the whole work. The autobiography was to be the basis of a narrative dealing with her generation of Nisei—their background in the early years of the century, and their struggle to achieve the full rights of citizenship as native-born Canadians. This manuscript is referred to as an Unpublished Autobiography in the Editor's "Introduction: The Life and Times of Muriel Kitagawa."

["Hills of Home."] *NC*, 3 March 1945: p. 7; published in the column, "Hello There"; signed "T.M.K."

["I Know the Nisei Well."] PAC, Kitagawa Papers, MG31 E26, circa

291

1943. This unpublished and untitled piece is a draft only, with comments by Muriel in the margins for intended revisions and additions; it appears to be a section of a book she planned to write on the internment.

["I Stand Here Tonight."] PAC Kitagawa Papers, MG31 E26, circa 1945-46. This untitled manuscript is a draft of a speech, date and place unknown. The essay may have been the basis of a number of speechs Muriel gave to Caucasian groups in Toronto.

["Letter to Friends."] *NC*, 12 August 1944: p. 7; published in the column "Hello There"; signed "T.M.K.".

["Letters to Wes: December 1941-May 1942."] The originals are in the private manuscript collection of Dr. Wesley Fujiwara; copies in PAC, Kitagawa Papers, MG31 E26.

["Looking Back."] Untitled manuscript in the private collection of Dr. Wesley Fujiwara, circa 1945. This manuscript is another excerpt from the Unpublished Autobiography (see note above with "Growing Up Nisei").

["On Loyalty."] *NC*, 4 February 1942: p. 3; untitled and unsigned in a regular column, "Water 'Neath the Bridge."

"Problem of the Japanese in Canada, The." *NC*, 2 June 1948: p. 3. This essay is the text of a speech delivered 31 March 1948 at the Sherbourne House Club to the Executive Conference of the Toronto Council of Women. A manuscript version is located in PAC, Kitagawa Papers, MG31 E26.

"Racialism is a Disease." *NC*, 26 January 1946: p. 7; signed "T.M.K."

"Record of Dignity, A." *NC*, 5 March 1942: p. 2; signed "T.M.K."

"Series of Three Letters on the Property Issue, A." In *The Canadian Japanese and World War II: A Sociological and Psychological Account*, by Forrest E. La Violette, pp. 302-304. Toronto: University of Toronto Press, 1948.

["Solemn Mockery."] *NC*, 31 March 1945: p. 2; untitled, written for the column, "Hello There," signed "T.M.K."

["Story of the Japanese in Canada"]. Untitled manuscript, PAC, Kitagawa Papers, MG31 E26, circa 1947. The essay is a rough draft only, with numerous corrections by Muriel throughout.

["This is My Own, My Native Land!"] Untitled manuscript, PAC, Kitagawa Papers, MG31 E26.

"Today the Japanese—Tomorrow?" *Nisei Affairs*, vol. 2, no. 3 (April 1947): pp. 5-7; signed "S.S.," the initials for a pen name "Sue

Sada." The name belonged to Muriel's grandmother on her mother Tsuru Toyofuku Fujiwara's side.

"We'll Fight for Home!" *NC*, 9 January 1942: p. 4; written for the column, "For A' That," signed "T.M.K."

"Weep, Canadians!" *NC*, 2 March 1946: p. 2; also published in *Nisei Affairs*, vol. 1, no. 8 (March 1946): p. 6; signed "Dana." The poem was a reaction to a newspaper headline on the Supreme Court decision authorizing the government to deport Japanese Canadians who had not committed a crime—nor had even been charged with a crime. The original manuscript, written immediately after Muriel saw the newspaper, is attached to a letter (dated 21 February 1946) to George Tanaka in PAC, National Japanese Canadian Citizen's Association Papers, MG28 V7, vol. 1, file 1-19, *Nisei Affairs*, Correspondence 1945-48.

"Who Was the Custodian." *NC*, 16 August 1947: p. 2; signed "Sue Sada."

"Year 1942, The." *NC*, 31 December 1941: p. 2; written for a regular column, "For A' That," signed "T.M.K."

II. Selected Secondary Sources

Adachi, Ken. *The Enemy That Never Was: A History of the Japanese Canadians*. Toronto: McClelland and Stewart, 1976.

Fowke, Edith. *They Made Democracy Work: The Story of the Co-operative Committee on Japanese Canadians*. Toronto: Garden City Press Co-operative, n.d.

Ito, Roy. *We Went to War: The Story of the Japanese Canadians Who Served During the First and Second World Wars*. Stittsville, Ontario: Canada's Wings, 1984.

Japanese Canadian Centennial Project. *A Dream of Riches: The Japanese Canadians 1877-1977*. Vancouver: Japanese Canadian Centennial Project, 1978.

Kogawa, Joy. *Obasan*. Toronto: Lester and Orpen Dennys, 1981.

La Violette, Forrest E. *The Canadian Japanese and World War II*. Toronto: University of Toronto, 1948.

Nakano, Takeo Ujo, with Leatrice Nakano. *Within the Barbed Wire Fence: A Japanese Man's Account of his Internment in Canada*. Toronto: University of Toronto Press, 1980.

Nakayama, Gordon G. *Issei: Stories of Japanese Canadian Pioneers*. Toronto: NC Press, 1984.

National Association of Japanese Canadians. *Democracy Betrayed: The Case for Redress*. Winnipeg: National Association of Japanese Canadians, 1984.

Sumida, Rigenda. *The Japanese in British Columbia*. Unpublished MA thesis, University of British Columbia, 1935.

Sunahara, Ann Gomer. *The Politics of Racism: The Uprooting of Japanese Canadians During the Second World War*. Toronto: James Lorimer, 1981.

Takashima, Shizuye. *A Child in Prison Camp*. Montreal: Tundra Books, 1971.

Takata, Toyo. *Nikkei Legacy: The Story of Japanese Canadians From Settlement to Today*. Toronto: NC Press, 1983.

Vancouver Japanese Canadian Citizens' Association Redress Committee. *Redress for Japanese Canadians: A Community Forum*. Vancouver: Vancouver JCCA Redress Committee, 1984.

Manuscript Collections

British Columbia Security Papers, Public Archives of Canada (PAC).
Department of External Affairs Papers, PAC.
Department of Labour Papers, PAC.
Department of National Defense Papers, PAC.
Ian Alistair Mackenzie Papers, PAC.
Japanese Canadian Citizen's Association (JCCA) Papers, PAC.
Muriel Fujiwara Kitagawa Papers, PAC.
Royal Canadian Mounted Police Papers, PAC.
William Lyon Mackenzie King Papers, PAC.

Newspapers and Periodicals

New Age, The (Vancouver). 1932-1933.
New Canadian, The (Vancouver, Kaslo, Winnipeg, Toronto). 1938-1952.
Nisei Affairs (Toronto). 1945-1947.
Vancouver *Daily Province*. 1941-1942.
Vancouver *Sun*. 1941-1942.
Young People, The Young People's Society, United Church (Vancouver). 1931.

Index

E

Acknowledgements

My thanks to Ann Sunahara for her ground-breaking study of the unjust treatment of Japanese Canadians during and after World War II. Her book, *The Politics of Racism*, cleared a path to the abundance of documents on Japanese Canadians in the Public Archives of Canada. She has also provided much appreciated encouragement for this collection of Muriel Kitagawa's writings. To Joy Kogawa, I owe the pleasure of spending one quiet afternoon in her house reading, for the first time, the originals of the letters. I also thank Joy for many conversations on the fragile future of our community— and how writers like Muriel have made it possible for us to re-envision our history.

For interviews on Muriel Kitagawa and the social and political background to her writing, I thank Kay Kato Shimizu in Ottawa, Ed Ouchi in Vernon, Tom Shoyama in Victoria, and Roger Obata in Toronto; and for their comments on my all-too-brief visits, I thank two of Muriel's oldest friends, Hide Hyodo Shimizu in Toronto and Eiko Henmi Etheridge in Montreal.

My deepest gratitude to Ed Kitagawa and Dr. Wes Fujiwara for their generosity and support from the initial stage of research to the final stage of publication. They have graciously given me free access to all relevant manuscripts and material belonging to Muriel; they have patiently answered all my pestering questions; and they have extended their warm hospitality to me in each of my visits to Toronto. I also thank Douglas Fujiwara and Kathleen Fujiwara Sano for much appreciated information on Muriel's childhood and their family's early history.

The staff of the Public Archives of Canada have been wonderfully patient and helpful. For guiding a novice through the intricacies of research in the Public Archives, I thank them all, but especially Paulette Dozois, Judy Roberts-Moore, and Robert Hayward. Thanks also are due to the staff of the University of British Columbia, Special Collections, for assistance.

I thank Barbara Barnett from the Office of the Dean of Arts, Simon Fraser University, for her expertise as a word processing operator in typing and preparing the manuscript for publication. Without her assistance, this publication would not have proceeded as smoothly as it did.

I wish to acknowledge the Social Sciences Humanities Research Council for a Leave Fellowship to undertake this publication project during a Research Leave from Simon Fraser University.

I thank my children, Waylen and Elisse, for being a source of inspiration and for their curiosity. Finally, I thank my wife Slavia for her patience and constant support. Her comments have helped me navigate the invisible boundary that joins history and experience—which is to say, in those moments when scholarship threatened to divorce itself from actual lives, she provided a touchstone.